ARCHBISHOP
CORRIGAN
AND THE
ITALIAN
IMMIGRANTS

ARCHBISHOP CORRIGAN
AND THE
ITALIAN IMMIGRANTS

Stephen Michael DiGiovanni

Our Sunday Visitor Publishing Division
Our Sunday Visitor, Inc.
Huntington, Indiana 46750

The author and publisher are grateful for material contained in this work that has been gleaned (or adapted to one extent or another) from various sources. If any copyrighted materials have been inadvertently used in this work without proper credit being given in one form or another, please notify Our Sunday Visitor in writing so that future printings of this work may be corrected accordingly.

Dedicated to Our Lady of Guadalupe, at whose altar in the chapel of the North American College Michael Augustine Corrigan celebrated his first Mass of thanksgiving as a newly ordained priest, on September 20, 1863.

TABLE OF CONTENTS

Acknowledgments ✦ My thanks must go to many people who have assisted me during these years of research and composition.

First and foremost, I am grateful to Bishop Edward M. Egan and Bishop Walter W. Curtis, who gave me the opportunity to research and write this work. Monsignor Andrew T. Cusack of Seton Hall University also supported my studies and encouraged me to complete this book. Father Giacomo Martina, S.J., of the Pontifical Gregorian University, directed the original research and version of this work, to whom I am forever grateful. Monsignor Florence Cohalan supplied insights and observations that were invaluable. Doctor Brian Butler and Ms. Mary McNiff of the United States Catholic Historical Society and Mr. Henry F. O'Brien of Our Sunday Visitor generously supported and guided me through the publication process.

The archivists at the various ecclesiastical archives in Italy and in the United States deserve much praise and my gratitude for their generosity and dedication. In particular, I am grateful to Father Josef Metzler, O.M.I., Prefect of the Vatican Archives, who assisted me during his time as the Prefect of the Archives of Propaganda Fide, and to Monsignor Charles Burns of the Vatican Secret Archives, who guided me through the labyrinth of the Vatican's archival holdings during my years of research. Sister Marguerita Smith, O.P., whose vast knowledge of the Archdiocese of New York and generosity to me during my research, made my task easy during the months of work at Dunwoodie. I also wish to thank Monsignor Edwin O'Brien, who was Rector of Saint Joseph Seminary at Dunwoodie during my years of research, for his generous hospitality to me during my time there.

I am grateful also to Reverend Robert Wister of the Archdiocese of Newark, to Monsignor Joseph Martino, and to Brother Randal Riede, C.F.X., of the Pontifical North American College, for their moral support and guidance in methodology. In addition, I am obliged to Maureen Eisenman and Rose Sullivan for their great assistance. Finally, I would like to thank Mr. Michael Madden, a deacon of the Diocese of Bridgeport, who graciously assisted me in the painstaking task of proofreading and editing this work.

Introduction ✧ Italian mass immigration to the United States began in 1880 and continued through the end of the century

and into the 1920's. The majority of these immigrants entered the country by way of the port of New York which, by 1892, had become the only government port of entry into the United States. Along with the millions of other European immigrants, the Italians required assistance and protection, both material and spiritual, and called upon the Church in America to provide that assistance, as a familiar institution in an otherwise foreign land. The majority of the Italian immigrants arriving in the United States shared the poverty and illiteracy of many other Catholic immigrants. However, the Italians were distinguished from other Catholic immigrants because of the insistence by the Holy See that they receive special care from the Church in the various countries to which they migrated.

In 1979, the Vatican Archives, and those of the Sacred Congregation for the Evangelization of Peoples (Propaganda Fide) in Rome, opened the documents dealing with the reign of Pope Leo XIII. His reign, from 1878 until his death in 1903, included the beginning of Italian mass immigration to the United States, and the formulation of the Church's plan in their regard. The opening of the archives of the Holy See — as well as the use of the Roman archives of various religious congregations involved in the Italian apostolate in the Archdiocese of New York — has made this study possible. This work relies chiefly upon the hitherto unpublished documents found in these Roman archives and also on material from numerous archives here in the United States. The material provided in the Roman archives sheds light upon the complexity of the Holy See's call for the special efforts in favor of the Italian immigrants, as well as the practical problems and tensions that resulted from an attempt to obey those instructions by the Church authorities in the United States.

New York received the majority of the Italian immigrants. This work, therefore, deals with the Church's efforts for the Catholic Italians in the Archdiocese of New York during the administration of Michael Augustine Corrigan, who served as the Archbishop of New York from October 10, 1885, until his death on May 5, 1902.

11

Corrigan was born on October 13, 1839. He was of Irish immigrant stock, his parents (Thomas Corrigan and his wife, Mary English) having emigrated to the United States as children. Corrigan was a perspicacious youth and was given a good preparatory school education at Saint Mary's College in Wilmington, Delaware, followed by collegiate studies at Mount Saint Mary's College at Emmitsburg, Maryland. In the summer of 1859, Michael Augustine began his seminary preparation as a member of the first class of the newly inaugurated North American College in Rome. His studies were taken at Propaganda Fide, where he perfected his linguistic abilities as well as his studies in philosophy and theology. He was ordained a priest in the fall of 1863, and was awarded a doctorate in theology with honors in August the following year. Upon his return home, Corrigan was appointed professor of dogmatic theology and scripture, and the seminary director at Seton Hall College in South Orange, New Jersey, then under the administration of Bernard McQuaid. In 1868, he was named vice-president of the college, and then as college president and vicar general of the Diocese of Newark.

Corrigan acquired a reputation throughout the country as an authority on moral, rubrical, and canonical questions, and was consulted by various bishops for assistance in these fields. By 1871, Corrigan was considered for the vacant see of Cleveland by the bishops of the Cincinnati Province. James Roosevelt Bayley, Bishop of Newark, vehemently opposed the nomination and succeeded in removing his vicar general's name from the terna, or list of three nominees. Upon Bayley's promotion to the metropolitan see of Baltimore as its eighth archbishop the following year, Corrigan's name again appeared as an episcopal candidate, this time for Newark. He received the unanimous approval of the bishops of the province as *dignissimus*, and was noted in the terna for his educational background, academic credentials, professorial experience, and linguistic abilities in Latin, Greek, Hebrew, English, French, and Italian, as well as his seminary and administrative experience.[1] On May 4, 1873, Michael Augustine Corrigan was consecrated at Saint Patrick's Cathedral in Newark, the youngest bishop in the country at the age of thirty-four years.[2]

His years in Newark were marked by the centralization and reorganization of the entire diocese by means of pastoral visitations, the incorporation of ecclesiastical property, and the standardization of the discipline and professional competency of his clergy.[3] He presided over the Third Diocesan Synod of Newark in April, 1878, instituted regular clergy conferences for the continued standardized theological education of his priests, and began regular examinations for the younger clergy. The number of churches in the diocese increased from 121 to 182 during Corrigan's administration, while the number of parochial schools more than doubled, and numerous academies, orphanages, and asylums were founded.[4]

During his years as the Ordinary of Newark, he assisted the Italians and other Catholic immigrants whenever needed.[5] Corrigan was one of the few priests in his diocese who could speak Italian, owing to his Roman training. One instance of his pastoral solicitude toward Catholic immigrants dealt with the Italians in 1875.

In that year, Corrigan requested the Reverend Joseph Borghese, then an assistant at the cathedral church, to take a census of the Catholic Italians in Newark.[6] Borghese reported that the Italian immigrants were arriving in ever-increasing numbers. As a result, Corrigan began Saint Paul of the Cross Church in North Vineland, which was blessed in June, 1880, the first church in the diocese established primarily to assist the Italians. Within four months of that blessing, on October 1, Corrigan was named the Titular Archbishop of Petra and coadjutor to Cardinal John McCloskey, succeeding him as the Archbishop of New York in 1885. Corrigan would be called upon to apply the same administrative abilities and pastoral zeal in New York that he had manifested in Newark, among American-born Catholics as well as among their arriving European coreligionists. This work traces the formulation of a general project in favor of the Catholic Italian immigrants by the Church authorities in Rome, to the administrative and practical applications of that project in the Archdiocese of New York during the years Michael Augustine Corrigan served as the ordinary of the Archdiocese.

CHAPTER ONE

The Huddled Masses

Immigration to the United States: 1880-1900

Europe's "huddled masses yearning to breathe free"[1] looked to America as a land offering a way of life free from the sporadic economic and political disturbances plaguing their continent during the last century. The visions and reports flooding back to Europe from family members, ticket companies, and shipping agents painted a world filled with opportunities, riches, and freedom. The flow of European immigrants to the United States during the nineteenth century was continuous, increasing and decreasing in relation to the economic, political, and — to a lesser extent — religious conditions of the respective nations.[2] In 1880, the total white population in the United States was approximately 43,403,000 persons. The Catholic population is estimated to have been 6,259,000 persons. Natural increases and conversions to the faith added to these numbers. An unexpected increase in the membership of the Roman Catholic Church in the United States during the latter nineteenth century was due to the millions of immigrants who arrived at the various American ports. During the period of 1881-1900, approximately 9,000,000 immigrants arrived in the United States from various countries. Of these, some 2,475,000 were Catholic, at least in name. By 1900, the total white population in the United States was estimated to be 66,809,000 persons, of which approximately 12,041,000 persons were Catholic.[3]

These Catholic immigrants presented themselves to the Church in America as its spiritual charges. They expected to receive some aid, both spiritual and material, and to be greeted in this strange world by a Church truly catholic and familiar to them. They found the Church, but its customs, ritual manifestations, and language were not always familiar, nor were the priests and fellow Catholics always welcoming.

The bulk of these immigrants were from southern and eastern

Europe. They would soon be labeled "new" by the progeny of the preceding generations of immigrants, predominantly Irish and German. These earlier immigrants had fought for the Church before a hostile society, proudly bore their battle scars earned in defense of the faith, and had built up the young Church in America. They felt it to be their Church, and they took a dim view of the intrusion of these newer immigrants.

The Church had never been a welcome institution in the United States that grew out of the English colonies. When, in 1790, the American hierarchy was established with the episcopal consecration of John Carroll, the Church already had a long history of persecution in the New World. During the nineteenth century, the anti-Catholic sentiment of the Protestant majority in America flared up at various times, often in verbal and printed attacks, while at other times in violent, destructive manifestations or political action, since the Roman Church was regarded as the enemy of the freedom, institutions, and ideals of the growing American Republic.[4]

The waves of Catholic European immigrants were not looked upon with delight by the Protestant majority of the American populace. It was generally held that the immigrants could be welcomed, if they could be converted and "Christianized." Since these unskilled masses could provide the manpower needed for the growing industries of America, it was America's duty, so the argument ran, to transform them into Americans: productive and Protestant, in accord with God's plan to convert the world.[5]

The Catholic Church could be welcomed if its doctrines were purified by the free Protestant society of the United States. Commenting on the pastoral letter of the Third Plenary Council of Baltimore, the *New York Times* editorialized that "the Church must be Americanized if it is not to remain an alien on our soil, chiefly sustained and maintained by the membership of persons of foreign birth."[6]

Of all the "membership of foreign birth" then constituting the Catholic Church in the United States, the Italian immigrants were seen as racially and religiously reprehensible by a number of Catholics and non-Catholics alike. One priest of the Archdiocese of New York posited the question concerning the Italian immigrants in prejudiced terms when he wrote: ". . . where do all these dark-eyed, olive-tinted men and women come from," whose main trait, according to the author, was "money-getting," who came lacking "especially what we call spirit," totally devoid of a sense of respectability, "certainly on the score of personal independence and manliness"[7]? Whether they were welcomed by their coreligionists or not, the Italian immigrants continued to arrive in ever-increasing numbers.

Causes of Italian Immigration

The unification of the Italian peninsula was accomplished in the autumn of 1870 with the seizure of Rome and the unseating of the pope from his temporal throne. The effects of the formation of one Italian nation from many Italian states, however, were not so satisfactory as had been envisaged by its leaders and by much of the world press. The American press took much delight in the fall of Rome, and prophesied great things for the future of a united Italy.[8]

Within a decade, any Italian peasant of the *mezzogiorno* (southern Italy) could bear witness to the fact that the triumph of the Savoyard government had produced few of the promised benefits. Enormous fiscal expenditure by the centralized government and the maintenance of a massive standing army led to inordinate taxation.[9] Since the youth of the nation were being drawn off for military service, less and less of the land could be cultivated, thus forcing prices up. The few natural resources Italy possessed were also being appropriated for the military. Thus, with higher taxes, rising prices, mandatory military service, and a growing scarcity of work and opportunities, more and more of the population of southern Italy chose to emigrate.[10]

By the 1880's, the Italian mass immigration to the United States had begun in earnest and continued into the 1920's. In 1879, according to the United States Census Bureau, 5,791 Italians entered the United States. This number more than doubled in the following year, with a total Italian immigration of 12,354 persons entering the United States. For the years 1880-1902, approximately 1,286,000 Italians entered through the various ports of the United States.[11]

The Italian in America

The motivating force that led the majority of Italian immigrants to leave their native land was, indeed, economic. By 1880, Italian immigration was composed primarily of those from the *mezzogiorno* and southern Italy, chiefly from the Abruzzi, the Campagna, Calabria, and Sicily.

17

The majority of the Italians coming to America were young: sixty-five to eighty-five percent being between the ages of fourteen and forty-four years, with three times as many men immigrating as women.[12] By 1896, the Italians formed the largest single group of immigrants arriving and settling, at least temporarily, in New York City.[13] Most settled in the large cities of the industrial northeast and in the midwest. Others scattered, having accepted contracts in Italy for work along new railroad lines as well as mine and canal excavations throughout the country.[14]

The Italian immigrants were mainly unskilled laborers or farmers who had no desire to continue farming. They were usually willing to take on any type of work at low wages, often incurring the opprobrium of American-born laborers as a result. Many fell victims to the *padroni*, or labor bosses, who would contract the Italians in Italy and pay their passage to America, assuring them employment upon arrival. For this service the Italians were paid the lowest possible wages, while they themselves were required to pay a percentage of their wages to the labor bosses. The *padroni* also received payment for the Italians' passage to America, along with a kickback for food and lodging while the immigrants were under their control. Very often the labor boss was also a banker, or else joined forces with a banker, thus furthering his profits while reducing the Italian immigrant to grinding poverty and near slavery.[15]

The family was of prime importance in the life of the Italian immigrant. When he arrived at the port of New York, the Italian immigrant was often met by relatives or friends, unless he was under the care of a labor boss.[16] He endured long working hours and a frugal way of life in order to support his family in America, or to send money to his family in Italy.[17]

Most Italians who arrived in New York were illiterate and ignorant of the customs and language of America, often speaking only the dialect of their province or town. They, therefore, settled in colonies in the larger cities, forming "Little Italies," composed of other members of their family and province, re-creating, as best they could, their village life with its customs, language, and relationships.[18]

The Italians had no real national identity, unlike the other immigrant groups. They identified themselves, not as Italians, but as Neapolitans, Sicilians, or Abruzzesi.[19]

The percentage of Italian immigrants who returned to Italy from the United States was also high. Of the total Italian immigration to the United States from 1882-1896, 47.92% returned to Italy; from 1897-1901, 30.93%; from 1902-1906, 37.9%.[20]

Regardless of the fact that all Catholic immigrants who arrived in America claimed a common faith with American Catholics, it was the Italian who found himself isolated by his language, his beliefs, and his rituals that were not commonly held by Catholics in America. The majority of Italian immigrants in America were definitely religious. But their religious beliefs and practices were not always in keeping with the Catholic faith as professed and practiced by the hierarchy, clergy, and faithful in the United States.

The culture and beliefs of southern Italy were a combination of extreme provincialism, loyalty to family, a blending of Christian beliefs, ritual and sacraments with popular superstition, and remnants of the beliefs of earlier generations. Their beliefs represented the individual's life as controlled both by good and evil forces.[21] These beliefs were merely the distillation of Church doctrine by the uneducated inhabitants of the small world formed by the confines of town or village. There was only one religion for these people — Roman Catholicism. But there were two forms: the pure, doctrinal form of the official Church, and the popular interpretation and practice of the truths of that faith.[22] The religious education of most of the Italian immigrants reflected this, being a distillation of the lives of the saints, stories of miracles, and some prayers, along with protective incantations, passed down from generation to generation.[23] The Church was in many ways the center of Italian village life, as both a religious and social force. "The people came to the priest, . . . not as a binding moral force but as a friend, often the only educated man in the community."[24]

During the latter nineteenth century, the relationship between the priests and their people, though previously far from perfect, would be seriously damaged by the growing influence of Freemasonry and anticlericalism encouraged by the Italian government.[25] The Church become impoverished because of the confiscation of ecclesiastical lands by the state and due to a lack of government funding for the maintenance of the clergy, churches, and charitable institutions. Once the Church required support from those who had previously received her aid, her influence diminished.[26]

The center of life in any village during the year was the *festa* in honor of the village patron saint. This provided one of the few occasions for entertainment, with abundant food, colored lights, fireworks, the religious pageantry with processions accompanying the image of the local patron, and the opportunity to socialize with neighbors rarely seen in the everyday life of an isolated agricultural community.

The worldview held by many southern Italians was religious in nature, one very much aware of the concrete presence of good and evil in creation. This was fostered by the isolated life and myopic worldview of the small village, the hardships of poverty, and the inability of the uneducated and unlettered to come into contact with a way of life or culture other than their own. Therefore, the *festa*, prayers, rituals, and even the incantations and magical cures can be seen as infrequent intrusions of the sacred goodness of God breaking into the monotony of a life overburdened with fear, suffering, and poverty: the products of real evil in the world.[27]

The Italian immigrants brought all this with them to America. The physical surroundings had changed, from Italian village to New York ghetto, but the evil was still as pervasive, if not more painful and immediate, since their suffering and poverty were now clothed in the strange forms of the New World.[28]

The Church in the United States and the Italian Immigrant

The Church in the United States was faced with the challenge of ministering to these immigrants who were, for the most part, ignorant of the language and customs of their new home. The Italians' practice of religion was scandalous to many American Catholics and Protestants alike, since it was a mixture of Christian belief and superstitious practices. Because their religious beliefs and practices often were contrary to American Catholic practices, most Italians were judged to be irreligious.

Because the anniversary of the twentieth of September — the fall of Rome and the temporal deposition of the pope — was usually celebrated in most Italian colonies in America, the Italians were usually considered to be anticlerical, since such celebrations were repulsive to most American Catholics.

The majority of the Italians were not well educated religiously, did not frequent Mass or receive the sacraments, and did not contribute to the Church as did most American Catholics and their coreligionists of other ethnic origins. These "new immigrants," those from southern and eastern Europe, and especially the Italians, were seen to emphasize the "foreignness" of a Church desperately desiring to prove the political loyalty of its members as Americans. The Italian immigrant seemed to undermine all such efforts, and presented the American Church with a pastoral dilemma usually referred to as the Italian Problem.

The authorities of the Congregation of Propaganda Fide, the central Roman agency in charge of the Church's missions throughout the world, were not totally unaware of the problems facing the Church in America.[29] To deal with the extant problems, an invitation was extended to all the metropolitans of the United States in May, 1883, requesting them, or their representatives, to attend meetings in Rome the following November in preparation for the Third Plenary Council of Baltimore, desired by Pope Leo XIII.[30]

The Third Plenary Council of Baltimore: Preparations

In October of that year, members of Propaganda Fide met to discuss the state of the Church in the United States and to propose a preliminary draft of chapters to be presented to the assembled American prelates at their November meetings.

Cardinal Johannes Battista Franzelin, charged with the task of presenting the *ponenza*, or report, on the American Church, gave a rather negative view. He pointed out that despite its apparent growth and flourishing in America, the Church was greatly hindered by many serious problems. The causes of these difficulties were seen to be a result of poor financial administration and clerical laxity. Among the pastoral efforts to be studied prior to the Baltimore Council were parish schools, the conversion of Negroes (as African-Americans were then called), and Italian emigration, as mentioned in article eight of the first chapter of Franzelin's *ponenza*.[31]

Propaganda Fide had written to Archbishop James Gibbons of Baltimore and to other American prelates earlier in the year requesting possible topics for discussion, as well as for information about the Church in America. The Vatican was particularly interested in the condition of the Italians who had so recently begun to immigrate to America in large numbers.[32] Most of the information sent to Rome concerning the material and spiritual state of the Italian immigrants pointed to their miserable condition.

Propaganda took special interest in the letter of Bishop John Lancaster Spalding of Peoria, Illinois, who suggested that "it might not be bad if the council were to occupy itself with emigration in general, to try to stop Catholics from dispersing themselves among non-Catholics, thus being impeded in the practice of their religious duties."[33]

Spalding emphasized the fact that the Italians were in the worst condition of all immigrant groups then arriving. He observed that there were few Italian priests and no bishops in the United States. The Italians were left unaided upon their arrival in America, he continued, since they, of all the immigrant groups, had no Catholic emigrant society. The Italians would be helped to regain their religion, honesty, and material stability, the Bishop concluded, if an Italian center or colony were established. The concluding point of Spalding's letter confirmed Propaganda Fide's fear of Protestant proselytizers among the Italians. He suggested that unless the Church acted swiftly in aiding the Italians, the pope could be greatly criticized for the lack of care exercised on behalf of his own countrymen. Spalding warned that the question of Italian emigrants "is even greater since the Head of the Church is in Italy, which fact could bring those ill-disposed towards the Church to maintain that the abandoned condition of this portion of our population is due to the Church itself."[34]

Propaganda's decision was to place before the American prelates a chapter entitled *De Colonis in America immigrantibus*, in which they called for the establishment of committees in both America and Italy to undertake the care of the Italian immigrants. They would also insist upon the institution of Italian colonies wherever possible. Bishops were to seek out zealous Italian missionaries who would build churches for the Italians and watch over them.[35]

The meetings of the American prelates and Propaganda Fide representatives were held in Rome from November 13 through December 13, 1883. The Americans were presented with a preliminary draft prepared by Propaganda consisting of thirteen headings. During the eighth session, held on the first of December, the twelfth chapter dealing with the care of immigrants was discussed.[36]

The Americans agreed that immigrant committees should be established in America. They suggested, however, that there should be corresponding committees in Italy. The plan to assign Italian priests to direct the care of the Italians in the United States was approved. Archbishop James Gibbons of Baltimore added that committees should be established for all other national groups as well. He also stated that there already existed churches in America for the care of Italians, thus obviating any need for national Italian parishes.[37]

Archbishop Michael Augustine Corrigan of New York made the rather impolitic yet accurate observation that it was very difficult to care for the Italians or to establish churches for them, since the greater number of them did not attend church, were dispersed in small colonies throughout the various cities, and made no offerings for the maintenance of church or priests. Corrigan's observation was the first attempt to point out to the Roman officials that the spiritual deprivations of the Italian immigrants were not entirely due to a lack of pastoral efforts on the part of the American clergy.

Archbishop Patrick Ryan, coadjutor of St. Louis, supported Corrigan's views and suggested that the care of the Italians be entrusted to priests in the major churches of various cities, who would be charged "with the duty of seeking out [the Italians], inviting them to attend church, and giving them religious instruction."

Officials of Propaganda Fide agreed with Ryan, with the stipulation that the priests engaged in such work could teach and preach in Italian. Propaganda judged this solution acceptable "as long as it was not possible to provide them [the Italians] with their own churches." It was impossible at that moment to provide a specific plan for the care of the Italians, but Propaganda concluded that "the zeal of bishops and priests should be stimulated in the interest of their eternal salvation, especially in the care of the children."

Rome did not seem to be satisfied with mixed parishes — parishes that served a community of various nationalities. Rome preferred the establishment of individual national churches, already proved successful in America among the Irish and German communities. This provision for the "salvation of souls" according to national differences and language seemed natural and necessary to the Propaganda officials, but was not overly welcomed by the Americans. Ever aware of the foreign appearance of the Roman Catholic Church in Protestant America, and of the apparent financial inability of the "new immigrants" to build, support, and maintain independent parishes, the American prelates disdained such national churches, preferring the establishment of immigrant committees to assist the arriving Catholic immigrants. Rome also favored such committees, but viewed them as only a part of the Church's work for the immigrants, especially for the Italians.

The Saint Raphaelsverein for German immigrants was suggested as a model for the future immigrant committees. Letters would be sent by Propaganda to the Archbishops of Naples and Genoa with the statutes of the society to guide them in the establishment of similar committees.

Following his return to the United States in March, 1884, Gibbons began preparations for the upcoming plenary council to be celebrated the following November. The chapters of the proposed Roman schema were to be prepared by individual metropolitans in consultation with their suffragans.

Chapter twelve on immigrants was assigned by Gibbons to Archbishop William Henry Elder of Cincinnati. Elder asked Gibbons to be relieved of the task in favor of an East Coast bishop who would be more knowledgeable in the area of immigration than he. Gibbons responded that it was too late to change, and "besides, there is very little to be said about it, & its study involves very little labor. I will make all the suggestions that occur to me on the subject."[38]

But there was much to say on the subject. Rome had already reminded Gibbons and the other American archbishops by letter of the importance of the work and emphasized the pope's growing interest in the welfare of his countrymen who continued to arrive in America and, reportedly, were being lost to the faith in ever-increasing numbers.[39]

Gibbons responded to Propaganda's letter on the fourth of April. He began briefly contrasting the newer immigrants, especially the French and Italians, with the Germans and Irish, who had arrived in such large numbers earlier in the century. He wrote, ". . . among the many Italians who migrate here to the United States of America are not a few who are deceived in their hopes, but this, in numerous cases, is attributed to their own negligence and apathy."[40]

The Germans and the Irish, he continued, "according to their own nature and aptitude," adjusted well to the language of the country and were able to make a good living for themselves. The Italians and the French, however, found greater difficulty in adjusting. But, the Archbishop continued, if they were willing to work hard, they would find that they too could make a suitable enough living. He felt that for the good of all immigrants, so that they might fulfill their Catholic duties, and if the local priest were to deem it necessary, their native languages could be permitted in church, in the preparations for the sacraments, and in their parish schools, wherever they might exist.

Cardinal Giovanni Simeoni, Prefect of Propaganda Fide, responded on the twenty-ninth of April. In his rather long and impassioned reply, he stated that Gibbons had not appreciated the gravity of the sad situation in which the Italians found themselves in America. The Italians were without their own priests and churches, unlike the earlier European immigrants to America. They were in the worst possible danger of losing the faith because of their move to the United States. He again asked Gibbons to bring their plight to the attention of the council fathers at Baltimore.[41]

Corrigan had written to Simeoni in January, 1884, asking the Congregation's advice concerning foreign priests, especially Italian priests, who had come to his diocese in order to escape the poverty and the want of their own countries. He referred to a "dozen" (*dozzina* is how he put it) Italian priests who had arrived and simply celebrated Mass and administered some sacraments wherever needed, but who refused to learn English. They had neither the desire nor "the vocation to work for the Italians, among the poor." Some, he continued, came only for money and then would return to their country, while the others were truly "hangers-on."[42] Rome responded that this problem should be brought to the attention of the upcoming Baltimore Council.[43]

In his response to Rome's letter of the sixth of March requesting information on the Italian immigrants from the American prelates, Corrigan went into some detail researching and reporting the facts concerning the Italians in New York City. Whether or not he was anxious to justify his rather bold remarks made during the meetings in Rome the previous fall, his research did support his observations about the Italians and the Church in America.[44] Attached to Corrigan's report were three other reports from priests working with Italians in New York City, who had prepared the reports at Corrigan's request.[45]

Corrigan began with the statistics that between 1847 and 1884, 7,522,072 European immigrants had arrived through the port of New York. Over the previous ten years, more than 100,000 Italians had entered. All immigration was under the control of the state government, which had various immigrant aid committees working to protect the immigrants, to help them arrive safely at their destinations, and to assist them in finding employment, if possible. There also were four immigrant societies at work in Castle Garden itself, the port of entry for the city: the German Society, working primarily with non-Catholics; the Irish Society, founded by Archbishop John Hughes; the Saint Raphaelsverein for Catholic German immigrants, founded by Peter Paul Cahensly; and the Mission of the Holy Rosary, founded in 1883 and run by New York diocesan priests, for all Catholic immigrants. Corrigan restated the familiar cry that the Italians were in the most deplorable spiritual and material condition of all the immigrants; the religious education they had received in Italy was inadequate; and the problems faced by the Church in New York regarding the Italians stemmed from a lack of good Italian priests needed to educate these people. This was compounded by the different dialects and customs of the Italians, and by the growing threat of Protestant proselytizing.

The three attached reports supported Corrigan's statements. They considered the problem of the Italians' religious practice and poor education according to the provinces from which they came, and concluded that the majority of the northern Italians were more faithful to traditional Catholic faith and practice, and better educated religiously, than were the southern Italians. The reports spoke of the type of work the Italians found in America, and of their transient habits, moving from job to job, or simply coming to America long enough to earn money, and then returning to Italy. All of these factors, they concluded, contributed to the Church's difficulty providing for the spiritual and material needs of these poor people.

The solution unanimously suggested by these reports was to provide zealous Italian priests who would come to the United States as missionaries. It would also be necessary to impress upon the pastors in Italy the importance of adequately educating their people religiously, and to stress the necessity of the Catholic faith and Church in the lives of the Italians once they arrived in America.[46]

Corrigan received no response from Rome. So, on August the fourth, he repeated the basic details of his March report in an abbreviated form, adding a scathing report on the conduct of the fifteen Italian priests in his diocese, including a short biography of each. All, save one, had arrived with good letters of recommendation from their Italian ordinaries. Since their arrival in New York City, Corrigan had discovered that, with the exception of two, all had been guilty of grave crimes or immoral conduct in their own dioceses, and were forced to emigrate. Others had begun to live dishonest if not profligate lives upon arrival in America. Needless to say, their conduct did not aid in the spiritual amelioration of their fellow countrymen in New York. Corrigan also sent along a report on the Italians written by the Reverend Thomas Lynch, rector of Transfiguration Church, substantiating Corrigan's earlier reports.[47]

The Immigrants

The Third Plenary Council of Baltimore was held from the ninth of November through the seventh of December, 1884. The chapter of the Roman schema concerning Italian immigrants was discussed heatedly on the first of December, during the twenty-first private congregation of the Council. Its reception by the council fathers was less than favorable. The committee, headed by Archbishop Elder, charged with preparing the chapter, had not changed the form agreed upon during the Roman meetings the previous year.

When the proposal was made by Bishop Joseph Dwenger of Fort Wayne to accept the chapter as it stood, Archbishop Corrigan vehemently objected, recommending the rejection of the entire chapter, since, as he stated, it was both useless and untrue.[48] Armed with the clear information from the reports of his priests and other sources in New York City, Corrigan maintained that the Italians were not free to live as they would, since most had bound themselves to *padroni*, or labor bosses, as contract laborers in exchange for passage to America. Because of this, they were unable to practice their religion as freely as other immigrant groups, since they were either totally bound by their contracts or forced to work continuously as the result of their abject poverty. He related much of the information he had sent to Rome concerning the religious practice of the Italians, the work of the Italian priests, and the damage done by Protestant missions to the Italians' Catholic faith. He also mentioned having written to Don Bosco, asking for priests to help the Italians, but without success.[49]

It was decided that the chapter should be rewritten by a new committee composed of Archbishops Corrigan and Riordan and

Bishops McQuaid, Spalding, and Leray. After three days' work, the committee proposed a total rejection of the chapter and the composition of a new one entitled *De Colonis et Advenis.* The chapter made no specific mention of the Italians, but limited itself to recommending care for all Catholic immigrants arriving at American ports. The immigrants, the chapter said, should be aided by immigrant societies and priests who would assist them and direct them to rural colonies, if possible.[50] It was further recommended that a strong letter be written to the pope informing him of the actual condition of the Italian immigrants in America. After some discussion it was deemed more prudent to address Propaganda Fide on such a delicate matter instead of the pope.[51] Bishop Thomas Becker of Wilmington was entrusted with the task of drafting the letter.[52]

The Ides of January

It was no easy task to convey to the Holy See the nearly unanimous opinion of the council fathers that the Italians who had come to the United States were woefully ignorant of, and faithless to, the religion of their fathers. Becker was quite aware of this and expressed as much to Gibbons: "My letter should be carefully worded, yet quite as firmly as usual. It is a very delicate matter to tell the Sovereign Pontiff how utterly faithless the specimens of his country coming here really are. Ignorance of their religion and a depth of vice little known to us yet, are their prominent characteristics. The fault lies far higher up than the poor people. The clergy are sadly remiss in their duty."[53]

Becker's source of information was Corrigan. In three letters to Becker, the Archbishop sent along the information he had gathered for his reports to Rome of the previous March and August, from his priests, New York bankers, immigration officials, and others working with the Italians.[54]

In his first letter to Becker, Corrigan reported a recent conversation with the Reverend Emiliano Kirner, the rector of the then new Italian church in Harlem, Our Lady of Mount Carmel.[55] Kirner spoke of the Italians' poverty, their lack of religious education, their greed for money, that seemed to inspire their every action, and which led to apostasy and exploitation by *padroni.* He also spoke of their distrust of priests, who had given so many bad examples to the Italians: "They [Italian immigrants] see no one [priest] here, [who is] not drawn by love for money. They speak openly of said scandals. . . . Besides, their religion at home was both too cheap and too mercenary, to make them esteem it as they ought, or be willing to make sacrifices for it here."[56] Becker acknowledged receipt of this letter and expressed his own belief "that the poor *paesani* are infinitely less to be blamed than the clergy about the southern parts of the [Italian] Peninsula."[57]

Corrigan's second letter dealt with Protestant activity among the Italian colonies of New York. The American government supported various Protestant schools working with Italian immigrants, the most effective being that of the Children's Aid Society. According to the 1883 New York Board of Education report, the Society received $35,014 in government funds for the instruction of 13,968 students by sixty-nine teachers. A number of these students were Italians. There were three other Protestant missions with schools for Italians in New York City, "but the majority [of Italian children] do not attend any school, or at least not a Catholic one."[58]

The third letter from Corrigan referred to information he had previously sent to Rome, along with information from a Catholic reporter on Protestants from the Commissioner of Immigration.[59]

America's View

Becker's letter, which was sent to Propaganda in the name of the council fathers, was far from earth-shattering. It merely reiterated everything the Roman authorities already knew about the Italians in America and had already expressed in various letters written to American prelates on the subject. Regardless of this, the council fathers felt "it was evident that Rome was unaware of the fact that the Italians suffered a spiritual destitution greater than that of all other immigrant groups."

The Becker letter also accused the Italian clergy of being responsible for their countrymen's apparent lack of faith: "The Bishops of the southern provinces of Italy should be pushed over and over to show pastoral concern in giving religious instructions to the poor and ignorant peasants. It cannot be denied that nowhere among other Catholic groups in our midst is there such crass and listless ignorance of the faith as among the Italian immigrants."[60] The immigrants, especially those of southern Italy, the letter continued, should receive solid religious instruction before they leave Italy.

"Such a task cannot be accomplished here, both because of the lack of Italian-speaking priests and because the number [of priests] is inadequate to the size of the task."

The letter provided no solution or plan to the immense problem of the pastoral care for the Italian immigrants. For the Third Plenary Council of Baltimore, the question of the Church's pastoral response to Catholic immigration to America in general, and Italian immigration in particular, was left unanswered. For the Americans, the solution to the growing Italian Problem lay in Italy, where they saw its roots in the poor religious training of the people and in clerical laxity.

The Holy See seemed to care little for any discussion of the causes for the Italians' alleged lack of faith. The possible loss of their Catholic faith by millions of Italians after migrating to the United States pointed out clearly to Rome that the solution, as well as the problem, was now to be found in the New World.

CHAPTER TWO

Rome and the Catholic Immigrants

Ferragosto

The officials of Propaganda Fide met during the hot days of late August, 1885, to review the decrees of the Third Plenary Council of Baltimore. The American representatives, sent to explain the legislation to the Congregation, were Bishops Joseph Dwenger of Fort Wayne and John Moore of St. Augustine. They arrived in Rome on March 17, 1885, to join forces with Denis J. O'Connell, Rector of the North American College, close friend and Roman agent of Archbishop Gibbons, who had appointed him procurator. The fourth member was Bishop Richard Gilmour of Cleveland, who arrived in Rome on June 5, 1885.

The Americans had anticipated opposition to some of the conciliar decrees, especially concerning diocesan consultors, which the Americans preferred to the establishment of cathedral chapters. Their major opponent would be Cardinal Johannes Battista Franzelin, who was to serve as the cardinal *ponens* for Propaganda's meetings concerning the Baltimore decrees.[1]

Franzelin summarized the information that the Congregation had received concerning the Italians in the United States in a brief history of the 1883 preparatory meetings over which he had presided. Presenting the various opinions then aired concerning the pastoral care of the Italians in America, he concluded: "In most [Italian immigrants] the Faith is weakened, diminished, enfeebled, while in others it is totally dead. . . . Saddened by such evils and inspired by a true or Christian patriotism, the Holy See has sought to provide some remedy."[2]

Franzelin had little good to say about the comments voiced by members of the American hierarchy concerning the Italian immigrants. He was particularly displeased by Corrigan's curt remarks and commented that "the manner of Mons. Corrigan's reasoning seems strange, if not illogical." The Cardinal believed one should not simply cease to act when problems arose, as he suspected Corrigan of suggesting. Franzelin went on to say that the Italians needed protection against the speculators, and their faith revived, lest they apostatize. The condition of the Italians, he continued, was not hopeless: "Many preserve the Faith. In nearly everyone there is the seed of religion; it is therefore necessary to cultivate that seed, that it might sprout and produce much good fruit."

During the conciliar meetings, Bishops John Lancaster Spalding of Peoria and Francis Silas Chatard of Vincennes both maintained that the Italians were not in such a terrible condition as Corrigan would have had the Council believe. The number of Italians in either the Diocese of Vincennes or Peoria was relatively small, compared to that in New York City, and the circumstances in which the Italians in the midwest lived were radically different from those in Corrigan's Archdiocese. These two bishops called for the establishment of Catholic agricultural colonies for the Italians. The salutary effect of such colonies was proved, so they maintained, by the numerous German Catholic settlements in the midwest.

The problem with this suggestion, however, was to be found in the fact that the majority of Italians refused to farm upon arrival in America, even though many were from the agricultural regions of Italy. The majority of Italian immigrants preferred to remain in the larger eastern cities. The problems, dangers, and difficulties encountered by the Italian immigrants in New York City were vastly different from those encountered in the midwest by their conationals.

Regardless of this, Franzelin gave more credence to the comments of the Bishops of Peoria and Vincennes than to those of the Archbishop of New York. Comments on Becker's letter to Propaganda of January, 1885, concerning the Italian immigrants, completed Franzelin's brief history of the views of the American episcopate on the Church's pastoral response. Becker had mentioned in his letter that the Italian bishops should be encouraged to teach their people the fundamentals of the faith before they left Italy. Franzelin's response to this was, "Good! But these provisions are insufficient. The danger of evil is there in America. . . . A strong will, inflamed by Christian charity overcomes all obstacles; its power shows itself even more splendidly when the obstacles to be overcome are great."

Since the American Council had neither remedied the situation of the Italian immigrants in America nor proposed a satisfactory plan of action in this regard, Franzelin concluded, then "with the most solid foundation the Consultor expresses his desire that the S. Con. de Prop[aganda] study by itself the practical manner to remedy such evils, and provide, by itself the necessary solution."[3]

The decision of Propaganda concerning the pastoral care for the Italian immigrants had four parts: (1) to send a circular letter to the established committees in Italy concerning emigration; (2) to contact the Superior of the Pallotines to arrange for the sending of a priest to New York to work with the Italians resident there; (3) to write to the Prefect of the Congregation of the Council to remind the bishops of southern Italy to take serious measures for the improvement of the clergy; (4) to ask the pope to write an encyclical on emigration, dealing especially with the Italians, and touching upon the necessity for the evangelization of Negroes and Indians.[4]

The pastoral solution to the growing number of Italians in America was seen by the Baltimore Council to be the provision of good Italian priests, emigrant societies, and agricultural colonies. Becker's letter to Rome expressed the Council's views:

> If the Supreme Authority . . . were to send here and to those regions of Italy from which the peasants migrate, priests prominent for their good behaviour and doctrine and fired by zeal for souls, priests who, having rejected the sordid desire for temporal gain, might devote themselves fully and permanently to the spiritual care of the Italians, . . . then, by such auspices, in due time such a work will achieve full results.[5]

The chapter entitled *De Colonis et Advenis* of the Baltimore decrees praised the extant Irish and German Catholic emigrant societies, and commended the founding of emigrant colonies that would be supplied with "prudent priests" who would be able to minister to the arriving immigrants in their native tongue and also protect them "from the fraudulent dealings and plots of evil men who abound . . . in such places."[6]

Independent national parishes, the establishment of which the chapter after next will narrate, were not, however, considered by the council fathers as a possible remedy. The opposition to such parishes came, not so much from the bishops, as from members of their clergy. This priestly opposition was based in part on the fact that few Italians attended Mass with regularity; fewer contributed financially to the churches. Other priests opposed the erection of national parishes, which would be independent and distinct from territorial parishes, since such parishes by necessity would be established within the already existing parish boundaries of the territorial churches. This could pose a considerable and lasting threat to the existing territorial churches. Another factor was the belief held by many New York rectors that Italian priests should be assistants to the rectors of existing territorial churches and not rectors of national churches, since the Italian clerics were unfamiliar with the language and customs of America and were thought to be incompetent administrators.

Growing National Tensions

Tensions between the various national groups arriving in the United States continued to grow during the latter decades of the nineteenth century. Rome received numerous letters and petitions from groups of Catholic immigrants, and from individuals explaining these growing tensions, asking for help to establish national churches, requesting priests, and, especially, petitioning to be allowed the use of their native language and customs in religious education and liturgical ceremonies.

There was also a growing number of complaints against the so-called "Irish" clergy by various national groups.[7] Reports of "Irish" prejudice, especially against non-English speaking groups such as the Germans, Poles, and Italians, flooded into Propaganda Fide. These "new" immigrants felt discriminated against because of their language, customs, and clannishness that kept them outside the mainstream of American, English-speaking life.

An article was published in July, 1883, by John Gilmary Shea, entitled "Converts — Their Influence and Work in This Country." Shea claimed that converts among the foreign-born Catholics in America were isolated, especially among the Germans, since they learned the language and customs of that foreign group and identified with them alone. Such fostering of national feeling breeds animosity, Shea contended, since the next generation would grow up as Americans having America, and not Germany, as their home.

Religion could not be bound up exclusively with one nationality, for with the death of that nation would come the death of religion. Nationalism in America, Shea maintained, was a "canker eating away the life of the Church in the United States." He continued, "A Protestant will point to the map and say: 'where are your American Catholics? The whole country is laid off in dioceses, as though you owned it, but how is it that your Popes have never found an American Catholic fit to occupy a see west of the Mississippi and Lake St. Clair? There are thousands of miles where no American-born bishop has ever been seen.' "[8]

The majority of the German immigrants who had come to the United States settled in the midwest, forming strong enclaves, preserving their language and culture in order to protect their Catholic faith. The most powerful center of German culture was located in what was known as the German Triangle, formed by the areas centering on Milwaukee, St. Louis, and Cincinnati.

The German response to Shea's article, and complaints to Rome about alleged "Irish" persecution, came primarily from the German Triangle. For the German Catholic, who had fled the anti-Catholic atmosphere of Bismarck's regime, the desire to preserve the Catholic faith in Protestant America was very strong. Equally strong was the Germans' sense of national pride, manifested in their desire to preserve their language and customs. This love of faith and cultural heritage led invariably to the foundation of German Catholic colonies — and local American animosity. Not only did the German Catholics find themselves unwanted by the Protestant majority in America because of their Catholicism, they also found themselves unaccepted by their American coreligionists because of the "foreignness" of their Catholicism. In spite of this seemingly universal opposition, the German Catholic immigrants succeeded in building a strong and effective means of preserving both their culture and their faith in the United States.

They built churches and parochial schools, founded societies and newspapers, and supported German priests and bishops, who preached and educated their children in the language of their homeland. Their faith was strong, they believed, because they had maintained a strong German culture. The fear of many American non-German ecclesiastics was that the Germans were growing too strong and too German to be good for the growing "American" Church.

Shea's article of July, 1883, against national sentiment in religion, was answered in two articles in the *Pastoral Blatt*, by the Reverend William Färber, a rector in St. Louis, and by the Reverend Innocent Wapelhorst, O.F.M., professor and rector of Saint Francis Seminary in Milwaukee. These articles explained that the primary concern motivating the retention of German culture in America was the salvation of souls. All fears put forth that Germans would create a new Germany in America were groundless, they maintained. The Catholic immigrants who arrive in the United States should not be forced to give up their culture too quickly, since forced and rapid Americanization was dangerous and detrimental to the immigrants. They stated that the Germans had the greatest love of America and were quick to learn English. The varied nationalities found in America would unite naturally, without being forced to reject their individual heritage and culture.

The article continued: "Forcible, premature interference is always dangerous. In nature there is no leap; this also holds good in the national development of things, social, political and religious. Let us cheerfully permit our descendants to settle those questions. When once immigration has entirely ceased, and there lives a generation that has been reared up with its priests, the English language will also be gradually adopted in the Churches. The best policy for the present would be . . . that all bishops, priests, and people, should become large hearted; that they should not be Americans, Irish, or Germans, and then Catholics; that they should be more solicitous for the salvation of souls than for the preservation of the German or English language; and that no one should disregard the words of the Chief Pastor of souls, Jesus Christ: 'Quaerite PRIMUM regnum Dei et justitiam ejus et reliqua adjicientur vobis.' It would be dangerous, through zeal for one's mother tongue, to disregard this admonition of the Eternal Wisdom; it would be DANGEROUS and FOOLISH to wish, at present, forcibly to solve these delicate questions and complications by suppressing, slighting, disfranchising the people of any nationality."[9]

Wapelhorst stated that 18,000,000 souls had been lost to the Church in the United States. The primary cause of this great loss was America's "godless public school system" to which Catholic children were allowed to be subjected. If Catholic children only had a strong Catholic upbringing and education, all other problems would clear up naturally. For the German Catholics in the United States, the safeguarding of their Catholic schools was of the utmost importance for the preservation of the faith and culture of subsequent generations.

On July 31, 1884, a petition was sent to the Prefect of Propaganda Fide, Cardinal Giovanni Simeoni, from eighty-two diocesan and religious priests of St. Louis dealing with succursal (that is, auxiliary) churches, established for individual national groups. It had been prepared by the Very Reverend Henry Mühlsiepen, Vicar General for German, Bohemian, and Polish Catholics in St. Louis. Its major complaint dealt with the apparent second-class status of German churches in St. Louis, viewed by many an English-speaking rector as under his jurisdiction. These German priests requested that parochial status be granted these German churches, and that they be independent of English-speaking congregations, with rights equal to those enjoyed by English-speaking churches.[10]

Färber was in Rome during the summer of 1884, and did his utmost to strengthen the claims of the German petitioners, as did Mühlsiepen, who wrote Archbishop Anton Maria Graselli, a consultor at Propaganda Fide.

One of the most influential prelates at Propaganda who strongly supported the German cause in America was the same man who had opposed so many of the American innovations and decisions of the Baltimore Council: Cardinal Johannes Battista Franzelin. In a letter of March, 1885, Bishop Bernard McQuaid of Rochester wrote Bishop Gilmour, "It is evident that we have to dread Franzelin more than anyone else, he is German and Jesuit; his prejudices against us are very strong; he needs to be taught a lesson or two."[11]

The fears of the American hierarchy were heightened when, during one of the conferences held concerning the Baltimore decrees, Franzelin told Bishop Moore that the German Catholics in America were "neglected and the priests opposed."[12] Their fears were confirmed when Archbishop Domenico Jacobini, the Secretary of Propaganda, addressed a public letter to the president of the German Central Verein in the United States, promising that a cardinal protector would be named for the various German societies. Gilmour wrote Gibbons: "The Holy Father has not concluded whether it will be Card. Franzelin or Melchers."[13]

Bishops Moore and Gilmour quickly drew up a memorial, or

report, on the entire German question in America in the fall of 1885, sending copies to Propaganda and to the Vatican Secretary of State, Cardinal Ludovico Jacobini, with a request that it be presented to the pope. They also sent copies to all the curial cardinals, to Bernard Smith, Abbot of Saint Paul's Outside-the-Walls, to Denis O'Connell, newly appointed Rector of the North American College, and to the ordinaries of New York, Baltimore, Louisville, and Rochester.

The memorial defended the American Church against the German accusations of anti-German prejudice. It claimed that a spirit of nationalism was dividing the Church in America. The writers, who believed the Germans were forming a distinct national movement in America that would do immense harm to the unity of Catholicism in the United States, pointed out: "This perpetual discussion among the Germans is not limited to any class: bishops, priests, laity, all have their part, thusly showing that if one cannot say that there is an ORGANIZED action, then there is nonetheless a well-defined INTELLIGENCE of that subject."[14]

While the Congregation had been studying the decrees of the Baltimore Council, a letter was received from a "certain bishop" in the United States asking about the relationship of these succursal churches, or quasi-parishes, to independent or territorial churches. The author of this letter was Bishop Kilian Flasch of La Crosse, Wisconsin. He asked (1) whether several independent parishes, distinct from territorial parishes because of language and national groups, could exist in the same neighborhood; (2) whether a local ordinary would offend "the mind and law of the Church" if he were to require the children of immigrants to remain as members of their parents' parish until they attained their legal majority or married.[15]

Simeoni wrote to sixteen American prelates, asking them to give due consideration to his request for information concerning the German Catholics in America, and to relay their views concerning the existence of quasi-parishes established for the various national groups. He referred Flasch's questions to them as guides for their consideration, but did not reveal their author to them. According to the report of the Congregation, all sixteen American prelates answered the questions in unanimous agreement. In response to the first *dubium*, the prelates agreed that there could exist a number of different churches within the same neighborhood, distinct and independent of one another because of language and national groups.

Unless total independence were granted these national groups, many would refuse to attend church rather than be subject to a priest of another nationality. They would also feel humiliated if their priest were forced to be the curate to a rector of another nationality. In such a case the faithful might refuse to receive the sacraments in protest and shame. Because of this, the already existing territorial parishes could die, since support for the church would be divided.

In response to the second *dubium*, the bishops answered in the negative: the local ordinary would not be acting against the mind and law of the Church if he were to require the children of immigrants to attend their parents' church. The bishops observed that the parents have a responsibility to look after their children. They could do this only if their offspring attended the same church as their parents. If they were allowed to go to another church, the children could easily elude their parents and not attend church at all.

Gibbons observed that there already existed national churches in a number of American dioceses. Such churches were effective means of aiding the immigrants.[16] He answered the second *dubium* by describing the process of assimilation of many of the immigrants' children who very often tended to leave their parents' national church in order to learn English. Many enjoyed socializing with children of other national groups while at school and felt neither the need nor the desire to segregate themselves from these other groups in the matter of religion. The practice in Baltimore, the Archbishop continued, was that children could be baptized or married in either a German- or an English-speaking church, if one of the parents was German. It was very difficult, however, to enforce this strictly.

Corrigan answered Simeoni's letter on January 3, 1886. He wrote that national churches could be established in the same neighborhood as other churches. The great number of immigrants of various nationalities made the existence of national churches essential. They existed as independent churches in practically all parts of the United States, except St. Louis. The faithful could receive the sacraments in any church they wished, except for baptism and matrimony. In his answer to the second *dubium*, however, Corrigan responded by making the distinction that even though the local ordinary had the right to determine where baptism and matrimony were to be performed, prudence should reign in the application of such an episcopal right. He continued, "It is not prudent to restrict the making of confession where one pleases, or to make cast-iron laws that would only bring trouble."[17]

While the Americans' letters were being digested at Propaganda, and before any decision could be reached concerning national churches, the Reverend Peter Abbelen, a priest of the Archdiocese of Milwaukee, arrived bearing letters of recommendation from Archbishops Gibbons of Baltimore[18] and Michael Heiss of Milwaukee.[19] He was also armed with a document that would magnify the German Catholic battle, the growing animosity between national groups in America, and the question of Catholic immigration to the United States.

The Abbelen Memorial

During the fall of 1886, a noteworthy collection of American ecclesiastics was assembled in Rome. Bishops John Ireland of St. Paul and John Keane of Richmond arrived to discuss plans for the new Catholic University of America, to gain Propaganda's approval of the Knights of Labor, and to discuss the rumors of an Apostolic Delegate for the Church in America. All were welcomed as guests at the North American College by the Rector, Denis J. O'Connell, who had also received the Reverend Peter Abbelen as a guest a few weeks earlier. Gibbons would join this group on February 13, 1887, arriving for the March consistory, and in response to the invitation he had received from Cardinal Jacobini, relaying the pope's desire that Gibbons come as soon as possible to treat of important matters.

In a letter dated March 9, 1886, the Reverend William Färber of St. Louis had written to Monsignor Antonio Grasselli stating that he had been advised by the Reverend Henry Mühlsiepen, Vicar General of the Archdiocese of St. Louis and President of the German-American Priests' Society, to write confidentially, "for the salvation of souls," concerning "the ecclesiastical relationship between the Germans and the English." Recently, Färber continued, Propaganda had received various letters from American bishops. Archbishop Heiss, being concerned lest the entire business drag on too long, "has been given counsel that a representative be sent to Rome, who would express the state of things 'viva voce,' not just according to the archbishop of St. Louis, but in general." Heiss had found such a worthy representative. Färber continued, ". . . there is a priest here, equally endowed with piety and doctrine, with a full sense of the Church and who at the same time enjoys the trust of his bishop and of the German clergy. He is the Reverend P. M. Abbelen of Milwaukee, who took such a part in the preparatory works of our last Plenary Council, being a theologian."

Färber went on to say that Heiss personally wanted Abbelen to go to Rome, "if His Eminence the Prefect of the S. Congregation of Propaganda would insinuate to Heiss that a representative should be sent to Rome 'ad hoc' to treat the subject of 'viva voce.' "[20]

Abbelen, accordingly, was sent to Rome, and in November, 1886, he presented Propaganda a document later known as the Abbelen Memorial, dated September 28, 1886, and signed by Archbishop Heiss on October 3, 1886.

There were eight points in the memorial: (1) all parishes should be equal to English-speaking (Irish) parishes with no canonical distinction; (2) German parishes should be granted irremovable rectors according to the decrees of Baltimore III (Titulus II, Caput V); (3) members of national parishes should be inscribed in those national parishes, and their children should be under the authority of their parents; (4) children who learn English should be free to attend English-speaking churches with written permission from their rector or local ordinary; (5) bishops and priests should be reminded that customs and traditions are not prohibited unless dangerous to the Church and that English was to be taught in the schools; (6) both languages were to be respected in mixed parishes; (7) in a diocese having a number of national groups, there should be a vicar general for each group; (8) if, because of the end of immigration, English dominates in a parish, the parish is to be split, and separate parochial facilities would be given to the German and English congregations.[21]

Before Propaganda could consider the memorial, Ireland secured a copy, printed other copies, and, with the Congregation's approval, sent these copies to the American prelates with a letter signed by Keane and himself, presenting Abbelen's memorial as a part of "a conspiracy wide-spread and well-organized against English-speaking bishops and priests." As the result of the intervention by Ireland and Keane, the letter continued, the discussion of the matter had been delayed by Propaganda. They requested the American Archbishops to cable Rome immediately with their protests against the German claims, and then to send letters from them to submit to Propaganda, "sustaining our request, not mentioning, however, how or from whom your information has come. If you can trust other bishops, give them word, and get them also to send telegrams and letters."[22]

O'Connell added his voice to the frenzied cry of Ireland and Keane, cabling to the American Archbishops to ensure the quickest response in order to provide a solid defense before Propaganda Fide officials.[23] He also wrote the Archbishop of New York, underscoring the strength of the German position in Rome: "It required the strictest kind of protest to have the matter delayed even for a little while. Rome is full of disapproval for the inequality at which the Germans are placed, . . ."[24]

Ireland and Keane protested to Propaganda, presenting their own memorial dated December 9, 1886, denying Abbelen's allegations that German Catholics received prejudicial treatment from the "Irish" clergy and hierarchy. They insisted the only question to be dealt with was one of German parishes in relation to "Irish" parishes. They stated, "The only question that can be considered is this: the question between the English language, which is the language of the United States, and the German language, which emigrants from Germany have brought to the United States. Why Germans so often give to this question another form, as to indicate that there is a conflict of races in America between the Germans and the Irish, we do not know."[25]

Ireland and Keane presented Abbelen's memorial as a type of secret mission, organized by the Germans in the United States. This is clear both in their memorial to Propaganda[26] and in their letter to the American bishops.[27] Gibbons convoked a meeting of the Archbishops of New York, Baltimore, Philadelphia, and Boston in Philadelphia on December 16, 1886. Elder of Cincinnati had also been invited. Being unable to attend, however, he sent his observations. The Archbishops composed a letter drafted by Corrigan.

The Archbishops stated that they knew of Abbelen's actions in Rome and denied his charges of unfair treatment of the Germans, or of any other Catholics of any national group, by the Church in America. National churches had existed in the United States for these groups, with succursal parishes existing only in St. Louis. The Germans had had every opportunity to air their complaints to the other members of the American hierarchy during the Baltimore

Council, which had provided a committee to discuss new material, a member of which had been Heiss himself. Why had the Germans remained silent if there had existed such prejudice in America? Special care had been given to the Germans, at least on the East Coast, where German parishes, German sermons, and the opportunity to confess in German were provided. The Church in the United States was already seen as a foreign institution by the American Protestant majority, the letter continued. If concessions were made to the Germans, then these anti-Catholic charges would be proven true, and the Church would suffer. The Archbishops concluded:

> If the Church of God wishes to make true progress among us [in America], it cannot depend exclusively upon European emigration, but must fix deeply its roots elsewhere than this alone. Therefore, the Church will be neither Irish, nor will it be German, but AMERICAN, and even more, ROMAN; since there is neither Jew, nor Greek, . . . but all are one in Christ Jesus.[28]

Corrigan reiterated these sentiments in his own letter to Simeoni sent later that same month.[29] He began by accusing Abbelen of not taking into consideration the Catholic population of the East Coast of the United States — which composed nearly one-half the total Catholic population of the country. He continued, "I say that no 'ponenza' that ignores this major portion of the Church could have the right to include the whole United States of America in their [sic] laments."[30] He condemned Abbelen and the calumnies intimated by him against the Province of New York. Corrigan insisted on the absurdity of Abbelen's assertion that there existed in New York City the common belief that Irish rectors had jurisdiction over all, whether born in America or elsewhere. Corrigan went on: "Our Brothers [the German Bishops] made an enormous error in drawing a universal conclusion from a particular fact. . . . The Germans have always jealously guarded the spirit of Nationalism or of the tribe, as they say, by which they do not assimilate themselves to the customs of the country, but hold fast to their own ways, and thus, they desire their own German schools, as well as their own newspapers, Churches, Priests and Bishops."

Corrigan continued his harangue of the Germans, pointing out that they built schools, "as Cardinal McCloskey once told me, not so much because of education, as to preserve their people, and to retain their mother-tongue." The Germans, he continued, would only accept German priests, "and not finding a German Priest, they easily go to listen to a good Lutheran (German)." If Corrigan intended to disprove the Germans' claim of "Irish" prejudice, he did not succeed in this letter. He revealed the belief strongly held by many Americans: "Until today the Bishops of the United States of America were in agreement, as brothers. It grieves me greatly that our [German] brothers have desired to scatter the seeds of discord, and that they have wanted to 'Germanize' the Church of these States. If we were to go to Germany, we would not expect the English language to prevail. But thus do they want it here."

Corrigan totally opposed the idea of vicars general for individual national groups in each diocese, and was insulted by Abbelen's insinuation that all Americans who spoke English were Irish. Abbelen had suggested that all the Germans attending a German church should be inscribed in that parish. Corrigan held that if this were approved, it should be the practice for all nationalities, so no preference would be shown to any group. All nationalities should be inscribed, including the Irish, who had contributed generously to all other national groups to build their churches and schools.

The Archbishop concluded his rather heated letter by warning the German bishops to remember that the German Catholic population in America was only 1,500,000 persons. There were another 6,000,000 Catholics in the United States, whose total population was 55,000,000 persons. They could not Germanize the entire country! He continued: "But they can render irreparable damage to Holy Mother Church, and the Sacred Congregation will have to give precisely the same rights that they give to the Germans to everyone else."

Propaganda settled down to discuss a possible solution to the problems of providing pastoral care for the Catholic immigrants in April, 1887. The meetings combined the postponed discussion of the 1884 memorial of the St. Louis German clergy, the 1885 memorial of Bishops Gilmour and Moore, the responses to Propaganda's inquiries concerning national parishes, based on the questions of Bishop Flasch, and the letters and memorials recently received as a result of the Abbelen Memorial.

The *relatio* of the Congregation recognized Abbelen's memorial to be nothing more than an elaborated form of the two questions put before Propaganda by Flasch in 1885. According to the replies of the Americans to Flasch's questions, such "quasi-parishes" — established for language groups, distinct and independent of territorial parishes — could exist according to the canon law then applying to the United States. In reality, the legal problems of establishing such missions were nullified by the mission status of the Church in the United States, thus rendering all churches missions and not canonical parishes. Since the United States was composed of various groups and peoples of diverse national origins, who did not always coexist peacefully, and who were distinguished one from another by language and national custom, there was seen a true necessity for the establishment of such national missions.

The final decisions of the April meeting of Propaganda officials took the form of answers to Bishop Flasch's questions: (1) national missions, or quasi-parishes, were to be erected for the salvation of souls; (2) these could be independent of other churches even when in the same territory as another church, and could have the same rights as enjoyed by the territorial missions; (3) the local ordinary could legitimately establish that the children of families belong to the quasi-parish of their parents while living under their parents' roof.[31] There were other questions discussed but never decided upon or published. The most important of these dealt with the questionable necessity of such national parishes once immigration ceased. There was no response to this one question, which is still problematic today.

The Abbelen intervention and subsequent decision concerning national churches in the United States did little to allay the fears of many concerning the growing nationalistic spirit found in a number of immigrant groups in America. The episode had served to unite the members of the American hierarchy against the national rivalries they saw as threatening the unity of the Catholic Church in the United States. Those who were Catholic immigrants to the United States could not be allowed to remain foreigners, but were to be assimilated and Americanized.

For the Roman authorities, and for others interested in the welfare of the Catholic immigrants in the United States, the question of assimilation and Americanization was one of secondary import. For Rome, the salvation of souls as well as the preservation of the

Catholic faith of the immigrant was primary. This concern is reflected in the plans and provisions, approved by the Holy See, of Peter Paul Cahensly, a Catholic merchant from Limburg, and of Giovanni Battista Scalabrini, Bishop of Piacenza. Both men were moved to devote their lives to the aid of Catholic immigrants. Both men were deeply devoted to their Catholic faith, obedient to the Church, and in love with their respective countries. More than any other individuals in the nineteenth century, these two men influenced the formation of the Church's programs instituted in response to the growing Catholic immigration to the Americas.

Immigrant Aid: Peter Paul Cahensly

Simon Peter Paul Cahensly (1838-1923) was the youngest of four children, born in Limburg, on October 28, 1838. His family was involved in the mercantile wholesale grocery business, to which he himself was destined by his father. His education was good, if geared primarily toward his entry into the family business, and brought him throughout Germany, Switzerland, France, England, Belgium, and Holland studying freight and shipping techniques. He inherited the family business at the death of his mother in 1868, and built up a flourishing trade.

In 1861, at the Port of Le Havre, Cahensly began to take interest in the plight of European immigrants. While visiting the various European ports he saw firsthand the conditions of the emigrants and the lack of protection and aid they received during their journey. During the subsequent years, he collected data concerning emigrant conditions and initiated programs to provide aid and protection for the emigrants.

In 1871, the Saint Raphael Society for the Protection of German Catholic Emigrants was founded in Mainz. This attempted to provide material and spiritual assistance to the Catholic emigrants at the ports of departure, on board ship, and at the ports of entry, especially in the United States. Over the years the Society grew, with branches in Italy, Belgium, France, and other European countries, and with an office in New York City, which opened in 1883. Cahensly was elected its first secretary and nominated president of the Society in 1899. He also served as a member of the Prussian House of Delegates from 1885 to 1915, and as a member of the Reichstag from 1898 until 1903.

During these years, Cahensly fought for reforms and emigration laws to aid his Catholic countrymen who were leaving for the New World. His work brought him into conflict with various groups having vested interests in emigration, and with the German government itself. He was not afraid to address his government or the members of the Catholic hierarchy, both in Germany and in the United States, reminding them of the sufferings of their coreligionists and fellow countrymen.

In 1872, the Saint Raphaelsverein addressed a petition to Bismarck, requesting him to aid the German emigrants. The government, however, refused any assistance to those whom it considered traitors to the fatherland. Not content merely to provide aid to the emigrants at the port of departure, the Society addressed memorials to the President of the United States, Ulysses S. Grant, in January, 1873,[32] and to the American hierarchy in March of the same year.[33] Neither the United States government nor the hierarchy replied. These two documents are the first formal attempts made on behalf of the European emigrants.[34]

It was during these early years of the Saint Raphaelsverein that Cahensly began his statements concerning the loss of Catholic immigrants to the Church in the United States — statements and statistics that eventually would lead to the nationalistic explosion and subsequent American panic brought about by the *Lucerne Memorial* of 1891.

In 1881, during the Catholic Congress held in Bonn, Cahensly claimed that one-third of all German Catholics had lost their faith after arriving in America. This was, he claimed, because "they settled in areas where there were no German churches and schools." He suggested that German immigrants go to the midwestern colonies, citing especially those organized by Bishop John Ireland, who would later be his major opponent, and by the German Benedictines, rather than settle in the cities of the East Coast.[35]

Cahensly's dedication to the cause of Catholic emigrant protection was not limited to his fellow countrymen alone. In September, 1882, he visited Italy to attempt the founding of an Italian Saint Raphael Society for Italian Catholic emigrants. He met with Leo XIII and with Cardinal Simeoni, both of whom applauded his efforts and blessed his work, encouraging him to expand on an international level. While in Italy, he contacted various prominent Catholics who promised to assist in the founding of such a society. Nothing came of any of these meetings.

Acting upon his belief that one of the solutions to the emigrants' sufferings was to be found in the United States, and in the assistance that country might afford, both governmental and ecclesiastical, he requested letters of recommendation from Simeoni to the Archbishop of New York and to various influential American Catholics.[36]

In August, 1883, Cahensly visited New York City, where he met with Archbishop Corrigan who, according to Cahensly, showed himself to be very interested in the Society for emigrant protection. Cahensly also met with Winand Wigger, Bishop of Newark, and later the first president of the American branch of the Saint Raphael Society for the Protection of German Immigrants.

Cahensly was amazed by the organization of the various Protestant churches working among the arriving immigrants at the port of New York. The Methodists, for example, passed out little informational booklets to all immigrants, directing them to places and people who would assist them. There were twelve Protestant ministers at Castle Garden, the city's immigrant station, distributing free Bibles and booklets to all immigrants from Germany, England, Norway, and Sweden. The Protestants also had a house at Castle Garden providing free food, lodging, and other forms of assistance. The Catholics had only one old man, "who acts as he pleases," having little effect.[37]

The remainder of Cahensly's eighty-day American excursion was spent traveling west, visiting various cities with large German populations. He was appalled by the supposed losses to the faith, estimating them to be as high as 5,500,000 persons, which he believed resulted from the neglect of the Catholic officials who failed to guide Catholic immigrants to areas where they could receive pastoral care.

Corrigan was the only influential ecclesiastic Cahensly spoke with during his visit who was not of German extraction. Cahensly met with no other leading American Archbishop, and restricted his observations to the German communities and German immigrants. Because of this, Cahensly's views of the United States and Catholic immigrant care in that country were limited and inaccurate. Such inaccuracies, and the conclusions he drew from them, led him into conflict with the American hierarchy, and cast a shadow of suspicion over his work and the work of others in favor of the various European immigrants in America.

Giovanni Battista Scalabrini

Even though Cahensly's first attempts to organize an emigrant protective society in Italy failed, there were others hard at work to provide Church assistance for the growing number of Italians leaving Italy for America. First and foremost among these was the Bishop of Piacenza.

Giovanni Battista Scalabrini, who died in 1905, was born in Fino Mornasco (Como) on July 8, 1839, the youngest of three children. He was ordained a priest for the Diocese of Como in May, 1863. He taught history and Greek at the Seminary of San Abondio in Como until 1867, when he was named the seminary rector, a post he held until 1870, when he was named pastor of San Bartolomeo Church in Como. In 1875, he was named the Bishop of Piacenza. He was an exemplary bishop, celebrated a number of diocesan synods, and frequently visited the parishes throughout his diocese. He instituted the first catechetical congress at Piacenza and the first catechetical magazine in Italy, the *Catholic Catechist*.[38]

On December 18, 1876, Scalabrini embarked upon his first pastoral visitation of the diocese. It was during this visitation, as he mentioned in his 1887 proposed plan for aiding the Italian emigrants, that he became aware of the lack of assistance provided, either by Church or state, for the protection of the emigrants. He observed correctly that besides methods to bring back to the Church those who had lost their faith in the New World, ways of preventing the moral ruin of those going to America were needed.[39]

While Scalabrini was developing his project to aid the emigrants, his first method of assistance was an attempt to prevent emigration. This could be effected, he believed, only by the local pastors employing every possible means to dissuade their parishioners from leaving Italy. In a letter to Cardinal Simeoni, he admitted this was usually impossible because of the impoverished state of many Italians. He wrote, "To rob or to emigrate, this is the terrible dilemma heard spoken of more than once from the mouths of poor artisans and peasants. The local pastors must not allow anyone to leave without a letter of recommendation from him to the clergy of the place in the New World to which he is going to live."[40]

Scalabrini would become the most outspoken Italian ecclesiastic on the subject of aid to the Italians emigrating to America, stressing the obligation of both Church and state to protect their fellow coreligionists and countrymen. Unfortunately, his views on the subject embarrassed and infuriated the anticlerical Italian government, which passed no laws aiding the emigrants between 1876 and 1888.[41] His work also ruffled the sensibilities of the Vatican, ever sensitive of too close a link between the Church and the Italian state, and about the pope's temporal sovereignty, still denied by the Italian government.

The Roman Question, as the problem of Italo-papal relations came to be known, entered into most of the Vatican's relationships with various European governments, and colored some of the pastoral programs developed at this time. Italian emigration was one such example. As Bishop John Lancaster Spalding had warned Propaganda Fide in 1883, unless the Church came to the aid of the Italian immigrants, those ill-disposed toward the Church would hold the Church responsible for their desperate state in America. The Roman officials were very much aware of the existence of those ill-disposed toward the Church, both in Protestant America and in the unified Kingdom of Italy.

The Vatican, the Italian Government, and the Immigrants

The taking of Rome on September 20, 1870 by the troops of the Savoyard government effected the final unification of the Italian states. The last temporal domain to resist unification in the peninsula was the Papal States. The fall of Rome also brought into high relief the Roman Question that had existed since the decree of March 26, 1861 of the Italian Chamber of Deputies, proclaiming Rome to be the capital of the new Kingdom — a rather bold and tactless pronouncement, when one realizes that the one-thousand-year-old Papal States were then still in existence. Pope Pius IX responded to the conquest of the Church's lands in his encyclical *Respicientes ea omnia* of November 1, 1870, in which he excommunicated those who ordered or participated in the usurpation of the States of the Church.

Pius's battle with the new Italian government, his resolute refusal to recognize its sovereignty, his self-imposed imprisonment in the Vatican, and his rejection of the government's plan for some type of settlement in the Law of Guarantees, were based ultimately on his belief that the Church's lands had been illegally seized and, most importantly, that the freedom and security guaranteed by the inherent sovereignty of the head of the Universal Church could not be denied him by a government that existed only by right of violence and conquest.

The *London Times*, in reporting a supposed conversation of Cardinal Antonelli, the Vatican Secretary of State, with a member of the Italian Parliament, reflected the Vatican's lack of trust in the promises of the Italian government. Antonelli is reported to have stated: "I am loath to suspect the good intention of your King or even of his Ministry, but how long are these men likely to remain in office? Who can answer for their successors? Was not the Government the first to promise us protection and was it not the first to invade our territory? . . . [N]either your Sovereign nor his Ministers are able to make us any promise on which we can rely. . . . We had far better wait patiently 'till circumstances allow us to regain possession of what belongs to us, or 'till time shall have arranged matters [otherwise]."[42]

On May 13, 1871, the Italian government manifested in its Laws of Guarantees its desire to reassure the Catholics of the world that the freedom of the pope, the full communication of the Holy See with the diplomatic corps, the hierarchy, and the Catholic faithful, would be respected and preserved. Pius IX solemnly declared this to be unacceptable in his encyclical *Ubi nos* of May 15, 1871. The government's proposal was solely a unilateral one, the pope stated, not taking into account the rights and authority of the pope as a sovereign in his own right, but treating him rather as a subject of the Italian state. If accepted, the pope would be subject to the whim of a changing state, which could, in its subsequent regimes, revoke or radically alter its Laws of Guarantees.[43] The Roman Question was not resolved with the death of Pius IX on February 7, 1878. It was part of the legacy he left to his successors, along with the growing liberalism, secularism, and anticlericalism that challenged the Church in Italy and throughout Europe.

On February 20, 1878, Vincenzo Gioacchino Pecci, Archbishop of Perugia and camerlengo under Pius IX, ascended the papal throne, taking the name Leo XIII. He believed, with the rest of the College of Cardinals, that the Vatican could do little else than continue its campaign to recover the lost temporal power. But he believed there were ways to go about this other than those employed by his volatile predecessor: open war with the recently united Italian state could be avoided while still maintaining one's principles.

This is especially evident in Leo's first encyclical of April 21, 1878, *Inscrutabili Dei Consilio*, in which he stated that a corrupt government is one that rejects the Church and her moral teachings. He emphasized that the rights and freedom of the Holy See must be maintained. The Church would continue to strive that "we may be restored to the condition of things in which the design of God's wisdom had long ago placed the Roman Pontiffs. We are moved to demand this restoration . . . not by any feeling of ambition or desire of supremacy, but by the nature of Our office and by Our sacred promise confirmed by oath; and further, not only because this sovereignty is essential to protect and preserve the full liberty of the supernatural power, but also because . . . when the temporal sovereignty of the apostolic see is in question, the cause of the public good and the well-being of all human society in general are also at stake. We cannot omit, . . . to renew and confirm in every particular by this Our letter those declarations and protests which Pius IX . . . published against the seizure of the civil sovereignty and the infringement of rights belonging to the Catholic Church."[44]

Unflinching in his resolve to uphold the principles of his predecessor in regard to the inherent sovereignty and authority of the Holy See, Leo nevertheless was willing to search for a conciliatory resolution to the Roman Question. He realized the impossibility of regaining the entire domain that had once been papal. But he did hope for a suitable solution that would grant the Holy See "only as much territory as would suffice to ensure its complete freedom. The Holy See must be so endowed as to be freed from the worries of the administration of a large state, which would distract from its spiritual duties."[45]

A few weeks prior to the successful entry into Rome by the Italian forces through the Porta Pia on September 20, 1870, the Italian Cabinet, in a memorandum to the European governments, suggested, among other things, the granting of the Leonine City to the pope, under whose sole authority it would be subject. The project was not pursued, since Pius IX was not overly keen about any Italian government plan dealing with the future of his temporal domain. The plan was dropped, and after the fall of Rome, the Italian government allowed the pope the use of the Leonine City. Leo wanted this situation changed to a legal reality.[46]

However, the rising anticlericalism and secularism of the Italian government and its ministers, combined with the shifting loyalties and illusory political promises made to the Holy See by Germany and Austria-Hungary, led, not to a territorial settlement, but only to a stronger entrenchment of both sides. The Roman Question was not to be resolved until the reign of Pius XI and the establishment of the Vatican City State as a result of the Lateran Treaty of 1929. As will be seen in a later chapter, the question of Italo-papal relations would even affect the pastoral work of the Italian missionary priests working among their conationals in the United States.

That the Vatican desired to aid the Italian immigrants because of a sense of spiritual responsibility was a fact. But the line was drawn very boldly by the Church authorities stressing that the Church's work was to be clearly differentiated from any Italian state effort to aid the Italian emigrants. This differentiation was to be preserved with all vigilance on the part of the Vatican. Scalabrini was himself questioned by the Vatican whose officials were fearful that he might intimate official Church recognition of the Italian state by his emigrant work.

Scalabrini thought the faith of the Italians could not be maintained if stripped of its cultural expressions. Thus, he saw the possibility for joining the forces of the Italian government with those of the Church in order to aid the emigrants more effectively. He expressed this in a letter written to Adriano Zenchini, a consultor for the Congregation for Ceremonies, who, in turn, reported Scalabrini to Simeoni and Jacobini for this seemingly pro-governmental stand. Scalabrini had written Zenchini, ". . . it seems that the help of the secular arm is indispensable, to which a lay committee, or quasi-clerical one, would be able to have recourse more freely and with greater hope of being heard, than would an ecclesiastical committee."[47]

In 1889, Propaganda again was fearful lest Scalabrini compromise the Vatican's principles on Italo-papal relations. The cause of the reprimand was a rumor concerning Scalabrini's brother, Angelo, who was to leave on a South American tour. Rumors had circulated that Scalabrini's brother, a supposed government employee, had received a secret mission from the Bishop of Piacenza to inspect the religious condition of the Italian colonies in relation to the intended aim of the Sacred Congregation.[48]

The accusations were both false, as Scalabrini was quick to point out in a letter to Simeoni, reassuring the Prefect of Propaganda that he worked only to please the pope. He continued, "Is it possible, Eminence, that you believe me to be a child and an imbecile to the point of supposing me capable of sending a layman . . . to report about things that are the duty exclusively of the clergy? I, who am so jealous of the principle of hierarchical authority? I would be worthy of a lunatic asylum if this were true."[49]

Scalabrini sent his projected plan for an institute of missionary priests to Propaganda in response to Simeoni's request of February, 1887. He outlined for Propaganda authorities a short history of Italian emigration to the Americas, and listed the numerous dangers to the faithful abounding in the New World, not least of which were "heresy, unbelief, and above all Freemasonry, which in America is most powerful."[50] These were aggravated by a lack of zealous priests willing to work for the emigrants.

The first provision to be made was the sending of Italian priests who would be without a fixed residence, assigned to search out the Italians scattered throughout America, who would give fifteen- to twenty-day missions and exhort the people to build chapels. These priests would send reports back to the head of the institute. The wandering missionaries would serve as precursors of the stable missionaries who would follow and who would be under the special protection of the Holy See, dispensed from the obligations of permanent residence, either canonical or beneficed. Here was a case for Scalabrini in which the Church's universal canon law could be adapted to the "new conditions of the social world and of the Church." These non-beneficed clergy would be lent by their own respective Italian ordinaries and considered members of the local American diocesan clergy. The Holy See, he continued, should order the Italian bishops not to oppose such vocations, since in actuality they would care for their own diocesan subjects who had gone to America in search of a better life.

The advantages of such a system, according to Scalabrini, would be: (1) to prepare immediately a number of good, zealous priests who would respond to the needs of the Italian emigrants; (2) to shed light, by way of the missionary reports, on how best to meet the needs of the emigrants; (3) to protect the young priests from the dangers of the non-Catholic American society and culture by establishing a mutual fraternity; (4) to prepare the way more effectively for future missionaries.

The Institute would be open to any Italian diocesan priest in good standing with his diocese, who was at least thirty years of age, with at least three years active ministerial service. "It is absolutely necessary," Scalabrini wrote, "that the aspirants be known for their piety, for their good character, irreproachable conduct and for their apostolic zeal for souls." They would be required to stay in the Italian colonies in America only one year, with the option to remain longer. Prior to departure for the missions, the missionaries would spend one month together in retreat, and receive instructions in moral theology relative to the special conditions and needs of the emigrants in America. They would take a vow not to keep any money or gifts offered them, but to render all to their superior, thus "returning to their own diocese in the same condition as they left." This provision would discourage attracting those priests who only sought their own fortunes in America.

The missionaries would direct themselves solely to catechesis, preaching, teaching, and the administration of the sacraments and associated ministerial duties. They would be immediately recalled to Italy if they were discovered doing anything contrary to the wishes of the Holy See. The priests would be entirely dependent upon the American ordinary of the place in which they were to minister, receiving faculties from him alone. The missionaries were to gather every three months in groups of three or six for spiritual exercises, in order to strengthen, advise, and comfort one another. Upon returning to Italy the missionaries would make a full report to their respective Italian bishops.

The work would begin in Italy by sending letters to the Italian bishops who, in turn, would invite members of their clergy to participate in the new institute. Interested priests were to send their requests and letters of recommendation from their respective bishops to the head of the association. To ensure the proper collection and distribution of goods and funds, emigration committees would be established at the principal Italian ports.

To prepare for the work in America, a circular letter would be sent to the American bishops asking them to indicate the needs of the Italian emigrants in their dioceses and the manner in which they might provide for missionary priests to be sent to them. They should assist the work of the institute by gathering offerings, and by founding Italian seminaries in some large American cities for the formation of native Italian clergy who would work only with the Italian community resident in America. Scalabrini saw a vast number of potential priestly vocations in the children of the Italian immigrants. By his estimation, in 1885 alone, 15,642 Italian children had emigrated to America.

The best possible way to protect the emigrants' faith was to direct them to colonies, similar to those established by the Irish and Germans, where the Italians could mutually support one another, since "it would be like living in a part of Italy amongst other Catholics."

Scalabrini did not only work for the founding of an institute of missionary priests. Through his numerous writings and public addresses he attempted to inform public opinion in Italy concerning the emigrants and emigration. His most famous work was published in June, 1887, entitled *Italian Emigration in America: the Observations of Giovanni Battista Scalabrini, Bishop of Piacenza*. In this pamphlet he presented his view of emigration as an inalienable right, since most did not choose to emigrate, but left their native homeland because of necessity.

For Scalabrini, the Italian state had three options in its relationship with the Italian citizen and emigrant: (1) to remove the cause that forced Italians to emigrate, thus providing employment or at least a means of ensuring the Italian a better life by restricting his migration to within the boundaries of his native homeland; (2) the state could give direction to emigration, by guiding the emigrants to colonies established outside Italy, where Italian culture and identity could be preserved; (3) the state could effect laws designed to protect Italian citizens from being forced to leave their country. Man has the right to emigrate but must not be forced to emigrate. Rather, he must be allowed by law to search for his own well-being and that of his family.

Scalabrini believed that emigration, the movement of vast numbers of individuals, if directed, could be an extremely powerful tool.[51] The state should, therefore, guide emigration, not by forcing the poor to flee their homeland, but by assisting them to establish colonies throughout the world. Scalabrini viewed such colonies as the perfect blending of Italian patriotism and the Catholic faith. The prosperity of the Italian emigrants would depend upon the character of their religious life united to their identity as Italians. This communion of religious and patriotic sentiments would provide the Italian emigrants with a motivation far above the purely material desire for gain, and would unite them as one people bound by a common love of God and of their far-off homeland.[52] The Bishop of Piacenza ended his pamphlet with a call for reconciliation between the Holy See and the Kingdom of Italy, so that "Italy might be able to emulate those ancient glories . . . sending forth her distant children upon the il-lumined paths of true civilization and progress."[53]

On July 9, 1887, Scalabrini established a committee at Piacenza for the protection of Italian emigrants, patterned after the German Saint Raphael Society, with the Marchese Giovanni Battista Volpe-Landi as its president. The main purpose of this lay committee was to provide protection for the Italian emigrants at the ports of em-barkation, during the crossing, and at the port of arrival in America. This central committee established local committees in a number of Italian cities. However, those established in the major Italian ports had no productive effects, except in Genoa.

Scalabrini's hopes for a united effort of Church and state in emigrant aid were illusory at best. The Italian government was equally unrealistic about the Italian emigrants, even though its min-isters felt that the state alone understood the needs of the Italians abroad. The government approached the emigrant as if he had a deep-rooted patriotic love for the united Italy. According to the government, the emigrants, as all Italians, were the heirs of the ar-tistic, literary, and cultural heritage of Italy's glorious past. The Italian emigrant was one who longed to work the land, as he had in his far-off homeland.

The Italian government had little understanding of the strength of *campanelismo*, the provincial nature and loyalty of the Italian, whose identity extended no farther than the frontiers of the province or town in which he was born. Most Italian emigrants knew little of the richness of their country's cultural past, since they were usually uneducated, had never traveled to the cultural centers of the United Kingdom of Italy, and had little interest beyond the welfare of their family. Their life was usually spent within the confines of their small town, where they eked out a living as poor farmers. The last thing they wanted to do in America was farm.

The representatives of the Italian government who presented themselves to the Italian emigrants, who had fled their country to the Americas, were usually ex-teachers, students, newspapermen, government employees, and intellectuals who looked down on their poor conationals. Consequently, they were unwelcome in the Italian emigrants' lives. Only the *padroni* and the priest had any lasting effect on the lives of the Italians in America.[54]

The Church's Plan

Propaganda Fide was itself collecting information on Italian emigrants in America from various sources and devising a plan to assist them, as had been decided in the *relatio* dealing with the acts of the Third Plenary Council of Baltimore.[55]

In November, 1887, Propaganda officials discussed a report on Italian emigration.[56] The report gave a description of the hardships endured by the emigrants and a brief historical summary of the beginning of Propaganda's charitable works in favor of the Italian emigrants. In 1883 and 1884, Propaganda wrote to the various bishops in the principal Italian port cities requesting studies of the means with which to aid the Italian emigrants, and instructing the establishment of emigrant committees wherever possible, based on the model of the German Saint Raphael Society.[57] The Archbishops of Naples and Genoa responded that they had established commissions of four laymen and four clerics whose main task was to dissuade Italians from emigrating, and to assist those who did emigrate. The Archbishop of Palermo promised to assist in whatever way possible.[58] None of these reports or committees was worth the effort, since they produced no satisfactory results.

What had become evident from the experiment with these various committees was that in order to help the emigrants, the assistance of the various shipping lines had to be secured so that the conditions aboard ship could be improved and zealous priests could be provided during the crossing. There was also the need to provide information centers at the American ports, staffed by dedicated people who would protect the arriving immigrants.[59] Since the work of so many Protestant ministers and *padroni* in the various

American ports was seen to increase the danger to the faithful, such centers would be indispensable.[60]

Most Italians emigrated to South America, the Vatican report continued, and to the United States. The northern Italians preferred to settle in South American countries because of the availability of arable land at very low prices. There were few priests and the enormous distances between Italian settlements made the founding of parishes nearly impossible.

The condition of the Italians in the United States was much worse, as was reported by the fathers of the Baltimore Council, and according to "authoritative and confidential information contained in Sommario #7" of the Vatican report. The source of this information was the Reverend Agostino Morini, Vicar General of the Servants of Mary (Servites) in North America. His letter related all the familiar accusations against the Italians as faithless to the Church. However, he gave his opinion as to the causes of this alleged infidelity. First, education was neglected in the past in certain parts of Italy, and, second, since the Italians were indolent by nature, they desired to be neither artisans nor farmers. Because of this, the Italians were the only national group without agricultural colonies in the United States.

In spite of Morini's low opinion of his own countrymen, he had an interesting observation concerning language in his postscript. Since the majority of the Italian emigrants coming to the United States were from Genoa and Naples, speaking only their local dialects, it was imperative that Genoese and Neapolitan priests be sent for them. If immigration continued, Morini went on, then the Italian parish would become English-speaking naturally, since the children of the immigrants would learn English. Morini concluded, ". . . it seems to me . . . that one of the great obstacles of the well-being of the Italians here, is the language, that great element of nationality that is connected so strongly to the Faith." He saw little practical sense in teaching the Italian language to the immigrants' children, since Americans spoke English. If Propaganda Fide officials were to send Italian priests to the United States, they must also speak English.[61]

The Propaganda report added that the United States was mainly a Protestant country. There was a scarcity of Italian priests, who, because of the great number of Italian emigrants, were continually busy but were unable to meet the demand of so large a number of people.[62] However, it continued,

> . . . the lack of priests is not so much the complaint as is the absolute sterility of the priestly ministry for the welfare of the Italians: and the gathered information, unfortunately, attests to this.

There were two causes for this sterility of the priestly ministry among the Italians in the United States, according to the Propaganda report. The first was the economic situation of the Italians that prohibited them from contributing generously for the maintenance and upkeep of churches and priests. The grinding poverty of the people likewise rendered their lives callous to the work and preaching of the Church. The report noted, "It is humbling to remember that after the disappearance of the Indian of the United States and the emancipation of the Negroes, it is the Italian emigrants who represent, in such large numbers, the PARIAH of the Great American Republic."

The Italians in New York City were so poor, the report went on, that the Irish allowed them the gratuitous use of the basement of Transfiguration Church for Mass. The report also noted that the Italians were not welcome in the main church. The reason was explained in blunt terms by Corrigan, "Forgive me, Excellency, if I state frankly, that these poor Italians are not extraordinarily clean, so the others [American parishioners] don't want them in the upper church, otherwise they will go elsewhere, and then farewell to the income."[63]

The report also pointed out that the Italians who emigrated to the United States differed from their fellow countrymen who went to South America, in that they were not farmers. Those who had any professional skills generally settled in the far west of the United States. Another difference was that a number of those Italians who went to the United States had already "mortgaged their work to a Protestant labor boss, who pays the expense of the crossing and then controls the lives of his slaves — and these labor bosses are often times fanatical proselytizers."[64]

The second cause of the sterility of priestly ministry was the alleged religious indifference of the Italian emigrant. There was almost total religious ignorance among those in the United States according to the report. Their habits, termed anti-Christian by many in America, as well as the material preoccupations that encumbered them, aided in weakening their already debilitated faith. "The lack of esteem that they [the Italians] show to the Religious, to the priests of their own country, the blasphemies and their lack of contributing to the Church" were commonly cited as proof of the religious apathy of the Italians in America, Propaganda observed.

Another barrier to their faith, according to the report, was the Italians' lack of English, which deprived them of the help of American Catholics. This material deprivation was aggravated by their spiritual deprivation caused by their dispersion throughout the country that made priestly visitation nearly impossible. "The poor Italians remain condemned individuals within the multitude of Americans," since they do not speak English and thereby are isolated from the political and economic life of the country. This linguistic isolation of the Italians in America was heightened by their provincialism, which limited their contacts, even with other Italians, to those of their own district who spoke their dialect. Their provincial isolation prevented the Italians from attending local churches established by Italians of other provinces, or by Americans, neither of whom would welcome one they considered a foreigner. Many of the Italian families, the report observed, were slowly being transformed, and thereby ceased to be Italian, except in name.

The conclusion of the report was that the Italian emigrants were truly in the worst condition of all emigrant groups in the United States, partly because of their own fault, and partly because of their poverty, and the lack of good Italian priests dedicated to the well-being of their countrymen. The documents received by Propaganda pointed to the need for Italian priests to meet the immigrants at the United States ports and to direct them to Italian settlements where there would be priests capable of speaking their language. Such a Catholic presence and organized Catholic activity would be of the greatest importance in the United States, since the activities of the Protestant churches and of Freemasonry were thought to be so intense there.

The various projects already attempted to meet the spiritual and material needs of the Italian emigrants had failed, the report continued. They failed, since their purpose (which was so intimately linked to the united Italy) did not correspond precisely to that of

Propaganda, whose aim was "primarily religious and Catholic." Propaganda stated it could not favor any particular mission supported by an individual nation, since such an association might be detrimental to the universal nature of the work of the Sacred Congregation, which had to be safeguarded so as "not to destroy the sublime universal and Catholic concept of its work with any limited national interests." The only emigrant society then satisfactorily seeking to preserve the faith of the Catholic emigrants was the Saint Raphael Society founded in 1871 at Mainz, whose secretary general was Peter Paul Cahensly. In Propaganda's view, this society alone was able to preserve national culture and nationalistic sentiment without doing harm to the faith and religious practice of the emigrants.

It is here in the report that Scalabrini's plan is proposed and considered as a possible remedy for the sufferings of the Italian emigrants. His pamphlet, *Italian Emigration in America*, published in 1887, was also treated here, pointing out Scalabrini's five major suggestions to aid the emigrants.

First, active committees should be formed in Italian ports to assist the emigrants. Second, an office to coordinate the work would be established, with the aid of the United States and Italian governments. Third, priests should travel with the emigrants in case of any crisis. Fourth, a war against the speculators and *padroni* would be begun, again with the help of the various governments. Fifth, religious assistance would be provided for the emigrants during the crossing.

During the audience of November 14, 1887, Leo XIII approved the following decisions: (1) the erection of Scalabrini's institute in Piacenza was to be encouraged and placed under the care of Propaganda Fide, which was to approve its rule. A house was to be established by Scalabrini, paid for by gifts and offerings from those who were interested in his work; (2) a bishop *in partibus* was to be sent to America to study the needs of the emigrants as well as the discipline of the Italian clergy working in America, and was to submit a report on his findings; (3) a letter was to be sent to the American bishops informing them of the pope's desire to remedy the evils of emigration. The Italian bishops were also to be asked to send pious, zealous priests to Piacenza; (4) a letter was to be sent to Scalabrini praising his ideas and his project; (5) a house was to be established in America as headquarters for the traveling missionaries; (6) the institution of committees in the United States and Italy was to be deferred for the moment; (7) Italian youths from America were to be admitted to the Piacenzan institute to be ordained for the Italian colonies from which they came.[65]

Rome's plan was formulated as a result of the overwhelming testimony from both North and South America, attesting to the sufferings, poverty, and indifference of the Italian emigrants to the institutional Church. This indifference could not be overlooked, or attributed solely to the alleged pastoral apathy or "Irish" prejudice of the American hierarchy. The reports of the prelates bore witness to the reality that most of the Italians who arrived found it impossible to be faithful to the Catholic faith in the predominately non-Catholic United States, so radically different from the predominately Catholic environment of the country from which they came.

The plan formulated and approved by Propaganda was basically that which had been sent by Scalabrini, with certain deletions and alterations, adapted to the practical realities and circumstances of the New World. It also emphasized the right and ability of the Church to provide, exclusively and effectively, for the Italian immigrants without the unnecessary interference or assistance of the Italian government. The Vatican's plan for the Italian immigrants was based upon the Church's desire to preserve their Catholic faith and to work for the salvation of souls. In order to succeed, Italian priests and national parishes would be needed to aid the Italian immigrants in America.

This, however, was not a provision made to nourish any shred of developing nationalism that might exist in the hearts of the Italian emigrants. The use of the language, feasts, ceremonies, prayers, and religious trappings familiar to the Italians would be provided for them in America only as a practical concession. Since they spoke no English, they must be sent priests who spoke their dialects; since they longed for the familiarity and comfort of their villages and its saints, national parishes would be erected so that the ancient Catholic faith of the Italians would provide a familiar welcome to them in a strange world.

According to this plan, the Church alone would provide for the Italian immigrants, so that none of the enemies of the Church might maintain that the abandoned condition of the Italians in America was due to the neglect of the Catholic Church or the Vatican. Scalabrini himself wrote of this in 1889: "It is useless, I repeat, that the formidable problem of Emigration, about which the various governments work and work always in vain, is, according to me, destined by Providence to acquire an immense social prestige for the Holy See, and to become for the Church a source of infinite consolations and of incalculable good. He who knows even a little of the tendencies of our times cannot doubt this. I say this in order that we might well convince ourselves that to undo this problem, as agreed upon, every sacrifice must be seen by us as light."[66]

Rome's concern, then, was not based primarily upon the nationality of the Catholic immigrant who was arriving in America, whether Italian, German, or Irish. Neither was it the primary concern of Rome whether or not these Catholic emigrants were Americanized. The salvation of souls was central to the Universal Church, whose work, as Propaganda's report had stated, so universal in its nature, could not be limited by the interests of any particular nation or group.

The Papal Letter

The primary importance given by the Church to the preservation of the Catholic faith, and not to the preservation of any nationalism or interests of national groups in America, is manifested in the Apostolic Letter of Leo XIII addressed to the American hierarchy, entitled *Quam Aerumnosa*, of December 10, 1888.[67] The basis for Leo's letter was information sent by Scalabrini in response to the Vatican's request for information in 1887.[68]

The letter spoke of the hardships endured by Italian immigrants, their sufferings in America because of their poverty, ignorance of the language, the dealings of the *padroni*, and the threat to the faith by Protestant proselytizing. Aware of all these evils, Leo continued, ". . . we have thought it our duty to render every possible help to them, . . . and to consult in every practical way for the good of their salvation." The primary concern of the pope was the salvation of the souls of these immigrants. However, his concern for the spiritual welfare of the Italians was also motivated, as he said, "because of our love for men sprung from the same soil as ourselves."

Leo attributed the hardships of the Italian immigrants to the lack of priests. To rectify this he approved Scalabrini's plans for clerical and lay institutes to assist the Italians. Leo's preoccupation with and solution to the problem of Italian immigration was to provide zealous Italian priests and religious who would willingly follow their countrymen to the land to which they migrated, working with them for the salvation of their souls by employing their language and customs.[69]

Leo made four proposals in his letter: (1) the children of Italian immigrants should be sent to the Piacenzan college to prepare for priestly ordination, and then sent back to America to work among the Italians; (2) Italian priests working among the Italian immigrants should be under the jurisdiction of the local bishop and guided by experienced parish priests; (3) missionary houses or centers should be established where Italians were numerous, from which a number of missionaries would go out and minister to the Italians; (4) information and suggestions from American bishops about the Italians should be sent to Propaganda.

In this one pronouncement, Leo XIII identified himself as the spiritual father of the poor Italian immigrants who had been forced to flee their homeland because of economic necessity. This spiritual bond and relationship was strengthened and magnified by his declaration that his concern for them went deeper still, since they had "sprung from the same soil as ourselves." This was a brilliant piece of statecraft, recalling the unity of the Italian people with the pope as fellow countrymen and Catholics.

The reactions to the pope's letter in Italy were mixed, as reported by Ella Edes in an article for the *Freeman's Journal*. The Italian Premier, Francesco Crispi, saw Leo XIII and Scalabrini as united in a plot to muster the Italian emigrants into Catholic legions who would be led by and dependent upon the priests. The Minister of the Interior, Agostino DePretis, praised the pope's plan and his concern that the emigrants be provided with "the bread of the body and of the soul in the New World." The newspaper *Italia* predicted the ultimate failure of the Holy See, since it was proceeding without the support and aid of the Italian government.[70]

Despite the grumblings of the Italian government against these ecclesiastical provisions, the Vatican maintained its position to provide for the Catholic immigrants in America primarily because they were Catholics. Allowances were to be made for the use of language, national customs, and preservation of cultures. But the Vatican could not risk identifying its efforts with any one national group or cause. The fact that Leo XIII singled out the Italians for special assistance may have had ties to the entire Roman Question. The fact that the Italians were in the worst condition of all other immigrant groups, however, must be seen as the basic motivating force for the Church's efforts on their behalf. Nonetheless, the coincidence that the Church's apostolic work might embarrass the government of the united Italy could not but have produced some satisfaction for certain Vatican officials.

National rivalries of immigrant groups in America were growing, and the Vatican knew well that its work could not succeed if identified with any particular nationalistic sentiments. Such rivalries and tensions would come to a head in the *Lucerne Memorial* of 1891.

The Lucerne Memorial

Regardless of Rome's desire to forge ahead with its pastoral plan for the Catholic immigrants in America, free from the limited interest of individual national groups, nationalistic sentiments played an increasingly important part in the maintenance of the faith of many Catholic immigrants. In some cases it was very difficult to distinguish the motivating forces for the various religious manifestations of numerous immigrant groups: were they manifestations of religious faith, or national sentiments with religious overtones? By the end of the 1880's, the national sentiments of various immigrant groups in the United States were seen as no longer serving religion, but as dividing the unity of the Catholic Church in America.

Corrigan expressed his fear of such division caused by nationalistic sentiments in a letter written in 1891 in response to questions from Propaganda Fide concerning the feasibility of a special Apostolic Delegate for Polish Catholics in the United States. Corrigan wrote, "I believe that we are dealing with more of a nationalistic sentiment than we are of a true love of Religion. And, if one were to accept the petition of the Poles, one would give the motivation to the other nationalities to do the same: that certainly cannot be allowed, since it would create divisions in America that sooner or later would be able to succeed in damaging the unity of Catholicism."[71]

The tensions between the various national groups, and the growing fear among many American ecclesiastics that these "foreign"

Catholics were adding a dangerous and unwanted alien element to the "American" Church, exploded with the publication of a document in May, 1891, that would come to be known as the *Lucerne Memorial.*

During the days of December 9 and 10, 1890, representatives of the boards of directors of the German and Italian emigrant societies of Saint Raphael, and delegates from the Swiss and nascent French societies, met in Lucerne to discuss and exchange ideas concerning the aid given to Catholic European emigrants. Among the delegates present were Peter Paul Cahensly, who represented the German Saint Raphael Society, and the Marchese Volpe-Landi, representing the Italian Saint Raphael Society. The United States had no representative.

The discussion of the first day's meetings centered on the need for measures to protect the emigrants at the ports of departure, during the voyage, and at the ports of entry in America. The second day's discussions were based upon the draft of a document presented by Volpe-Landi and approved by Scalabrini. The main point of the document was the means of protecting and safeguarding the practice of the faith by the immigrants after arriving and settling in the United States. Some minor changes were suggested in the text during the discussions, but on the whole the document was approved, and Cahensly and Volpe-Landi were named to present the Memorial to the pope as an expression of the thought of the congress.[72]

The following April, Volpe-Landi and Cahensly met in Piacenza to prepare for their audience with the pope. They arrived in Rome on April 6, 1891, and were granted an audience on the sixteenth of that month. On the fourteenth, Volpe-Landi was called back to Piacenza because of illness in his family, leaving Cahensly to present the Memorial to the pope.

The *Lucerne Memorial,* presented by Cahensly to Pope Leo XIII, was dated February, 1891, and stated that over 10,000,000 souls had been lost to the Catholic Church in the United States. It contained eight recommendations as essential to the preservation of the Catholic faith of the immigrants in America. These called for separate churches for each national group, the appointment of priests of the same nationality as their congregation, parochial schools, and catechism classes in which the immigrants' language would be spoken and taught.

The recommendation that would cause a violent eruption of nationalistic antipathies, jealousy, and fears was the seventh:

> It seems very desirable that the Catholics of each nationality, wherever it is deemed possible, have in the episcopacy of the country, where they emigrate, several bishops who are of the same origins. It seems that in this way the organization of the Church would be perfect, for in the assemblies of the bishops, every immigrant race would be represented, and its interests and needs would be protected.[73]

The reaction in the United States, both ecclesiastical and civil, was swift and negative. This was the result partly of the growing national rivalries between the immigrant groups, partly of the inordinately inflammatory reports of the American and European press, and partly of the scare tactics employed by the American ecclesiastics of the so-called "liberal" party, who carefully executed a plan to terrify the American public by feeding the country's paranoia concerning all things foreign.

Two groups of American ecclesiastical leaders had assembled themselves along distinctly drawn battle lines during the preceding years, defending their positions on such questions as Catholic schools and Catholic immigration. The so-called "liberals" were Cardinal James Gibbons of Baltimore, John Lancaster Spalding, Bishop of Peoria, John Keane, Bishop of Richmond, and Denis O'Connell, Rector of the North American College, led by John Ireland, Archbishop of St. Paul. This group favored, among other things, a rapid assimilation of Catholic immigrants to the American way of life.

The "conservative" party was formed by Bernard McQuaid, Bishop of Rochester, a number of German bishops of the midwest, Patrick Ryan, Archbishop of Philadelphia, and Patrick Feehan, Archbishop of Chicago, led by Michael Augustine Corrigan, Archbishop of New York. This group fought against the immediate Americanization of the immigrant Catholics. They believed it necessary to retard the process of Americanization as much as possible, since too rapid Americanization could demoralize the immigrants. They held that the shock of being forced to shed one's language, national customs, and traditions might result in the immigrants' shedding of their Catholic faith as well.

The mutual animosity of these two groups was made vividly manifest in March, 1890, when the archiepiscopal see of Milwaukee fell vacant with the death of Michael Heiss. Ireland and his followers immediately began work to prevent any German appointment, and to secure the post for one of their number, John Lancaster Spalding, whom they presented to the Roman authorities as the favorite of all the American archbishops.[74]

Propaganda, recalling the lesson learned from the Abbelen case, which made manifest the national antipathies at work in America, was wary of such an immediate endorsement by Ireland. Rome had also received condemnatory reports concerning Ireland's views on Catholic education in the United States, and had also been recently warned by Cardinal Camillo Mazzella of the growing power of Ireland's group. The source of Mazzella's information was Michael Augustine Corrigan.[75]

Corrigan had written Mazzella accusing Ireland and his group of "encroaching on the rights of bishops, and assuming to speak for the entire United States, in matters in which they had no rightful authority" by forcing the nomination of Spalding for the vacant see of Milwaukee. Their plan, Corrigan claimed, was "to put Gibbons' friends in every province . . . and so rule the country. In the ultra-Americanism of these [liberal] Prelates, I foresee danger, and sound the alarm." Continuing, he pointed out that "the plan of campaign is to rule Rome and at home." The incident clearly revealed the division of the American hierarchy, and put into relief their sentiments concerning immigration, Americanization, and the Church in America, all brought to the fore by the crisis of the *Lucerne Memorial.*

The *Moniteur de Rome* was the first to publish the *Lucerne Memorial* itself on May 8, 1891. The *New York Herald* was the first to publish an account of the *Memorial* in the United States on May 9. A translation of the *Memorial* was published in the *Herald* on May 28, in an article branding Cahensly the sole author of the document, which was treated as the fruit of the German Catholic machinations in America. Both the "conservative" party of the American hierarchy, led by Corrigan, and the "liberal" party, led by Ireland, reacted against the *Memorial,* and especially against its suggestion of national bishops in America.

Corrigan expressed his sincere dismay over the entire situation in a letter to Simeoni asking for clarification. The cables received from Rome, Corrigan reported, seemed to confirm the rumors that Cahensly had presented his *Memorial* to the pope, claiming the loss of faith of so many millions of immigrants in the United States. This was caused, so the reports went, by the "Irish" bishops who gave rectorates to the "Irish" priests who were ignorant of the respective languages of the various immigrants. Corrigan concluded his letter with a request for instructions from Propaganda.[76]

Ireland, far from being dismayed, since he and O'Connell were behind various bogus cables and press releases from Rome designed to inflame American opinion, put forward an attitude of defiance toward this alleged German intrusion. Ireland wrote Gibbons on May 30, 1891, stating, "We are American bishops, . . . an effort is being made to dethrone us, & to foreignize our country in the name of religion."[77] The Archbishop of St. Paul boldly reassured the American people that the Catholic Church would not take nationality into consideration when deciding the choice of bishops. He told the *New York Herald*, "The conditions for their elevation [to the episcopate] being their fitness, and for their fitness two things will be required: that they be strong in Catholicity and strong in Americanism."[78]

No foreign interference could be tolerated in the "American" Church, according to Ireland and his cohort. He desired to prove to America that the Catholic Church was not a foreign institution, but that it was one in full accord with American principles and freedom, and that the Church and her prelates would assist the United States government in "the struggle to assimilate the desirable and reject the undesirable elements of the immigration which is now pouring into our country."[79]

The Roman authorities, however, had learned enough from their experience of national rivalries in America to realize that the German Catholics in Europe and America were not attempting a coup in the Church in the United States. Simeoni communicated this to Corrigan in June, 1891, stating that the *Memorial* had been given an "exaggerated weightiness" in the United States. He himself had spoken with Cahensly and could openly say to Corrigan that "his projects of an international Episcopate in the United States were of impossible realization." He assured Corrigan that the pope was presently occupied with the problem and would soon speak out on it.[80]

The universally negative response from the American Catholic hierarchy and people produced by the *Lucerne Memorial* was nothing compared with that produced by the second *Memorial* of Cahensly and Volpe-Landi, presented to Propaganda in June, 1891. Cardinal Rampolla, Vatican Secretary of State, had asked Cahensly to supply details in support of his recommendations and observations made in the first *Memorial*. Cahensly and Volpe-Landi accepted full credit for this second *Memorial* as entirely their own work, presented independently of any of the European Saint Raphael Societies.

The second *Memorial* stated that according to reliable statistics, the Catholic population of North America should have been approximately 26,000,000. The actual number, however, according to the second *Memorial*, was hardly higher than 10,000,000. Therefore, they concluded, there had been a loss of approximately 16,000,000 souls in the United States. Cahensly and Volpe-Landi attributed this to a lack of adequate protection given the Catholic immigrants, a lack of priests and national parishes, a lack of Catholic societies to protect the working classes, a lack of immigrant representatives in the United States episcopate, exaggerated demands for money made upon the immigrants by the Church in America, and last but not least, the American public school system.

During the summer of 1891, both Corrigan and Winand Wigger, Bishop of Newark, wrote to Cahensly concerning the *Memorials* attributed to his authorship. They were the two American prelates who had encouraged and supported Cahensly in his work and who assisted him in establishing the New York branch of the Saint Raphaelsverein.

Wigger, as the president of the Society, wrote in conjunction with the board of directors of the German Saint Raphael Society in New York. He claimed the *Memorial* created the impression that the Society was a party to the national differences between the United States clergy and the desires to influence the Holy See in favor of the immigrant clergy. The United States bishops should have been questioned before the issuing of such a document, Wigger continued. The *Memorial* "insults United States pride and is detrimental to the foreign-born."[81]

Corrigan's letter was far less reserved than was that of the Bishop of Newark. He began by stating that the second *Memorial* "is based on a total misconception of the genius of the institution of this country, and . . . if adopted, it would result in incalculable harm to religion." If Cahensly were at all familiar with America, Corrigan

71

went on, he would have known the constant charges against the Catholic Church as a foreign institution. Catholics "are continually obliged to show that we are not opposed to the institution of this country; that we are not subjects of a foreign potentate." Corrigan then explained the impracticality of the *Memorial's* plan, using New York City as an example, in which could be found numerous immigrant groups. If the Archbishop of New York were chosen from one national group to rule such a diocese, should the other national groups not be cared for? The matter had caused great indignation among Catholics and Protestants alike.

Regarding Cahensly's estimate of Catholic losses, Corrigan stated that, according to a recent study, the greatest possible number of Catholic losses in the United States could not exceed 3,500,000 persons.[82] This, he claimed, was due primarily to the frequent intermarriage of Catholics with non-Catholics who, because of a lack of priests, had fallen away from the faith. Corrigan ended by requesting Cahensly to have the courtesy of consulting with the American hierarchy if ever he were to repeat such a project.[83]

Cahensly did not answer Corrigan's letter. Rather, he and Volpe-Landi wrote to Scalabrini, sending a copy of Corrigan's letter, and expressed that they "were mortified that such ideas were attributed to them," and asked Scalabrini to write Corrigan in their name.

"This is a tempest in a teacup. . . .," Scalabrini began in his response to Corrigan, and continued that Cahensly and Volpe-Landi never had any intention of offending the rights of the American episcopate. Their plan simply was to aid the immigrants by providing them with representative bishops in America. But these bishops were not to be foreigners; they would be American citizens, although of foreign birth. Scalabrini then pointed out that this idea was not something new, since it already existed in the United States; there were already German bishops representing the German Catholic immigrants in the midwest.[84]

Corrigan was not calmed by Scalabrini's letter. The offense of which Cahensly and Volpe-Landi were guilty, he wrote, was not simply that they had suggested an international episcopate in America. The fault was the manner in which the American bishops had been insulted and offended by their petition. The authors of the two *Memorials*, ignorant of the United States as they were, should have consulted with the American bishops before approaching the

Holy See. Corrigan continued, referring to Scalabrini's statement on the international nature of the American episcopate, asking why, if the practice of European representatives in the American episcopate already existed, as Scalabrini claimed, was it necessary that the *Memorials* demanded such a provision? Corrigan concluded by warning Scalabrini that

> . . . the question of emigration in America can have no solution by disregarding the American character and way of life. . . . The American people trains towards liberty and national independence, and moves towards Catholicism as it progresses in liberty; however, the idea of national independence is not left outside the door upon entering the church, and the American Episcopate must do its best that this independence not enter into the sphere of religion: it would carry with it the gravest harm: a people so formed by such an education would never resign itself to be subjected to a foreign bishop: and if one were to realize Cahensly's idea, without a doubt it would be the cause of division and dismembering among Catholic Americans: hence . . . fissures and discord to the damage of Catholicism and to the benefit of Protestantism.[85]

Cahensly's ideas concerning the episcopate were untenable, Corrigan contended, since they required the creation of foreign bishops as representatives of foreign nations. The American episcopate, Corrigan continued, required able men, first and foremost, "whether foreigners or Americans and more and more it wants bishops representative of the people entrusted to them, not just one foreign nation." The true concept of a bishop, Corrigan maintained, was that he "have the right over and direction of the entire flock, and that he must provide for all without distinction."[86]

If Cahensly's ideas were implemented, Corrigan went on, there would exist the possibility of double jurisdiction. Corrigan cited examples of various national groups who already had sought such representatives: the French-Canadians living in the United States had demanded their own bishop.[87] More recently the Italians had requested the same representation, especially when Monsignor Gennaro DeConcilio sent his pamphlet on Italian immigration to the Italian bishops and to members of the Sacred College.[88] The Greek immigrants also requested a bishop during the previous year, and the Poles requested that Bishop Koyniewiscki and two Polish priests be named vicars apostolic for the Polish Catholics in the United States.[89]

Corrigan did not approach the *Lucerne Memorial* or the national controversies as threats to defile the "American-ness" of Catholicism in the United States. Unlike Ireland and his Americanizing associates, Corrigan's main concern was the integrity of the Church in America as Catholic in the truest sense of the word, and the need to preserve the Catholic faith of the immigrants in America. The immigrants would be Americanized naturally, Corrigan felt. Because of this, the Church need not worry about that aspect of the immigrants' life in America. For Corrigan, the immigrants in America needed to be strengthened as Catholics in a non-Catholic, often hostile, society.

The difference between the liberal view concerning Americanization and that of the conservatives is clearly seen in the approach of Ireland and Corrigan concerning the qualities of a bishop in the United States. Ireland's concept of a bishop was that he would be strong in Americanism, and willing to assist the American government in the assimilation of the foreign-born, rejecting those who were undesirable or unfit for America. Corrigan's concept, on the other hand, as seen in his August 31, 1891 letter to Scalabrini, placed greater weight on the bishop's capabilities, whether foreign-born or American-born. The primary aspect of a bishop's ministry in America, according to Corrigan, was to provide for all without distinction. For Corrigan, the Catholic in America was first a Catholic, then an American.

On June 26, 1891, Rampolla relayed the pope's decision on the two *Memorials* of Cahensly and Volpe-Landi and on the question of national bishops in America, in a letter to Gibbons. The letter assured the Cardinal Archbishop of Baltimore that the Holy See considered the plans for the national representatives in the American hierarchy as "neither opportune nor necessary. . . ," and that the then present practice employed by the American bishops for the care of the immigrants, such as national parishes, should continue. Gibbons was instructed to calm his brother bishops with "the assurance that the August Head of the Church is not disposed to accept any proposal that would be the reason for disunity."[90] The immigrants of the various nations could be well provided for in national parishes, as already existed in numerous places in the United States.

Gibbons responded in July, thanking the Holy Father for his decision. He related his chance meeting with President Harrison while strolling along the boardwalk of Cape May, New Jersey, on the same day the pope's letter arrived. The President invited Gibbons to his house for a brief visit, during which the Chief Executive brought up the topic of Cahensly's *Memorial.* Gibbons wrote that the President expressed his "profound satisfaction in regard to the protests that I had made against the above-mentioned petition." Gibbons told the Chief Executive of the pope's decision not to accept Cahensly's plans. President Harrison expressed his delight and promised to write personally to the Holy Father, but changed his mind, since "he felt it would involve him in religious matters."[91]

In November, 1891, the American archbishops assembled in St. Louis for their annual meeting, combining it with the celebration in honor of the golden jubilee of Archbishop Kenrick. The Cahensly *Memorial* was discussed and summarily condemned, emphasizing the erroneous statistics on Catholic losses in America and the attempt of foreigners to interfere in American ecclesiastical affairs.

Cahensly had taken the brunt of the American accusations as the author of the two *Memorials* that were seen as part of a German plot to gain power in the Church in the United States. He wrote Simeoni in November, 1891, denying these changes. He alluded to the letter sent to Gibbons the past June, in which Rampolla conveyed the pope's decision, referring only to the German branch of the Saint Raphael Society. Cahensly expressed his dismay, since the Germans were blamed for the *Memorials*, especially because "the Memorial was not written to aid the German emigrants . . . nor the Belgians . . . but was written primarily for the Italians, and for the French Canadians." Cahensly reminded Simeoni that he and the pope had both been sympathetic toward the *Memorial,* having requested Cahensly to broaden his work by greater internationalization. The only scope of his work, Cahensly continued, was "the greater glory of God, the salvation of souls and the honor of the Holy See."[92]

Conclusions

During the years following the Roman meetings preparing the schema for the Third Plenary Council of Baltimore, the Holy See and the American hierarchy became much more aware of the sometimes volatile interrelations of the various Catholic immigrant groups in the United States, as well as of the need to spiritually, and on occasion materially, assist these groups in order that they might maintain their Catholic faith in the country they had chosen as their new home.

The general solutions and principles formulated under the guidance of the Roman authorities, with their emphasis on the maintenance of the faith at the expense of national interests of particular groups or nations, needed testing. In some cases, reformulation was required in order to meet the needs of the first and second generations of Catholic immigrants in the United States.

As a result of the nationalistic controversies of the previous decade, the Holy See, and at least some of the American bishops of the "conservative" faction, had discovered that in order to provide effectively for the spiritual needs of the Catholic immigrants in the United States, the Church could not be party to any national interests, American or otherwise. The primary goal of the Church's plan for the immigrants was the preservation of their Catholic faith, regardless of their nationality. Special arrangements and provisions were to be made for language differences and cultural expressions of the faith. However, the Church was not to align her preaching or apostolic work with any single national group or interest. The Church's duty was not to maintain or serve the national identity of any group — whether American or foreign.

This was reemphasized in 1892, in a circular letter to the bishops of the United States. The letter, dated May 15, from Cardinal Ledóchowski, the newly appointed Prefect of Propaganda, dealt with the nomination of bishops. He wrote that private interests could not be honored or served by the Church, especially in the nominations of bishops. He continued:

> The Holy See has in mind that in the United States the various nations of Europe that are seeking a new home should form one sole nation. This is the only viewpoint that the Holy Congregation [of Propaganda Fide] can approve, having studied the situation, and, therefore, it cannot encourage the maintenance of original national groups in their new home.[93]

Because of this, the Holy See did not deem it necessary to allow the nomination of bishops from the individual national groups. The practical application of the various Roman decisions was to be left to the prudent judgment of the local ordinaries in the United States.

By the 1880's, the majority of European immigrants entered the United States through the port of New York City. By 1892, the entire process of immigrant reception and processing had been turned over to the supervision of the Federal Government, and Ellis Island became the only government reception station for immigrants arriving in the United States. Because of this, the Archbishop of New York found his Archdiocese faced with the almost impossible task of alone helping those who were Catholic. By far those most in need were the Italians.

CHAPTER THREE

Italian Priests in New York City

Growing America

The United States grew rapidly during the last fifty years of the nineteenth century. The expansion of its industries, various technological, mining, and steel-production developments, new inventions, abundant natural resources, improved railroads and transportation systems that opened the entire continent as a prospective marketplace, a growing national pride and identity, and an immense population increase, primarily because of immigration, contributed to the rapid growth of the country.

Along with the developments in industry, science, and technology, and the rapid population increase, there was a growing movement from the countryside to the various cities. In 1860, in towns with over 2,500 inhabitants, there was an approximate total of 6,217,000 city or town residents out of an estimated total United States population of 31,500,000 persons. By 1880, the number of non-rural residents had jumped to 14,130,000 persons out of an estimated total population of 50,260,000 persons. By 1900, the number of non-rural residents had risen to 30,160,000 persons out of approximately 76,090,000 persons.[1]

As America was developing a sense of national identity, the nation also became aware of the ever-increasing number of southern and eastern European immigrants. These "new immigrants" settled primarily in the great industrial centers of the northeast and midwest, accepting work at the lowest wages, and became a thorn in the side of the growing American labor unions. These cheap laborers often were hired by strike breakers and management officials to undercut and break the demands of the striking unionized laborers during the last part of the century.[2]

Labor was not alone in taking a dim view of the new immigrants, nor was the objection to the immigrants of southern and eastern

79

Europe solely an economic one. Various Yankee blue bloods of old New England families were not satisfied with the America they saw before them at the turn of the century. Their thoughts were important, for they influenced the thought and sentiment of many in the country. Many wealthy and powerful men in government and industry took umbrage at the invasion of America by foreign intruders, whose breeding and education allegedly made them inferior to the citizens of American birth.[3]

Many of America's elite had been steeped in the evolutionary theories of Darwin and Spencer, and believed wholeheartedly in the Teutonic origins of America's institutions and in the supremacy of these people in government and learning.[4]

In 1894, the Immigration Restriction League was formed, taking upon itself the task of educating Americans in the danger of wanton admission of illiterate immigrants into the American Republic. Henry Cabot Lodge introduced a bill into Congress in 1896 proposing the restriction of admission into the country to literate immigrants only. Such a restriction, he said, would "bear most heavily upon the Italians, Russians, Poles, Hungarians, Greeks, and Asiatics . . . who are the most alien to the great body of the peoples in the United States."[5]

New York City

An example of this growth and development was New York City. The influx of people into the city as both residents and non-residents grew rapidly during the last quarter of a century. As a result, the city's methods of transportation also grew, linking smaller communities in New York State, New Jersey, and Connecticut with the city.

Along with a growing preoccupation with rapid transit during the 1880's and 1890's, a new class of individuals appeared in the city: the commuter. In an article in *Harper's Weekly*, it was pointed out that the number of daily commuters into Manhattan at the end of the century was greater than the total population of a city equal in size to Cincinnati, Ohio: 100,000 persons came by ferry and bridge from Brooklyn. Another 100,000 persons arrived by ferry from New Jersey, and more than 118,000 arrived daily at Grand Central Station from Westchester County and Connecticut.[6]

The development of public transportation also gave New Yorkers greater access to real estate developments, new housing, parks, and recreational areas. The city was expanding. By 1879, within the first year after the elevated trains were in operation, running the length of Manhattan from the Battery, along Sixth Avenue to Central Park, along Third and Ninth Avenues (and later along Second Avenue), uptown to the Harlem River, over five hundred houses were built north of 50th Street.[7] The blocks beyond Harlem were beginning to fill up with housing projects and row houses. In 1882, there were only a few houses on the corner of Sixth Avenue and 133rd Street, while the rest of the area was open land. By 1898, all the vacant property had been bought and developed.[8] Areas like Harlem, Brooklyn, the Oranges, and Yonkers became fashionable for the wealthy and upper middle class who could afford to leave the city and make their homes in the newer suburbs. However, along with the well-to-do went their tax dollars and their churches, thus leaving areas of the city to devolve into tenement and slum areas, which eventually filled with poor newly-arrived immigrants, abandoned by any real public assistance.

The Archdiocese of New York

The Church in New York was also rapidly changing during this period. During his audience with Pope Pius IX on September 20, 1874, John McCloskey, Archbishop of New York, requested a coadjutor to assist him in the ruling of his vast and growing Archdiocese during his declining years.[9] McCloskey's reason for this request was his poor health and age.

McCloskey was Archbishop of New York for twenty-one years and witnessed the rapid growth of the Catholic Church in that area of the country. The importance of the Church in New York was attested to by the nomination of McCloskey as America's first cardinal; its rapid growth by the completion of Saint Patrick's Cathedral in 1879. Both events received wide and favorable publicity. During McCloskey's rule, the number of Catholic churches, schools, and clergy in the Archdiocese more than doubled. Between 1864 and 1885, sixteen religious communities of men and women arrived in New York. During the same period, with the rise in population in the city, the number of Catholic charitable institutions also grew. In order to deal with the growth of the population and of the Church in New York, McCloskey convoked the Third and Fourth Diocesan

Synods, in 1868 and 1882 respectively, as well as the Second Provincial Synod in 1883.

Michael Augustine Corrigan had been the Bishop of Newark from 1873 until October 1, 1880, when he was named titular Archbishop of Petra and coadjutor with right of succession to the Cardinal Archbishop of New York.

Corrigan had been third on the terna, following Bishops Patrick Lynch of Charleston and John Loughlin of Brooklyn who were deemed *dignissimus* and *dignior*, respectively. He was not strongly favored by the bishops of the province, except by McCloskey. Even though Corrigan was only forty years of age, he was respected throughout the country, at least according to the report of the nomination, being pious, knowledgeable in doctrine, an able administrator, and a skilled linguist. The opposition saw him, however, as "Too Roman" for so important an American see as New York. For Rome, no one in the United States could ever be too Roman, and so, with McCloskey and other prelates supporting him, Corrigan was named.[10] Despite his nomination, Corrigan's authority was limited, and he exercised no greater influence than did any other upper-echelon functionary of the Cardinal in the ecclesiastical bureaucracy of the Archdiocese until 1885, when he succeeded McCloskey as the ordinary.

One of the major tasks facing Corrigan as Archbishop was the care of the Italian immigrants in New York. Various solutions to the practical problems of attending to their spiritual needs had been suggested during the years. The fathers of the Third Baltimore Council had suggested the sending of Italian priests to America who were willing to work with their countrymen. The Italians were the only Catholic immigrants who were not accompanied by their own priests in their travels to America. The solution suggested by Scalabrini, as seen in the plan he submitted to Propaganda for a missionary institute in 1887, and by Leo XIII in his apostolic letter of 1888, was to supply such Italian priests to work with the Italian immigrants. This conviction was strengthened by various petitions and reports sent from America to Propaganda and to various superiors of religious orders.

In New York, however, the problem was not simply a lack of Italian priests. By 1884, Corrigan could report that in New York City there were Italian religious and about twelve Italian diocesan priests who were working among the Italians, in one manner or another. In great part the problem was a lack of "good, zealous and pious priests ready to save souls," who had not come to America for "temporal gain."[11] The need was not simply to supply New York with warm bodies, ordained and possessed of the sacerdotal dignity. New York City and other parts of the country had a number of Italian priests as residents, but they usually had neither the desire nor the ecclesiastical permission to work among the Italians. Many had come to America in order to better their lives, seek their fortune, and then return to Italy. Others came to escape the jurisdiction of their local bishops, religious superiors, or Italian authorities, or to free themselves from the poverty of their villages.

The New World also provided a splendid opportunity for European bishops and religious superiors to rid themselves of not a few troublesome clerics, often providing them with fine letters of recommendation addressed to the unsuspecting bishops in the United States who needed priests, never referring in the slightest way that the arriving Italian clerics might be less than helpful, virtuous, or honest in their dealings with their countrymen. The number of these undesirable Italian priests had risen so high that, in 1886, Propaganda issued instructions to the American bishops prohibiting them from accepting any Italian clerics without the proper *exeat* from their individual bishops, and the express release of Propaganda itself.[12] In 1890, the Congregation of the Council extended this prohibition, requiring an Italian priest desiring to emigrate from Italy to secure a commendatory letter from his ordinary, and a letter of acceptance from the local bishop in the country to which he intended to migrate, along with the approval of the Holy See, prior to emigrating. The local bishop was to be morally certain that such a priest would not desert his mission and that he would be a blessing and not a hindrance to his people in the New World.

Even after Propaganda's restriction, numerous Italian *vagi*, or wandering priests, some of whom had apostatized and even married, presented themselves to various American bishops, without giving the slightest hint of their ecclesiastical irregularities,[13] often assuming false identities, producing forged papers, moving from diocese to diocese as they were discovered, or attempting to escape legal proceedings resulting from infractions of American laws or because of criminal offenses perpetrated in Italy. Unfortunately, because of the ever-growing number of Italian immigrants in the United States and the lack of capable, dedicated Italian priests, many American bishops found themselves forced to accept the ministrations of some of these priests of questionable reputation.[14]

As early as 1883, during the Roman preparatory meetings for the Third Baltimore Council, officials of Propaganda had promised Corrigan good Italian missionaries from the Collegio Brignole-Sale in Genoa "to interest Religious Orders in the welfare of the poor Italians. Then to write to the Propagation of the Faith [in Lyons] to furnish funds to pay said missionaries."[15] However, the preference of Propaganda and of McCloskey himself, at least immediately after the Baltimore Council, was to engage religious orders exclusively to work with the Italian immigrants.[16]

During Corrigan's years as coadjutor he was in no position to exercise any administrative power independently of the Cardinal. McCloskey, regardless of his age and precarious health, continued to rule his Archdiocese through the ministrations of his vicars general, Monsignors Quinn and Preston.[17]

McCloskey was not overly keen to accept Italian priests into his realm, whether religious or secular, nor was he supportive of any plans for the erection of exclusively Italian churches. It was only after the refusal of a number of religious orders to accept the work among the Italians in New York, and Propaganda's inability to supply the necessary religious, that Corrigan was allowed to write to the Brignole-Sale missionary college and to send representatives to Italian dioceses in search of priests.[18] Regardless of Corrigan's petitions and representations in Rome, the number of priests released by their respective ordinaries or superiors was insufficient. Italian bishops were loath to release their good and zealous priests to do missionary work in America,[19] especially since vocations to the priesthood, and priests themselves, were scarce — or at least not plentiful enough to send to the United States.[20]

This paucity of clerical subjects was aggravated by the Italian government's inclusion of seminarians into the ranks of military conscripts. The period of their military service could be shortened by paying between 1,800 and 2,000 francs per student — an enormous expense if a diocese had more than one prospective vocation.[21] Since the government also had suppressed all ecclesiastical benefices, the means of livelihood for many priests was reduced to a subsidy of approximately $3 to $4 per month — hardly enough to pay for living expenses let alone travel expenses to America for missionary work.[22] Money to send missionaries from the various Italian dioceses and religious orders, therefore, came primarily from Propaganda Fide, itself in fiscal straits as a result of the government's financial restrictions imposed on ecclesiastical institutions.[23]

Seminaries and Seminarians

The Fourth Provincial Council of Baltimore of 1840 had spoken of the need for priests, both immigrant and American-born, in order to minister to the then growing number of Irish and German immigrants arriving in the United States. The Council stated:

> At present, the tide of emigration is too copious to prevent our dispensing with the aid of an emigrant clergy. The people and the priest are derived from the same source; but gradually we must find our resources within ourselves, and we shall make timely preparations.[24]

In July, 1888, Corrigan betrayed a similar sentiment when he wrote to Simeoni protesting a proposed new church for the Carmelites in New York and the Order's desire to erect a novitiate in Dublin from which would come Carmelites to work in the United States. Corrigan wrote: "The day will come when the American people will request indigenous Priests. Will it be prudent to always and necessarily have foreigners?"[25]

In the search for priests to work among the Italians in New York City, a provisional supply had been found among those Americans who had studied in Rome at the North American College or at Propaganda. Since these Roman-trained priests proved to be a possible solution to this pastoral paradox, the idea of training men in Italy primarily for the Italian apostolate was not too far-fetched.

After having read newspaper accounts of the appointment of an alumnus of one of the Italian missionary colleges as a vicar apostolic to China in 1887, Corrigan, in exasperation, wrote Domenico Jacobini and asked why America received no missionaries. He suggested the sending of four or five American seminarians to be trained in Italy, if Italy could not provide Italian missionaries for America.[26]

Corrigan pursued his idea, writing in December, 1887, to Geremia Bonomelli, Bishop of Cremona, who was involved in assisting Italian immigrants in other European countries. Bonomelli, answering after the New Year, said that space would be available in his new seminary for the training of young men to go to New York. However, he felt the cost prohibitive; he would require at least $1,000 per year.[27] Corrigan sent Propaganda a copy of Bonomelli's reply, "since the letter might be nearly *indispensable* to us. . . ," and proposed paying for two alumni from New York to study with Bonomelli, if the Congregation would propose to help financially. Propaganda thought it preferable, however, that Corrigan apply to Piacenza,[28] since Scalabrini had developed the plan for the formation of his missionary institute, "which would gather together those priests who wish to dedicate themselves to the evangelization of the emigrants in America, and also those young men in the Italian colonies who show an inclination toward the clerical state."[29]

Scalabrini's plan, sent to Propaganda in February, 1887, also spoke of the establishment of Italo-American seminaries in various American cities, founded and supported by American bishops, exclusively for the Italian apostolate.[30]

Corrigan had heard of Scalabrini's institute and wrote in December, 1887, asking for priests, promising to cover their seminary costs if they would be sent to New York. If this were impossible, Corrigan suggested a plan proposed by the Reverend Marcellino Moroni, a member of Scalabrini's institute, in which Italian theological students would complete their last two years of theological studies in the New York seminary while studying English and the customs of America.[31] Scalabrini's plan, and that of the pope, were exactly the opposite of Corrigan's. They proposed teaching Italian and Latin to the sons of Italian immigrants in America and then sending them to Italy to begin their studies in philosophy and theology.[32]

Scalabrini's seminary plan never came into being, primarily because of the financial and organizational problems experienced by his missionaries in New York. Corrigan found it necessary, therefore, to enlist Italian clerics to work among the Italian immigrants while they were still in the midst of their seminary studies.[33] He also sponsored American students in the preparatory seminary in Genoa,[34] and continued to send his theological students to the North American College in Rome.[35] With the collapse both of the plan for an Italo-American seminary, and of the prospect of sending American seminarians to study at Piacenza for the Archdiocese, Corrigan insisted that the seminarians from New York at least study Italian.

Saint Joseph Seminary, Dunwoodie, the Archdiocesan seminary, opened in 1896. The course of studies included obligatory Italian courses for all students, with an Italian priest teaching the advanced students and giving instructions to those in Holy Orders for hearing confessions in Italian. The instruction continued with readings in Italian during supper in the refectory.[36]

Italian Priests and "Annex Parishes"

Since Italian priests were in short supply in the Archdiocese, and because of the lack of financial support from the Italian communities, a system of mixed or "annexed" parishes was developed in which two or more national groups worshipped in one church, with assistant priests of the respective nationalities ministering to their national groups, usually under the direction of an "Irish" (that is, American-born) rector.

The Italian priests assigned as assistants to such churches, as in Transfiguration, Our Lady of Mount Carmel in Harlem, or Old Saint Patrick's Cathedral, received from their rectors room and board along with approximately $500 annual salary, as well as Mass stipends ($1 per Mass) from the faithful.[37] The needs of the growing Italian community in New York, however, were not so effectively met under this system as had been hoped by the fathers of the Third Plenary Council of Baltimore and by a number of the American clergy.

For the Italians who did attend church, the frustration resulting from their inability to organize and raise sufficient funds to build and support an independent parish was compounded by the embarrassing necessity of worshipping in basement churches and of seeing their priests subjected to the authority of a non-Italian rector. Because of this, nationalistic tensions grew between the ethnic groups sharing such churches. Even tensions between northern and southern Italians developed, stressing the seeming impossibility of establishing independent churches capable of satisfying the spiritual needs of so diverse a group of immigrants.[38] By 1886, Corrigan expressed his opinion that, financially speaking, "It is impossible to erect an Italian national parish in that quarter of the city [lower Manhattan] or in any other section of New York City without the help of the Irish."[39] He added that Emiliano Kirner, rector of the Italian mission of Our Lady of Mount Carmel in Harlem, received no more than $7 per week from the Italian members of his congregation, while the debts of his small chapel were $20 per week, not to mention the expense of the church or maintenance of three exclusively Italian schools. "Because of this, this is the only manner in which one can work: to have an Italian priest, as Vicar, in already extant churches."[40]

By 1887, when Scalabrini's institute was approved, there were in Manhattan seven mixed or "annexed" parishes with Italian members, having either one Italian priest in residence, or at least one American-born, Roman-trained priest who spoke Italian and who was willing and able to respond to the needs of the Italians in his congregation or area.[41] Even with the labors of these priests, little progress had been made, and Corrigan wrote to Scalabrini in October, 1887, that few of the 50,000 Italians in the city frequented church. Of the sixty to seventy Italian priests in the city, only Emiliano Kirner, the Pallotine working in Harlem, had done anything significant for the Italian immigrants. The American Catholics could not financially support all the projects of the various nationalities, since they were themselves building churches and parish schools. Corrigan continued, relating how difficult it was to ask the Americans for funding for the Italian apostolate, especially when the Italians would do little or nothing themselves. Even Kirner, who had done so much, could do nothing without "Irish" help.[42] As a result of the scarcity of good Italian priests, the low attendance by the Italians in church, and the exorbitant land and construction costs both inside and outside the city, the thought of providing independent churches for the Italians — many of whom showed little interest in the church — was temporarily untenable.[43]

Despite these obvious practical problems, the insistence for independent parishes grew stronger as the ineffectiveness of the annex system became more clearly manifest. With Rome's approval of national parishes as a necessary, albeit temporary, means of aiding the Catholic immigrants in America, the approval of Scalabrini's institute, and with the pope's apostolic letter to the American hierarchy requesting complete and generous aid to the Italians, there arose a more public demand for greater efforts on behalf of the Italians, and especially for the founding of national churches for them. There also arose public opposition to such demands, especially among some of the American clergy. Greater efforts on behalf of the Italians were undeniably necessary. The dispute arose, however, over the manner of assisting them, either with national churches, or with a proliferation of annexed churches, with Italian vicars dependent upon American rectors. A consideration of some of the more widely acclaimed published pamphlets and articles of the period will give a clearer view of the pro's and con's of both positions.

Fiat Lux,[44] an anonymous pamphlet published in New York City in August, 1888, was an exposé on the causes of "the deplorable material and religious" state of Italians in America, accompanied by various proposed remedies.

The pamphlet began with certain observations about the Italian immigrants and their clergy in America. Those who came to America, according to the author, were "the dregs of Italy," who continued their bad way of life upon arrival in the United States. They were filled with hatred for the pope, the priests, and the Church, and were ignorant of religion, primarily because of the laxity of the clergy in Italy. Since the Italian priests did not accompany their people to America, the immigrants were without churches, forced to worship in basements. The author continued, "It seems to us that the American bishops and priests and Italian priests especially who have consecrated themselves to their conationals, would have had the right to expect that from the land of the Pope . . . would come, if not Catholics, at least Christians, and at least those who are Christianable [*sic*], but in vain."[45]

Remedies for the Italians' material destitution could be found, the author contended, if the Italian clergy and government joined efforts to educate the Italians, gave the immigrants money before they left Italy, and assisted in their protection and resettlement in America, especially in agricultural colonies. The American government was also urged to begin investigations into the health and morality of the Italians in order to limit the number admitted into the country.

Remedies for the Italians' spiritual needs were to begin by informing the Italian bishops of the spiritual destitution of their people. The hostility between the Church and the Italian state must cease, and the draft laws must be modified to exclude Italian clerics. All efforts by the Church to better the lot of the immigrants were to be subsidized by the Italian government. The Church, in return, was to be a national monument and center of Italian national zeal for those abroad. As the author so poetically described it, "She [the Church] is the indestructible golden ring that weds the Italians here [U.S.A.] to her mother country and conserves nationality, language and culture."[46]

The American hierarchy was to champion the Italian cause by appointing Italian vicars, and by encouraging the American "Irish" to help build Italian churches, or to rent places for divine worship for their brothers and sisters in the faith. Italian priests were to be allowed to collect money throughout the country, and be granted permission to speak any language necessary for the salvation of souls, besides English, which of course would be indispensable. The author concluded by suggesting that groups of roving missionaries be gathered to give missions to small settlements of Italians scattered throughout the country.

The tone of Bernard J. Lynch's article, "The Italians of New York,"[47] was set by his opening question, ". . . where do all these dark-eyed, olive-tinted men and women come from?" Within the previous years, Lynch maintained, Italians had begun to remain in America, investing their savings in real estate. For Lynch, the common trait of all Italians — both northern and southern — was "money getting." The Italians were shrewd, thrifty, and industrious, and replaced the Irish in their tenements in the city. He observed, "More Italian humanity can be packed into the cubic yard than any other kind. . . , the Chinese, perhaps, excepted. . . . Where no man can live, according to scientific theory, the Italian waxed fat according to actual reality."[48]

Lynch observed a distinct lack of what he termed "certain American traits" in the Italian immigrant, such as "spirit," being totally devoid of any sense of respectability, "certainly on the score of personal independence and manliness." Examples of this could be seen in what Lynch termed the lower-class Italian, who was always prepared to beg, whereas an American or Irishman would prefer starvation to such humiliation. Lynch also mentioned that Italians with money in the bank were known to commit their children to public institutions temporarily in order to save money.

The Italians arriving within the boundaries of Transfiguration Church in New York City were the most ignorant of their religion of all the arriving European immigrants, Lynch opined. The northern Italians were fairly well-educated, while some of the southern Italians did have a rudimentary education. But he felt the Italians of the old Neapolitan states were truly ignorant, and not well-educated enough in religion to receive the sacraments. Lynch believed that "if a priest should administer them [the sacraments] they would be invalidly administered for want of knowledge on the part of the recipients."[49]

Religious life as practiced in the immigrants' homes was based on devotions, miraculous pictures, and indulgences, "some peculiar kind of spiritual condition fed on the luxuries of religion without its substantials." He continued, "What good Catholics these people would be if they only had the qualities fitting them to be good Americans."[50] The poor state of Italians, Lynch contended, reflected the negligence of the Italian clergy. The sole remedy for this pitiful situation was to gather good Italian priests for the immigrants into the annex congregations of already extant English-speaking congregations.

Transfiguration Church, in Lynch's estimation, was a successful example of this fine experiment, in which the Italians were provided with all the services of any American church, except a school. Because Italians were unable to support their own church, this was the only practical solution. The weekly revenue from Mass for the Italians at Transfiguration was only $45 collected from nearly 2,000 Italians who attended Mass. (He also added that the center aisle seats in the church cost five cents, while those on the side aisles were free of charge.) Those who came to church, Lynch continued, did not mind worshipping in the basement, since "the Italians as a body are not humiliated by humiliation." Lynch observed that some Italians found Catholicism in America different than that of Italy, since "they have to readjust themselves to a religion lacking many things of a kind that to a half-instructed people makes up pretty much of the whole religious apparatus."[51]

Lynch concluded that in order to save the faith of the Italians, and especially that of their children, schools and good priests must be provided, thus forming an integral part in the necessary annex parish system.

Su lo Stato Religioso degl'Italiani negli Stati Uniti d'America [52] was written in 1888 by Gennaro DeConcilio, rector of Saint Michael Church in Jersey City, New Jersey. He dedicated it to Pope Leo XIII, and sent copies to all the members of the Italian hierarchy as well as to the Sacred College of Cardinals.[53] Provoked by various reports about the Italians in America, especially by that of Bernard Lynch, DeConcilio wrote in order to set the record straight about his fellow countrymen.

The subject of his work was the study of Italians as Catholics in America. He considered statistics concerning Italian immigrants in the United States, investigated the various causes producing the sad state of his conationals, and suggested remedies.

DeConcilio stated that there were forty priests of Italian origin in the United States who were charged with an apostolate to nearly 500,000 Italian immigrants. Even though his statistics were inflated, his point was abundantly clear: the poor religious state of his fellow countrymen in America was the result of the unexpected number of Italian immigrants arriving in the United States and the comparatively low number of Italian clergy among them.

He saw three difficulties that rendered religious assistance to the Italians a formidable task. The first was their lack of knowledge of the English language. The second was their unwillingness to support the Church, since they had never been educated to do so in Italy, as had other Catholics, especially in America. "The poor among them are convinced," he wrote, "that the Church should aid them in their needs instead of their aiding the Church."[54] Since many Italians immigrated temporarily to America, working for the lowest possible wages and indentured to their *padrone*, they had little interest, time, or money to spare for religion. Because of this, DeConcilio continued, the American bishops were saddled with the responsibility to assist these people spiritually and to provide financially for the churches, schools, and charitable institutions sorely needed by the Italians.

DeConcilio observed a common pattern he claimed was unwittingly followed whenever an Italian colony decided to erect an independent national parish. The Italians would express their desire to build a church and decide on the means to secure the needed land and to construct the building. Soon after, the Italians would lose interest, become indifferent to the plan, and refuse to contribute to the project. Naturally, the Italian priest involved became drawn to those who helped him, usually non-Italians, and slowly began to neglect his Italian charges, sometimes even speaking out disparagingly about them. The Italians would then become offended and react negatively to the priest and the project, leading the priest to report to the bishop that the Italians showed no interest whatsoever in the building of an Italian church, the plans for which, eventually, would be abandoned.[55] This was the reason, according to DeConcilio, why many bishops allowed exclusively Italian churches to become mixed congregations.

The third difficulty in providing religious assistance to the Italian immigrants was the separation of the middle-class educated Italians from the lower-class uneducated Italians in the various Italian colonies in America. The middle-class Italians usually attended the American-, or English-speaking, churches. This resulted in a total separation of the intellectual and monied classes of Italians, who possessed influence and some political power, from the lower, poorer, generally uneducated Italian workers. The lower classes were, therefore, deprived of their natural leaders, who would normally champion the causes of the poor or represent them in commerce or government.

DeConcilio saw two important conclusions to be drawn from this. First, the then present system of annexed parishes needed to be abolished.[56] Second, the system by which Italians would worship in church basements actually had the effect of abandoning them, expecting no change whatsoever as being possible in their lives, since they were seen as arriving already totally formed by their native culture and language. The only hope in the annex system, he continued, was directed toward those children of the immigrants born in America, who would one day join the American congregation in the upper church, thus removing the need for churches distinct according to nationality and language. The deeper problem with such a plan was the eventual abandonment of the parents by the children. Once the children become Americanized, divisions would arise in the family, leaving the older family members still foreigners and outsiders of the American culture and society.

DeConcilio felt it imperative that these systems be abolished, since they were neither necessary nor effective. What was needed was a system of independent national churches, and virtuous priests, encouraged and supported by ecclesiastical authority. De-Concilio praised Bishop Wigger of Newark who had allowed the Italians in New Jersey their own churches, and the efforts of Corrigan, who had tried to abolish the mixed system which had been introduced under McCloskey in New York.

In every large city, DeConcilio suggested, central "mother churches" should be erected that would have succursal chapels throughout the city. By this method, the Italians inside as well as outside the limits of the various large cities would be able to avail themselves of the ministrations of the Church. Each city should have one superior who would be familiar with the language and customs of the country, and who could direct the entire Italian apostolate in that area. To ensure good priests, Propaganda should restrict granting faculties to those Italian priests who would labor exclusively among their fellow countrymen.[57]

The Reverend Pacifico N. Capitano, rector of the first Italian church in Cleveland, Ohio, wrote a series of six articles in 1889 dealing with the Church's obligation to assist the Italian immigrants.[58] His articles, for the most part, were somewhat apologetic regarding the religious and material state of his fellow countrymen in the United States. They left Italy, he said, and arrived in America in a state similar to the Irish immigrants, except that they spoke no English.[59] Americans complained that Italy only sent her poor, Capitano continued. Since the wealthy rarely emigrate, this should not have surprised anyone. Yet, despite the outcry in America that only the dregs of Italian society appeared on the American scene, it was these dregs that were readily employed in order to satisfy America's need for a cheap labor force.[60]

Capitano felt the Italians were unjustly prohibited from founding national parishes by their ecclesiastical superiors, who, at the same time, treated the Italians with contempt because they had no churches.[61] That which was needed was a supply of good Italian priests. However, Capitano felt that the conditions of the Piacenzan institute rendered missionaries generally unfit for America. They arrived with no knowledge of English or of American customs, he observed, and lived within the isolated confines of their religious community, subject to the local American bishop as well as to a local religious superior, and returned to Italy after only five years.

The first step in solving the Italian Problem, Capitano concluded, was to help Americanize the Italians and to establish minor seminaries for them in America: "Let the Church raise up American-born children to be the future priesthood of America, thoroughly imbued with the principles of this country."[62]

Humphrey J. Desmond, who wrote *The Neglected Italians: A Memorial to the Italian Hierarchy*,[63] began his article by erroneously approximating the total number of Italians in New York City as 250,000 persons, served by five churches and nineteen priests. From this he calculated a ratio of about one Italian priest per 12,000 Catholic Italians. This was complicated by the number of Italians scattered in small towns who "do not seek the Church and the Church does not seek them."

The religious state of the Italians, in Desmond's view, resulted from this lack of Italian priests. The Italian priest did not usually accompany his people to America, Desmond observed, since "he loves too well the sunny skies of his fair Italy to venture into the missionary field."[64]

Desmond was exasperated by the existence of only twelve Italian churches in the entire country, so low a number being the direct result of the Italians' dislike for supporting the Church. Despite the low number of churches, he noted, there were two dozen Italian newspapers. He observed, "A people who will support a press will support the Church if they are rightly appealed to — if the true missionary comes among them."[65] Since the United States was under the jurisdiction of Propaganda, Desmond believed that Congregation should provide funding and good priests for the neglected Italians, rather than support the efforts of the Church among the Catholic Indians of America, who were, in his opinion, of infinitely less importance than his fellow Italians.[66]

The problem of Catholic education for Italian children was even greater. He continued, ". . . the little American-born Peccis, Rampollas, Parrochis and Bianchis are going en masse to the American public schools, while in Rome, grave diplomats are discussing the permissibility of an evanescent school adjustment far away in an American village called Faribault that concerns the educational welfare of a few dozen children only."[67]

The solution, according to Desmond, was to awaken Rome to the plight of the Italians, send good priests, and support the construction of Catholic schools.

All these pamphlets maintained the absolute necessity for dedicated, zealous Italian priests in America, who would work among their countrymen within the context of a parochial structure, in order to provide education, the sacraments, and spiritual counsel to the Italians. The development of effective parochial structures, and the establishment of these structures in New York, would result from practical necessity and open conflict between Corrigan, members of his clergy, and members of the Italian community in New York City.

The Emergence of Italian National Churches

Leo XIII's approbation of Scalabrini's Institute of Saint Charles Borromeo in November, 1887, appeared, at least to Corrigan, to be the precise solution to the Italian Problem. Upon hearing of the pope's approval, Corrigan wrote the Bishop of Piacenza, delighted and relieved that such an institute had been founded. He also sent his blessing, 1,000 francs, and a request for two missionaries for New York.[68]

Corrigan's hopes seemed well-founded, for in March, 1888, he received promising news from his secretary, the Reverend Charles McDonnell, who was Corrigan's representative to the pope's jubilee celebrations in Rome, and who had been instructed by Corrigan to seek out Italian priests willing to come to New York. McDonnell was Scalabrini's guest while in Piacenza, and reported to Corrigan Scalabrini's desire to establish a house for his priests within the Archdiocese. Such an establishment would serve as a center for the Italian apostolate from which his missionaries could visit parishes and dioceses as they were needed. Scalabrini promised to send two or three Italian priests of his congregation as well as Italian nuns to work in orphanages, nurseries, and schools, and to care for the sick. In fact, Scalabrini promised to take over the entire Italian apostolate within the Archdiocese if Corrigan approved.[69]

With the promise of Italian priests and women religious secured, the next obstacle to the founding of national churches for the Italians was the rather forceful opposition of some of the American rectors in New York City. It was not long before Corrigan felt the strength of their opposition, for by the end of March, 1888, he received a scathing letter from the Reverend Thomas Lynch, rector of Transfiguration Church, condemning Scalabrini's proposed project of a central house for Italian priests. The crux of his objection was the proposed independence of the Italian missionaries from the American rectors within whose parochial boundaries the missionaries would freely work.[70]

Lynch derived little pleasure from the project, and gave five reasons for his disapproval: (1) he felt a central missionary house was unnecessary, since the rectors who would employ Italian priests could accommodate them, as seen in existing churches and rectories; (2) the close presence of Italian priests to their work was imperative, since sick calls for them were at irregular hours. Lynch recalled the first five years of his rectorate at Transfiguration, when forced to direct many Italians across town to Sullivan Street, in order to find an Italian priest, since he himself spoke no Italian; (3) it was imperative, Lynch maintained, that the Italian assistants remain in constant contact with their rector in order to regulate their work. Such frequent consultation would be impossible if the assistants did not live with the rector. The only work the Italian priests should not be allowed to do would be with children. Such work should be restricted to English-speaking priests under the rector's supervision, "if we wish to make these children grow up with our (proper) notions of supporting the Church, and becoming useful members of congregations wherever they may settle"; (4) besides this restriction, the Italian priests received faculties from Lynch for Italian work in the church basement. He continued, "I treat these priests as brothers and their people as an integral part of my flock, and yet I WOULD OBJECT TO RENTING the basement, and allow their priests to take the offerings for seats, plate and perquisites"; (5) the perquisites and seat offerings in the basement on Sundays somewhat compensated for the falling off of collections in the upper church, Lynch continued, caused by the moving away of many of the Irish to other parts of the city, as the Italians moved in. Lynch mentioned a group of English-speaking Italians in his parish who objected to the "Italian crowd in the basement," and who willingly preferred to pay for seats in the upper church, rather than attend downstairs. Lynch continued his remarks stating, "The Italians are a fifth wheel to this coach. Thus you will please consider that when I came here they were not a wheel, but a load."[71]

Italians gave very little financial support to the church, he stated, especially the Neapolitans who contributed a total of $15 collected at four Masses. Lynch, therefore, expressed his preference for the then present "set-up with the Italian priests," whereby they were assistants to American rectors in mixed or annexed parishes.[72]

The relationship of Italian assistant priests with the rector of Transfiguration was not so idyllic as Lynch suggested in his letter. In March, 1888, two factions of the Italian money collectors of Transfiguration Church, empowered by the Italian colony to collect funds for the construction of an Italian church, wrote to Scalabrini and to the authorities at Propaganda. Both groups manifested a respect for the rector, especially since he had been instrumental in acquiring a priest from *Alta Italia* for the northern Italians.

The first petition, addressed to Scalabrini, requested Italian priests and asked him to intercede with Corrigan that he might allow the founding of an exclusively Italian church, even though, at present, only $5,000 had been collected. They had turned the money over to Corrigan, who deposited it in their name to be invested. They ended by stating, ". . . we are not rich, but with our strength and with the help of the Irish Catholics who are always ready to cooperate generously with holy works, a church for the Italians will soon rise."[73]

The second petition, addressed to Propaganda authorities, was signed by other members of the same committee of collectors, obviously not in full agreement with their confreres, concerning Lynch's administration in regard to the Italians.[74] The author of the petition was Mr. Antonio Casazza. He credited Corrigan as the author of the petition that had resulted in the assignment of the Reverend Marcellino Moroni to Transfiguration for the northern Italian community, mentioning nothing about the part played by Lynch.[75]

Casazza's petition referred to Moroni as being under "very restricted faculties," and strictly dependent upon Lynch, who allowed the Italians the use of the church basement only. Moroni, "by his submission," performed all the religious functions that the Italians had had in Italy. Their major concern, however, was the future of their children, which the committee thought had been rendered rather precarious because of the isolation of the few Italian priests employed in the various churches spread throughout the city, and because of Lynch's illusory promise that Transfiguration would become an exclusively Italian church. According to the petition, Lynch had mentioned this possibility in connection with the rapid departure of numerous Irish members of his congregation. The church could become exclusively Italian, according to Lynch, on two conditions: that the Italians be more generous in their offerings, and that they themselves procure two or three priests from Scalabrini.[76]

Lynch showed his true colors when Moroni, in accord with Scalabrini's plans, proposed a separate house for the Italian priests, and the exclusive use of the basement by the Italians until they could build their own church. Lynch was so fiercely opposed to this that even Corrigan had considered giving a house and chapel to the Piacenzan missionaries within the boundaries of Old Saint Patrick's Cathedral, instead of within those of Transfiguration, as he had originally intended.

The committee felt such a move would be useless, since the majority of Italians in the area of Old Saint Patrick's were Neapolitan, while the Italian priests at Transfiguration were northern Italians.[77] The committee clearly expressed the division within the Italian community between southern and northern Italians: "These days being only under one [united Italian] flag, we are all tied into one bundle, all judged by the same measure by those who make no distinction between one type and another, between those of upper and lower Italy, so very different because of diversity of climate, customs and education."[78]

Moroni also wrote to Scalabrini and to Simeoni in May, 1888, narrating his version of the entire situation at Transfiguration.[79] He reported that he had arrived in New York in October, 1887, and was received by Corrigan "with respect and love." There were two churches for which Corrigan was to provide priests, assigning Moroni to Transfiguration, the poorest and neediest. There were five priests then residing in the parish, two Irish priests, a Father Ansanelli, Lynch, and Moroni himself.

During his first day in the parish, Moroni's position was clearly defined by three events he described in his letter. The first took place in the church, which he had gone to visit after lunch. When Lynch saw him in the church, he came over to him, angrily judged him to be "a $5 priest," or one who did nothing but celebrate Mass, and then only for money. Having judged him thus, Lynch proceeded to order the priest out of the church. The second event dealt with the church funds, which he found to be controlled by the rector alone.

The Italian priests functioned only under the most rigid control of the rector, who took all the offerings and then distributed the stipends to the priests. Moroni surmised from this that Transfiguration was no church for Italians. The third event involved the other Italian assistant, who had been at Transfiguration for seven years. He instructed Moroni to serve as his personal secretary, unofficially, taking down the name, address, house number, and floor of anyone who might come to the rectory in search of him while he was absent from the rectory.

Lynch eventually treated Moroni civilly, having seen him to be respectful and submissive, and told him there had been other Italian priests who had offered to come to Transfiguration. However, Lynch continued, the Archbishop had not responded to them, since Lynch had made it quite clear that any Italian priest who wanted to come to his parish was expected to be a servant.

The Italians of northern Italy, Moroni continued in his letter, had been all but abandoned before he arrived, since most of the Italians in the congregation were Neapolitans. The rector refused to allow the celebration of great feast days, primarily because of the cramped quarters in the basement church. Moroni was, however, allowed to preach, sing vespers, hold "theological conferences," and, with some difficulty, teach Sunday catechism classes.

Lynch had forbidden him to prepare the first communion children or to teach any children who attended public schools. The rector felt that since the Irish were being replaced in the neighborhood by Italians, the offspring of this latter race should be encouraged to attend Catholic schools, and be taught in English, regardless of the fact that they were taught Italian at home and many would undoubtedly return to Italy. Lynch maintained that American children would be taught by educated, English-speaking priests, since Italian priests taught in a decidedly coarse manner. Lynch hired six teachers because of this, and forbade the teaching of Italian in his school.

Moroni claimed that Lynch ignored the Neapolitan majority of his congregation. Whenever they entered the upper church, where they were content to stand, they were always scorned, and the ushers usually abused them verbally.

In America one was expected to pay in order to enter or to sit in church, Moroni wrote, as well as contribute during the Mass itself.

These practices, Moroni observed, were both unfamiliar and infuriating to the majority of Italian immigrants. Regardless of these collections, the weekly income of the church was low. Lynch was unable to accept the radical changes then occurring in his congregation, and he resented the fact that the one-time Italian minority was quickly becoming the majority. Since these newcomers were settling in America, they would be treated like Americans, and must act as Americans, so Lynch decided. They would receive precious few concessions, while strict dependence of their Italian priests upon the American rectors would be fiercely insisted upon and enforced.

Lynch could not accept Scalabrini's plan for independent missionaries. Neither could he accept Corrigan's support of the plan, nor even of the requests of his own assistant Moroni, since Lynch demanded the Italian priests within his parish remain in his house, so as not to evade his jurisdiction and authority.[80] Lynch also made it quite clear, as Moroni pointed out, that the Irish would oppose any plan for Italian independence.

It had been thought practical to purchase a vacant Protestant church within the boundaries of Transfiguration, recently put up for sale. Corrigan, however, objected to the price of $70,000 as too high. He believed the rector of Old Saint Patrick's, Father John F. Kearney, who mentioned his intention of giving a chapel and a house to the Italians within his parish. Since the Italians in Kearney's jurisdiction were mainly southerners, the northern Italians of Transfiguration complained to Moroni, who withdrew from any discussion concerning the possible founding of an exclusively Italian church.

Moroni soon discovered the true reason for Corrigan's objections and cautious actions in regard to the purchase of the vacant Protestant church, and the founding of an Italian church. Ansanelli, the other Italian assistant at Transfiguration, had been told that the various rectors of New York were opposed to the coming of the Piacenzan priests. This was confirmed by a northern Italian priest, then residing at Old Saint Patrick's, who related various plans devised by some of these rectors to place obstacles in the way of any possible progress made by the arriving Italian missionaries in league with Corrigan.

The rectors were all too aware of the history of churches opened originally for Italians, but which eventually served the Americans because of the lack of Italian financial support. The result was the creation of new parishes within the territory of already extant churches, and the siphoning off of funds necessary for the maintenance of the American churches. Because of this, various city rectors were far from delighted by the presence and promise of future arrivals of Italian priests who would be independent of the rectors' territorial jurisdiction and free to collect money they considered rightfully belonging to their territorial churches.

As a result of the total lack of exclusively Italian churches in New York City, Moroni continued, many immigrants left the Church and attended various Protestant Italian missions. There was an Episcopal church within the confines of Old Saint Patrick's Cathedral, with eighty-nine Neapolitan children attending catechism class taught in Italian.[81] Likewise, the Italian Evangelical church had relatively good attendance in their infant asylum, which was exclusively for Italians. Moroni stated, "If I wanted to open a Catholic infant asylum, I would not be allowed to."

The priest concluded that the greatest need was for good, stable Italian priests. If Rome were to support the plans mentioned for independent missionaries and churches, they might possibly succeed. However, Moroni felt the opposition to be too strong and that "if he [Corrigan] encounters obstacles made by the Pastors, even he can do little."

Regardless of the intention of Corrigan to establish a national church for the Italians, the effectiveness and efficiency of many Italian priests was definitely marred by rivalries, ethnic jealousies, political differences, legal squabbles, and cultural clashes among the northern and southern Italians themselves, as well as with the American or "Irish" clergy, who formed the majority of New York's priests.

"Irish" and Italian Clergy in New York City

European immigration to the United States in the first half of the nineteenth century had been dominated by the arrival of great numbers of Catholic Irish and Germans. They arrived and settled in various rural and urban areas of the country, developed and prospered economically, socially, and politically as their numbers grew and as they adapted to their newly adopted country. The Irish and German immigrants also exerted an increasingly prominent influence upon the ecclesiastical life of the Catholics in America. By

1884, there were twenty Irish-born bishops in the United States. Out of a total of seventy-two bishops, only twenty-five had been born in the United States. The Germans had the highest Catholic percentage of the population at the time of the Third Plenary Council of Baltimore, but had only eight German-born bishops in the American hierarchy.

Since there was always a lack of clergy in the United States during these years, the bishops actively sought out clerical assistance from Europe to supplement the clergy who had arrived with their migrating conationals. It was, therefore, quite natural that the predominately Irish hierarchy would attract Irish priests to their American dioceses. Having no language problem in their new home, both the Irish clergy and laity became closely aligned with the American-born Catholics. As the number of non-English speaking immigrants grew, some of the Irish and American-born Catholics became more closely united, exercising a wariness toward their foreign-born coreligionists, both clerical and lay.[82]

The Italian priests who arrived in America during the beginning of the period of Italian mass migration did not always find themselves welcomed or trusted by the American clergy of Irish descent. The first strike against the arriving Italian cleric was that of being "foreign." The second, that of arriving with letters of introduction and recommendation from members of the Italian hierarchy and Propaganda. Because of these ecclesiastical credentials, the Italian priests were seen as possible secret agents of the Vatican, a tantalizing idea which was often given sensational emphasis by the American press. The accusation did not appear too far-fetched, especially when examples of the Italian clergy such as Gennaro Straniero and Ulysee Mori visited America. Despite the private nature of their visits, these Vatican functionaries posed as Church dignitaries, announcing their arrivals with a flourish of press notices and letters to bewildered American bishops and clergy. Such self-seeking clerics thrived on the publicity, and did little to allay the fears of their Irish-American coreligionists.[83] The third strike against Italian priests was the anti-papal political allegiance manifested by many of the Italian clergy and laity, to the outrage of other Catholics in America, who identified such sentiments as anti-religious.[84] As one writer of the period wrote, "Nothing more hateful to American Catholics could be named than the 20th of September, which the Italian colony celebrated as the consummation of national glory, the date of Victor Emmanuel's occupation of Rome and the downfall of the temporal power [of the pope]. For every slight cause the Irish would at any moment have attacked the annual procession, eager to drive the Garibaldians off the face of the earth, as in the case of the Orange-men. And as for considering them Catholics and aiding them to keep their faith alive, that is out of the question."[85]

For many Italians in the United States, the celebration of the fall of Rome on the twentieth of September was a national demonstration, an inevitable mixture of their nascent nationalism with a strong nostalgia for home. There were usually numerous Italian speakers ready and willing to hone to a finer edge that shadowy nationalism of the Italian expatriate by means of fiery anti-papal rhetoric, to the abhorrence of many American Catholics. The majority of the Italian clergy in New York City were not anti-papal. However, some still made the mistake of defying the orders of Propaganda by speaking on political subjects from the pulpit, thus infuriating members of their Italian congregations, the American Catholics, the local hierarchy, and Rome, while winning all Italian priests the false reputation of being anti-papal.

Scalabrini was very much aware of the complexity of the entire Roman Question, and wrote to his missionaries in America in 1892, "Continue to use all the talent and strength you have for the religious, moral and civil well-being of our countrymen, and while you try to keep alive their love for the mother country, be careful not to instigate among them anything that can separate them from their new fellow citizens or alienate them in any way from other believers."[86]

In 1895, the twenty-fifth anniversary of the fall of Rome was celebrated, and the Vatican sent a letter to the Apostolic Delegate in the United States, Archbishop Francesco Satolli, instructing him to communicate the Vatican's position on Italo-papal relations to the United States secretary of state and to the American press. The Vatican was very insistent that the world not forget the forcible occupation of the center of Christendom.[87]

Formal protests by various Catholic groups in America were sent to the press and to Rome expressing solidarity with the "August Prisoner of the Vatican."[88] Similarly, circular letters were ordered sent throughout the various American dioceses recalling the fall of

Rome. In New York, Corrigan's letter called all Catholics to "renew their fealty and devotion" to the pope, and "by their prayers seek to hasten the day when he shall be restored to unrestricted and necessary freedom." A triduum of prayer was to be held in all parish churches of the Archdiocese, on September 18th, 19th, and 20th, to implore God's mercy that the pope might be freed.[89]

The seemingly anti-papal attitude of many of the Italians, so popularly acclaimed as noisome to the burgeoning American Catholic spirit, was linked also with the feeling among Americans that Italian priests and missionaries sent to America were particularly unprepared for the task before them, especially in the area of parochial administration. Most arrived with little knowledge of English, and with a picture of America, and especially of New York City, that was sketchy at best. Their education seemed weak, not in theology or philosophy, but in the practical matters of church administration, such as the legal implications of the relationship of the Church and the state in America, and the responsibility of church financing and investment, which the Italian priests were not always willing to oversee.[90]

No matter how strong the anti-Italian sentiments were among some Americans, wrought by real or imagined irritating characteristics of the Italians in America, these alone were not the motivating forces behind the opposition of Italian national churches.[91]

Throughout the United States, there were national churches cropping up for various Catholic immigrant groups — except for the Italians: "not only for the Germans, but also for the French Canadians, Poles, Bohemians and Hungarians, . . . and one must search about with a little lantern for the Italian churches."[92]

These other groups were, for the most part, self-supporting, having arrived in the United States with their own priests, and with some bond between the Church and their homeland. These groups could afford to build and support their own churches, while the majority of the Italians could or would not. Therefore, to build exclusive churches for the Italians inevitably meant financial support from sources other than the Italian community. Most New York rectors were not in favor of losing their stipends and income to immigrants, the vast majority of whom were themselves unable, unwilling, unaccustomed, or uninterested in supporting any such project.

This fear of many of the New York clergy was not unfounded. Saint Anthony of Padua Church was the classic example of a church with Italian priests who worked primarily among the Americans and Irish — those who supported the church — instead of among the Italians for whom they had been allowed to found the church originally. This, combined with a dose of prejudice toward the Italians or any newly arriving immigrant group, oftentimes resulted in harm, both to the immigrants and to the Church itself.

While Italian priests were assistants in various churches in New York, their work was restricted by their rectors to the Italians alone.[93] Stipends for baptisms and weddings were to be turned over to the rectors of the church to which the Italian priest was assigned, or to the rector of the church in whose jurisdiction the Italian priest administered the sacraments, as was common practice in all parishes in New York.[94]

The opposition of so many "Irish" rectors to the erection of independent Italian churches was at least understandable from a practical and financial point of view. With so many of their parishioners moving away from the city, the life of their own parishes was considered jeopardized by the opening of new parishes within the same territory.

Also, the final twenty years of the nineteenth century saw a hitherto unprecedented rate of building in the Archdiocese of New York. The Third Plenary Council of Baltimore had decreed that each parish must build a school and each diocese a seminary.[95] By 1891, there was an Archdiocesan debt of $20,000,000. The new seminary at Dunwoodie, mandated by Baltimore III, was estimated to cost another $3,000,000.[96] Between 1884 and 1890, forty-five new Catholic schools opened within the Archdiocese, making a total of 177 elementary schools with 47,840 students, and forty high schools with 3,521 students. By 1900, there were 249 Catholic schools.[97] In the Archdiocese, Catholic children attended parochial schools free of charge, thus providing the individual parishes with the total bill for the construction, maintenance, teachers' salaries, and cost of educational materials.[98] Besides the construction and maintenance costs for the numerous schools throughout the Archdiocese, there were those for new churches, parish buildings, convents, and charitable institutions that were established, the bulk of which was to be paid by the generosity of the then extant territorial churches.

The Archdiocesan triennial financial report, covering the years 1889, 1890, and 1891, revealed the debts for such ecclesiastical construction projects in those years alone to have totaled $1,889,598.35. There were twenty-eight existing parishes that had incurred debts for the purchase of land and construction. Six new churches had been built within New York City, of which three were Italian; nine other churches were built outside the city.[99] These debts alone might have seemed a sensible enough justification to oppose any plan for the providing of Italian churches. This was precisely the justification required by some of the New York rectors to oppose Corrigan's plan, and to favor one promoting a more rapid Americanization of the Italians within already extant churches.[100]

Regardless of this, Corrigan wrote to Scalabrini by mid-May, 1888, stating his desire to establish a national church for the Italians in New York City, "where they will be truly independent. This is my firm will." He continued that he must act prudently in order to secure the necessary financial means. There were very many obstacles, but Corrigan promised he would not rest until the project was completed.[101] Bolstered by Scalabrini's offer to take control of the apostolate, and by Propaganda's decision of April, 1887, concerning the erection of independent national churches, Corrigan pursued his plan to establish an independent national church for the Italians, to be staffed by the Piacenzan missionaries.

Corrigan also offered positions and independent Italian missions to the Carmelites[102] as well as to the Jesuits,[103] following his decision to establish independent churches for the Italians. The Archbishop had decided to petition the various religious orders already working within the Archdiocese, in order to supply more priests to work among the Italians. In December, 1888, Corrigan wrote to the Jesuit superior general: "It has occurred to me that the Religious Orders, already established here, might well depute one or two members, each, to supplement the work of the Secular Clergy."[104]

Even with Corrigan's approval and active support, the project of founding and maintaining independent Italian churches was not secure. Such an ambitious design would require the support of the Italian immigrants themselves as well as a battery of dedicated Italian ecclesiastics and religious — commodities that would at times be in very short supply.

CHAPTER FOUR

Churches for the Italians in New York City

Edward McSweeney, the Commissioner of Immigration at the Port of New York, informed Archbishop Corrigan that approximately 705,000 Italians had entered the United States by way of New York during the years 1889 and 1900, of which 682,000 had given New York City as their final destination.[1] This was an obviously inflated estimate that did not reflect the actual number of Italians resident within the confines of the city, since it disregarded the appreciable factors of the numbers of Italians returning to Italy, those reentering the United States, and those settling elsewhere in the country after landing in New York City. However, it did reveal that for most of the Italians immigrating to the United States, whether contracted by *padroni* or not, New York City was synonymous with America.

Before these thousands of Catholic Italian immigrants, not to mention those additional thousands of other nationalities, the Catholic Church was caught off guard. The practical problem of providing for the spiritual needs of so vast a number of people was an awesome and near impossible task.[2]

Those who remained in New York City congregated in areas of the city where they found family, friends, and familiar dialects and customs recalling their far-off homeland. The Italians settled in various colonies throughout the city, on the Lower East Side of Manhattan, East Harlem, the South Bronx, and in Brooklyn. It was in the midst of these colonies that Italian churches were needed. The northern and southern Italians rarely intermingled, resulting in the rough groupings within the colonies of individuals of the same families, hailing from the same provinces, towns, or villages.[3]

The earliest of the "Little Italies" of New York City was formed in the Lower East Side of Manhattan in the fourteenth city ward. Its east-west boundary was from South 5th Avenue to the Bowery, a total of six city blocks, and its north-south boundary from Bleecker Street to Broome Street, a total of ten city blocks. The center of the colony was Mulberry Street, its inhabitants originally attending Old Saint Patrick's Cathedral. By 1896, there were 15,000 persons living within its confines.[4]

The densely populated slum housing of the Lower East Side was inhabited primarily by relatively young people, usually immigrants.[5] Despite the crowded quarters, its mortality rate was lower than areas of other large cities, such as the inner wards of Newark, downtown St. Louis, New Orleans, and the nineteenth ward of Chicago.[6] The area had been dominated originally by the Irish.[7] However, as the Italians moved into the neighborhood in increasing numbers, the Irish fled. One of the worst tenements in this area was the Mott Street Barracks, which was ultimately condemned by the city. In 1888, the infant mortality rate among the Italians in the Barracks was estimated at 325 per 1,000 children, or approximately one-third of all Italian infants died in that year. Between 1884 and 1888, in ninety-four of those apartments, 959 babies died, which was a death rate of 62.9%, compared to the general death rate for the city of 24.63%.[8]

A southeastern extension of this colony revolved around Chatham Square, Catherine and Monroe Streets, reaching into the fourth, sixth, and seventh wards. This area was composed primarily of immigrants from eastern Sicily and Basilicata. There were two notorious tenement areas in this portion of the Italian colony. The first, on Cherry Street in the fourth city ward, was known as Gotham Court. This was another tenement barracks, with a mixture of Irish and Italians forming the majority of the inhabitants. Jacob Riis, the great social reformer of the last century, described it as follows: "A double row of five-story tenements, back to back, under a common roof, extending back from the street two hundred and thirty-four feet, with barred openings in the dividing wall, so that the tenants may see but cannot get at each other from the stairs, make the 'court.' Alleys, one wider by a couple of feet than others, . . . skirt the barracks on either side."[9]

The Italian colony was continually expanding as newcomers arrived. Proof of this foreign growth was evident in Gotham Court. Riis continued, "Gotham Court has been the entering wedge for the

Italian element, who until recently had not attained a foothold in the fourth Ward, but is now trailing across Chatham Street from their stronghold in 'The Bend' in ever increasing numbers, seeking, according to their wont, the lowest level."[10]

Mulberry Bend was located in the "Bloody Sixth" city ward, on Mulberry Street, next to the old Five Points. "The Bend" was that section literally bent between Bayard and Park Streets, and Mulberry and Baxter Streets, forming one large city block. The "Bend District" was the entire area between Broadway and the Bowery, Canal, and Chatham Streets. The one city block forming "The Bend" had the highest crime rate of any comparable area in the city during this period.

The entire area was divided by small, narrow alleyways, sometimes no more than one or two feet wide, usually covered by more than one foot of garbage and refuse, leading to decrepit tenements and stale beer cellars, known as "two-cent restaurants," operated primarily by Italians. The entire section provided a refuge for the various street gangs fleeing the authorities in the intricate maze of alleyways.[11]

The infant mortality rate in "The Bend" was extremely high because of the closeness of the tenements, the overcrowding, and the poor sanitary conditions. On Baxter Street, in 1888, there were 315 children under 5 years of age, of whom 46 died, and 1,918 over 5 years of age, of whom 26 died. On Mulberry Street there were 629 children under 5 years of age, of whom 86 died, and 2,788, aged 5 and above, of whom 44 died within that same year.[12] An article in *Harper's Weekly* described "The Bend" as "the most picturesque, squalid, dilapidated, thoroughly interesting, and lively foreign colony in New York."[13] There was a small, offshoot Italian colony, located six blocks north of Mulberry Street, and it was attended to by Our Lady of Loretto Church and Old Saint Patrick's Cathedral.

The second major colony was situated in the west side of Manhattan, centering on Thompson, Sullivan, and Houston Streets, around Washington Square, and extending to the southern boundaries of Greenwich Village. It was populated primarily by immigrants from Genoa, Lombardy, Tuscany, Piedmont, Venice, and Emilia, having the Franciscan church of Saint Anthony of Padua as their parish on Sullivan Street.[14]

The third colony was in the northeast, or upper east section of

Manhattan, in East Harlem, known then as Italian Harlem. The tenements were originally brick flats or fine brownstone houses converted into multiple-family dwellings, housing between four and ten people in each two-room flat. The sections of the city from 96th Street south, and 125th Street north, from Lexington Avenue to the East River were "the abode of unutterable squalor, filth and human degradation."[15] The southern section of this area was composed mainly of Sicilians from Cinisi, while the area north of 125th Street was the territory of those Italians from Piedmont, Emilia, Lombardy, and Friuli-Venezia Giulia.[16] Riis commented on the Italians' attempts to reproduce in New York the life they had known in Italy which, when transported to America, was fruitless and destructive. He wrote, "The process can be observed in the Italian tenements in Harlem, which, since their occupation by these people, have been gradually sinking to the slum level."[17]

Because of the cultural diversity among the Italian colonies within the city, the establishment of churches for each group was a formidable task. Since the majority of the national Italian churches eventually were administered by the various religious orders working within the city, the remainder of this chapter will briefly study the development of such churches, with special emphasis on those churches in Manhattan in which the majority of the Italians within the jurisdiction of the Archdiocese of New York settled, at least temporarily, during the years of Corrigan's administration (1885-1902).

The churches will be studied in chronological order according to the date of the establishment of the respective religious order or society in New York specifically for work among the Italians. Annex parishes, which later became national Italian churches in the care of religious orders, such as Transfiguration Church, will be placed within the chronological schema from the time that the respective religious community undertook the administration of the church as an exclusively Italian establishment, and not in the chronological order according to the establishment of the parish per se.

Saint Anthony of Padua, Sullivan Street, Eighth City Ward

The Franciscans were the first to attend to the Italian immigrants in New York City, even though when their work first began, the Italian population was very small. The first group of Italians to arrive in New York City were political exiles, taking refuge after the

112

collapse of the Roman Republic. A large number of these early Italian immigrants settled in West Greenwich Village, which gave easy access to the garment district, to light manufacturing and stevedoring jobs on the west side wharfs, and to construction work in Greenwich Village.[18]

The first attempt to organize an Italian parish in this area of the city was in 1859, when the Reverend A. Sanguinetti leased a former French church on Canal Street, previously used by the Society of Saint Vincent de Paul, and renamed it the Church of Saint Anthony of Padua, in accord with the wishes of Archbishop John Hughes. However, because of a lack of financial support from the Italians, partially as a result of the fact that the chapel was not near the Italian colony, the mission closed after only a few months. The church was listed as "Italian" in *Sadlier's Catholic Almanac* in 1860, but was in reality a mixed congregation.[19]

The Church of Saint Anthony was reorganized in 1866, under the direction of the Reverend Leo Pacillo, a Neapolitan, and a member of the Allegheny community of Franciscans, who purchased a former Methodist church on Sullivan Street. Financial instability again threatened closure and Archbishop McCloskey was forced to draw parish boundaries to include nationalities other than Italian, thus making Saint Anthony's a mixed congregation, open to all Italians in the city while acting as a parish for any Catholic residing within its territorial boundaries.[20] The Order of Saint Francis was the only congregation involved in Italian work in New York City between 1866 and 1883.

A new church of Saint Anthony was dedicated by Archbishop Corrigan on June 10, 1888, built on an empty lot adjacent to the former Methodist church that had served as the parish church since 1866. A new rectory was built on Thompson Street, along with the new church on Sullivan Street, by the Very Reverend Anacletus De-Angelis, the fifth rector of Saint Anthony's, who held that position from 1880 until 1892.[21]

In an article describing the Church's work among the Italians in New York City, published in 1889, Monsignor Thomas Preston, the vicar general of the Archdiocese, gave a summary of the work of the Franciscans during the twenty-two years they had been at Saint Anthony's.[22] He wrote, "This church has been devoted to the interest of the Italians, who are the chief care of the Franciscan Fathers."

Religious instructions were given in Italian during the High Mass and at vespers. The parochial statistics were given for the period of 1866 until 1889, showing the number of baptisms to have been 2,054, weddings, 5,202, and confirmations, 3,717. Preston approximated the attendance at the church to be 5,000 Italians, with 700 children attending the parochial school.

The two-page article spoke of six churches then actively working with the Italians, of which Saint Anthony's, the oldest among them, received the shortest reference — one paragraph — and the least detail. The reason for this silence in a quasi-official report may have been rooted in the dissatisfaction felt by the Archdiocesan officials toward the Franciscans, whose work they felt to be inefficient and ineffective among the Italians of the city.

This official displeasure, at least in regard to their Italian work, was one of the factors that led Cardinal McCloskey to instruct Corrigan to petition the Salesians for Italian priests in 1883. In a letter to the coadjutor Archbishop, the Reverend John Farley, McCloskey's secretary, revealed the Cardinal's feelings: "Something more must be done for these poor unfortunate people [the Italians]: the children are being swallowed up by heretics everyday — and the Franciscans are utterly inefficient. The zeal of the young order of the Salesians is just the thing for the occasion."[23]

The principal reason for their purported ineffectiveness was that over the years the Franciscans of Saint Anthony's had found the "Irish" constituents of their congregation much more responsive to their ministrations than were the Italians.[24] Corrigan reported this to Propaganda in 1885 when he wrote, "Even though the Frati have the Church of St. Anthony for the Italians, and even though the Italians go there for Baptisms and Marriages, it is otherwise Italian only in name, seeing that at least three-fourths of the congregation is Irish."[25]

The work of the Franciscans among the Italians was further hindered, according to a report issued in 1897, by the growing number and influence of Irish Franciscans, and the resulting nationalistic tensions within the Franciscan Custody itself.[26] This began almost from the time of the founding of the friary at Saint Anthony's, when one of the newly arrived Italian Franciscans, Pamfilo da Magliano, began associating with Irish priests of the city. He spoke no English, and was unsuccessful in attracting vocations from the children of Italian immigrants, and so began to accept postulants of Irish descent.

As the number of Irish Franciscans grew, slowly outstripping the number of Italian friars, so too did the animosity between the Irish and Italian friars, thus undermining the unity of the Custody and causing many of the friars to transfer to other houses. The authority of the Custody was finally wrested from the Italian friars with the election of an Irishman as *custos regiminis*. The report concluded that the only solution to the nationalistic tensions within the Custody would be the establishment of two independent Custodies — one Irish, and the other Italian.

By 1885, Corrigan wrote to Propaganda officials to report that only one of the Franciscans of Saint Anthony's took any interest in the Italian immigrants.[27] The condition of both Franciscan houses in New York City was such that in 1886 Corrigan wrote the Franciscan Visitator General, requesting a tightening up of discipline.[28]

The Italian community itself had little faith in their Franciscan spiritual leaders, since they could see apostate Franciscans nearby who had opened Protestant missions for the Italians, while those who remained at Saint Anthony's reportedly harassed the people for money.[29]

The key to the possible success of the Italian apostolate in New York was the united action of the various religious orders, diocesan priests and authorities, as well as a pooling of available resources. However, such unity was very much wanting.

This was true, not only in New York City, but elsewhere in the country as well. Ethnic rivalries, jealousy, and distorted competitiveness between diocesan and religious clergy proved destructive.[30] Religious often used their superiors and the Sacred Congregation for Religious in Rome as a type of buffer between themselves and the local ordinaries. It was natural, therefore, that animosity could exist between the various orders and the members of the episcopate, with tensions and bitterness developing between the regular and the diocesan clergy.[31]

This is precisely what happened in New York in the case of the Franciscans involved in Italian work. Since they were the first religious to work among the Italians, they understandably felt themselves to be in exclusive possession of that apostolate.[32]

One example of this concerned money collected by the Franciscans from the Italian congregation then gathering in the basement of Transfiguration Church. The Franciscans had deposited money in a savings bank, refusing to turn it over to the rector of the church, the Reverend Thomas Lynch, in accord with diocesan practice. Lynch demanded the money, complaining to the vicar general that there was over $5,000 from collections, seat fees, money from various missions given for the Italians, and all the stipends from Italian baptisms and weddings, performed solely by the Franciscans of Sullivan Street.[33]

Another instance of such divisions among the clergy in New York working among the Italians was the animosity that developed between the Franciscans and the Piacenzan Missionaries. The origins of this tension were to be found in Boston's Italian colony in the city's North End, at the Italian Church of Saint Leonard, dedicated on February 23, 1876, and administered by the Franciscans.[34]

The church was frequented by a mixed congregation of Irish and Italians. In 1884, there was a movement among some of the members of the Italian colony, dissatisfied with Saint Leonard's, to form an exclusively Italian church, independent of the Franciscans. The cause of the dissatisfaction was the Franciscans' alleged misuse of parish funds. According to one report, some of the Italians of Saint Leonard had been refused absolution, and even the last sacraments, by the Franciscans, because the Italians had not paid their church tax. The Franciscans, the report continued, insulted the Italians from the altar in both English and Italian during the Masses. The Italians were scandalized further by the Boston Franciscans because of the apostasy of three priests over the previous few years, each of whom had taken up special collections in the church immediately prior to their flight from the premises, when they left both Church and order.[35] This proved to be too much for some members of the Italian community. A splinter group was formed, and broke from Saint Leonard's. They called themselves the San Marco Society and purchased a former Protestant meeting house, known as Fr. Taylor's Seaman's Bethel, located in North Square — one block away from, but still in full view of, Saint Leonard's Church! In 1885, the society petitioned Archbishop Williams to dedicate their new church. Williams, who supported the Franciscans, saw the society as a group of malcontents and rebels against legitimate ecclesiastical authority. He decided to allow the North Square building to be used as a church only if the society would transfer the property title to him as the ordinary, in accord with Church law.

To this they agreed, with one stipulation: "that the priest [assigned to their church] not be a Franciscan Father."[36] The condition was refused by the Archbishop, and the title remained in the group's possession, yet the society did not abandon their new church. They conducted their own religious services, gathering for prayer, the rosary, scripture readings, and exhortations, all conducted by their lay leaders.[37] Petitions were sent to Rome by the society requesting financial assistance and intervention with Williams on their behalf.[38]

To end the schism, Bishop Scalabrini was asked to send one of his priests to attempt a reconciliation between the society and the Archbishop of Boston. The Reverend Francesco Zaboglio was sent in the late fall of 1888, and, after opening a temporary chapel and negotiating with the society and the Archbishop, was allowed to open the society's chapel for public worship, as Sacred Heart Church.[39] The Franciscans were not pleased.

Shortly after the beginning of 1889, reports and complaints against the Scalabrini missionaries in Boston and in New York began to appear at Propaganda, accusing them of participating in twentieth of September ceremonies in Boston, and in an unveiling ceremony of a statue of Garibaldi in New York. The authors of these accusations were the Franciscan superiors of the Boston and New York houses.[40] The accusations were proven false by various testimonies stating that the priest involved in Boston was attending a parish picnic, and had walked in procession between an American flag and the standard of the San Marco Society, and not between the American and Italian flags as alleged.[41] The charges made against the New York missionary were also proven false, since the statue of Garibaldi was unveiled in New York on June 2, 1888, and not on July 23, 1889, as alleged. The Piacenzans could not have taken part in that ceremony, since they arrived in the United States on July 22, 1888.[42]

The accusations were seen by Corrigan to be more a vendetta than an attempt at uncovering the truth.[43] Scalabrini called the accusations "pharisaism," and nothing more than vindictive attempts on the part of the Franciscans to destroy the good done by his missionaries.[44] The truth of this was demonstrated by the Franciscan superior who wrote to the Reverend Bonafacio da Verona in 1889,

117

sending four letters condemning the Scalabrini missionaries and the Archbishop of Boston for their actions in regard to the North Square church. He wrote, ". . . we will show that we are not PUNY, . . . and that in Italy there is not only the Bishop of Piacenza."[45]

The work of the Franciscans of Saint Anthony of Padua Church among the Italians in New York, therefore, was very much affected as a result of these three factors: the lack of financial support given them by the Italians; nationalistic rivalries between the priests and the congregation, as well as within the Custody itself between the Irish and Italian constituents; and the growing tensions between the Franciscans in New York and the other clergy, both diocesan and regular, working among the Italians.

Their work at Saint Anthony's, however, was not fruitless. They organized various parish societies, attended the sick, administered the sacraments, presided over numerous devotions, and preached in Italian at all the principal Masses on Sundays and holy days.[46]

Our Lady of Mount Carmel, 115th Street, Twelfth City Ward

The procurator general of the Pious Society of the Missions, commonly known as the Pallotines, wrote Corrigan in May, 1884, informing him of the departure of the Reverend Doctor Emiliano Kirner from London on May 17, and of his assignment to take charge of the Italian mission in New York City, having received "powers from the Father General to represent our Congregation and to make any arrangement that may meet with Your Grace's and His Eminence's approval."[47] This arrangement had been precipitated by Corrigan's meeting with the procurator general, the Reverend William Whitmee, during the Archbishops' meetings in Rome in the fall of 1883, at which time Corrigan had requested the help of the Pallotines for the Italians in New York City.[48]

Kirner arrived in New York on May 26, 1884, to take charge of the Italian mission in Harlem, begun the previous Easter at 111th Street near the East River by the Reverend Domenico Vento, who left upon Kirner's arrival.[49]

Vento was a rather unsavory character, and his ministry in New York was not of the most inspirational quality. He hailed from the Archdiocese of Gaeta and was accorded temporary faculties by Corrigan to work among the Italians of the city. Vento subsequently traveled to Michigan where he found employment for a time as a logger in one of the camps around Lake Superior, then with some Italians working on the construction of the Canadian-Pacific Railroad.[50] Tiring of such physical labor, Vento applied for faculties from the Bishop of Marquette. After some investigations into the priest's past, the Bishop discovered that Vento had come to America with a woman and his own children, who had accompanied him through New York and the midwest during his varied and colorful career.[51]

The mission to which Kirner was assigned was housed in rented first-floor rooms, measuring eight feet by thirty feet, "in a poor house inhabited by several Italian families such as Sumer Street opposite the Italian church in London."[52] The entire house was leased by the Italians to whom the Confraternity of Our Lady of Mount Carmel paid rent for the chapel. Kirner described the location in his first report to his superiors, "Behind the altar window is a sorting yard, where all the rags collected during the day by the Italians all over the town are sorted, cleared and packed."[53]

By the time Kirner arrived, the mission was already more than $300 in debt, Vento having taken a loan from an Italian to purchase statues and benches. The colony was composed of approximately 3,000 Italians, chiefly Neapolitans, engaged in rag and bottle collecting. As Kirner quickly discovered, ". . . there exists a division among them, one faction refuses to go to the Chapel because it is in the hand [sic] of the other faction." This division of factionalism among the members of the congregation would plague the parish throughout its early history.

Kirner also discovered the Cardinal's plans to divide the local English-speaking parish in order to financially assist his new Italian mission, and that, to his amazement, the rector of the church was quite amenable to the idea. Although Corrigan was willing to allow the division, he was powerless to effect it, since he was only the coadjutor, and the decision was left to the vicar general who had been charged by the Cardinal with the responsibility of diocesan administration. The splitting of the parish, as Kirner admitted, would be beneficial to his young mission, since it would be a source of needed financial support. He conveyed his preference for the division in his report, in which he admitted, ". . . if he [the vicar general] is willing, all will be right — if we have charge of the Italians only, we could not keep a priest."[54]

On May 30, Kirner was taken by Monsignor Thomas Preston, the vicar general, to look at land for the proposed new church. They visited a "wooden villa," as Kirner described it in his report, measuring 55 feet by 100 feet, with vacant land measuring 75 feet by 100 feet, located on 114th Street near the East River. The asking price for the property was approximately $9,000. Kirner thought the building could serve the new congregation for about one year. He wrote, "The situation is very good, healthy and agreeable, close to the River. In the old maps of New York it is called 'Harlem,' but forms now a continuation of the City."[55]

By 1886, Kirner had already performed marvels among his divided Italian colony in Harlem,[56] having received the Cardinal's permission, Corrigan's support, and his superior's approval to build a rectory and church.[57]

The basement church was completed in 1885, and opened to the Italian congregation. The upper church was dedicated and opened in February, 1887. However, the church was not paid for entirely by either the moral or financial support of the Italian members of the congregation. Kirner found he could do nothing without the support of the "Irish."[58]

The church was located in a section of Harlem, housing a growing Italian colony, as well as substantial Irish and German communities. Kirner had been a wise choice for this post. Being of German birth, having lived a number of years in Piedmont, and later working among the Italians in London, he was able to speak German, English, and Italian. He was able to maintain peace in his very mixed congregation, building his new church with the assistance of all three groups. The Italians built the basement, after which they stopped their support, leaving the church proper to be financed and built by the Irish and German members of the congregation.

Besides the construction of the church and rectory, Kirner began a five-floor parish school, traveling to Italy in late 1887 in search of Italian religious to staff it. Kirner was killed during the building of the school when one of the newly constructed walls collapsed in late October, 1887.

The new parish had flourished under Kirner's administration with the aid of two assistant priests,[59] who convinced a large number of Italians to return to the Church.[60] During his years in New York, Kirner was also employed by the Archbishop to assist the arriving Italian immigrants at Castle Garden,[61] and to provide Corrigan with much detailed information concerning the Italians, as well as suggestions on how they might be better assisted by the Church.[62]

Kirner was succeeded in January, 1888, by the Reverend Michael Carmody, also a member of the Pious Society of the Missions. Under Carmody's administration the number of Italians continued to grow, as did the parochial services provided for them. One of Carmody's major concerns was Catholic education for the children of the Italian immigrants. He had provided a Sunday school and hoped to open a temporary parish school by October, 1888, until he could complete the school begun by Kirner. Plans were made to rent the convent of the Sisters of Saint Francis on 109th Street, which would serve as a school for 150 children as well as a residence for the five nuns, "enabling us to gather the Italian children off the street and form a nucleus for the new school."[63]

Pallotine sisters had been hired by March, 1889,[64] and the new school was completed and opened in 1890. The Pallotine nuns were all Italian, only one of whom, the superior, Sister Mary Fidelis, was able to speak English. The school grew and all progressed well for approximately two years, after which time the relationship between the Italian nuns and the Irish pastor became increasingly strained.

The situation worsened, coming to a head at the end of the school term of 1891, when Carmody arranged a ten-day vacation and retreat for the sisters at a Salesian convent, eighty miles outside New York City. When the nuns returned after their vacation, they found the convent shut and locked. Carmody refused to receive them, and sent them three miles across town on foot, carrying their luggage, to see Corrigan, who was as surprised as were the nuns, at 8:30 in the evening.[65] Carmody was led to this rather rash action by the nationalistic factional rivalries that had gathered strength in the parish over the previous year, in which the nuns played a major role.

Carmody and his three "Irish" assistants were not overly popular with their Italian constituents who, in 1891, accused them of favoring the Irish parishioners — primarily for personal financial gain. The priests were accused of having planned "outrages" against the Italian colony, and had persecuted and abused the Italian nuns, lately banished from the parish by Carmody himself, as were the Italian assistant priests, the Reverend Domenico Parozzo and the Reverend Victor Danesi.[66]

This was not the first occasion that the Italian colony felt offended as a result of their rector's actions. In 1888, the Italians celebrated their patronal feast of Our Lady of Mount Carmel in the usual elaborate fashion, with services, panegyrics, food, and fireworks. The sum of $1,600 had been collected to finance the annual extravaganza, with the agreement that the church would receive the profit. Carmody received only $60 and was furious, as was the Irish contingent of the parish, who sided with their pastor, since they had been paying all the parish construction and maintenance bills. Carmody thereupon addressed the Italians in not too complimentary terms, excoriating them for their apparent niggardly behavior.[67]

Regardless of Carmody's quarrels with the Italian colony, he was not entirely to blame for the unfortunate situation that had evolved. The culprit was actually his Italian assistant, the Reverend Domenico Parozzo, who, since his arrival at the parish, had stirred up the various Italian factions and secured the support of the Italian nuns against the English-speaking priests and parishioners in an attempt to seize the rectorate of this supposedly exclusive Italian church for himself.[68] Parozzo had made a name for himself throughout the Archdiocese and in Rome as one who provoked disturbances. He had been suspended in Rome while at the Church of San Salvatore in Onda. It was only after his arrival in New York that problems began in the parish of Mount Carmel. He was ultimately recalled by his superior general and suspended.[69]

The plot for the appropriation of the church by Parozzo and his Italian supporters was furthered by the leader of one of the Italian factions within the parish, Mr. Antonio Petrucci. He was a saloon owner and exercised some influence in Tammany Hall, since he controlled the Italian vote in the twelfth city ward.[70] The intention of Petrucci and his group was to establish Italian parochial schools in the city, administered by Italian Pallotine priests and sisters who, naturally, would be under the control of Petrucci and his associates. Petrucci, in other words, was trying to establish for himself a *padrone* system by which he could control the Italian lay, religious, and clerical elements of New York. The *modus agendi* chosen to begin the accomplishment of this task was the circulation of rumors throughout New York and Rome, relating the details of the alleged persecution of the Italian sisters by an Irish pastor. This was followed by the sending of petitions to Propaganda and to Corrigan demanding Carmody's removal.[71] As planned, the rumors were spread concerning Carmody and the persecuted nuns by means of petitions and by word of mouth from other Pallotine sisters. Carmody unwittingly cooperated by exiling the Italian sisters from their convent, thus dramatically confirming the otherwise false stories concerning his persecution of the sisters in the parish.[72]

Regardless of the disturbances and accusations, Corrigan defended the priests of the church as zealous, even though there was "ill-humor" between the rector and the Italians, which he was unable to judge as "just or unjust hatred by the people." Despite Corrigan's support, he did not condone Carmody's harsh actions against the nuns. By early spring, 1891, Corrigan ordered Carmody to reinstate the nuns or face removal as rector.[73] Carmody replied that he would reinstate them, observing both his ordinary's command and the decrees of the fifth diocesan synod.[74] He did not, however, reinstate them.

After repeated attempts to bring about a conciliatory settlement between Carmody and the nuns concerning the school, having arranged meetings with Carmody's superior general who visited New York, and meeting with Carmody himself, Corrigan had no alternative other than to remove him as the rector of the church, and accepted the priest's resignation in early September, 1891. That which decided Corrigan's action was Carmody's breaking of his promise to restore the school to the nuns, and his continued disobedience of Corrigan's demand that the nuns be treated justly and with equity.[75]

Corrigan reported the entire situation in detail to the Roman authorities in September, 1891, in response to Propaganda's request for information.[76] The petitions of the Italian parishioners, Corrigan stated, were not entirely truthful. They had claimed the population of the Italian colony of Harlem to have been 18,000 persons, while in reality it totaled only 10,000 persons. The Italians contributed nearly nothing to the building of the church, Corrigan continued, either in funds or labor, the bulk of the costs having been paid by the American members. The Archbishop expressed his belief that Carmody was not the ogre that the Italians had portrayed him to be. Carmody had given the Italians privileges they never had enjoyed before, granting them free seats at all the Masses in the upper church, while the other parishioners were required to pay for seats

123

and for standing room, as was common practice. He also had allowed them numerous solemn services in their downstairs church. The Italians, on the other hand, gave only $20 per month to the nuns, barely enough to rent them a small house. Carmody had been pleased with the teaching ability of the nuns, Corrigan continued. However, after two years, none could speak English, except the superior, and they could not write precisely, even in Italian.

Corrigan felt Carmody to be a zealous priest, although rather lively and fiery in temperament, which at times resulted in misunderstandings with his parishioners. The Archbishop closed by expressing his opinion that the rector of the Church of Our Lady of Mount Carmel must know English, even though the church was basically Italian, since the rector had daily dealings with city officials. Inasmuch as the Italian colony "wants to enjoy all the leisure, leaving the others to carry all the weight," the financial support of the church fell to the American members, and so the rector must be able to speak English.

The final solution to the problem at Our Lady of Mount Carmel was worked out between Corrigan and the Reverend Joseph Bannin, the general of the Pallotines, who arrived in New York in October, 1891, to deal specifically with the parish. The settlement reached was that Carmody would remain as rector until the end of his original three-year assignment. The Pallotine nuns were to return to their original residence, and three other nuns — a new superior and two teachers — were to be procured by the general himself. Classes in the school were to be taught in both English and Italian in order to accommodate both factions in the parish.[77]

By August, 1892, a new rector, the Reverend Luigi Monsella, had been chosen, thus ending the painful scandal of the previous year. Corrigan expressed his delight that there had been "rendered justice to the nuns," and that he had "regulated the discord in a peaceful way." In order to avoid further nationalistic conflicts, Corrigan gave specific instructions to Monsella stating, ". . .he would have to consider that his church was Italian and not American."[78]

The congregation continued to grow, as did its services and various social, religious, and benevolent societies. By 1897, there were fourteen such societies enlisting parishioners of all ages into their ranks.[79] However, Monsella's years of administration (1892-1896) were not free from disturbances. The Italian community, divided by provincial rivalries, was further alienated from the rector and the parish because of Monsella's extreme sympathies for the English-speaking community.

One of the major conflicts between the rector and members of his Italian congregation concerned the annual feast of Our Lady of Mount Carmel, usually presided over by the members of the Society of Santa Lucia. In 1893, due to the economic depression brought about by the drop in the price of silver, the society requested a reduction in the stipend for the church services accompanying the festal celebrations. The rector refused, and the members of the society referred the case to Corrigan, who sided with the Italians, forcing the rector to grant their requests. Monsella was not happy.

The following year, the rector changed the rules governing the feast, announcing the changes only twelve days before the celebrations, after the arrangements had been completed. The Italians protested, and, on the day of the feast, arrived at the church only to find the doors barred, with police guards in front of the church. The society again sought Corrigan's assistance, but the damage had already been done, and the split between rector and members of his congregation was irremediable.[80]

In addition to factional disturbances, a constant financial crisis plagued the parish.[81] The financial problems began under Carmody with the completion of the school, and were aggravated by the steady moving away of the Irish members of the congregation to other parts of the city, thus leaving the financial support of the church in the hands of the Italians.[82] The school also had its financial problems, especially since it maintained two separate departments and faculties, one English and one Italian, offering free education to the children of the parish.[83]

Under the administration of the Reverend John Dolan, who succeeded Monsella, disputes with local pastors arose over jurisdiction and stipends that posed another threat to the financial stability of the church.[84]

In 1900, the city decided to demolish four city blocks of tenements within the parish boundaries of Our Lady of Mount Carmel in order to develop the land into a park, further weakening the already precarious finances of the church. The obvious effect of the action was the drastic decrease in the number of members within the congregation, which in turn meant lower contributions for the debt-ridden church. This necessitated the extension of the church's parochial boundaries which then overlapped the territory of neighboring parishes.[85]

Saint Joachim, 22-24 Roosevelt Street, Fourth City Ward

Scalabrini's Congregation of Missionaries of Saint Charles Borromeo received papal approbation as the first religious congregation established exclusively for the spiritual assistance of the Italian immigrants in the Americas.

Corrigan immediately wrote Scalabrini requesting priests, sending money to support the new institute and praising Scalabrini's initiative as long overdue: "The Lord be praised a thousand times! Now I can breathe easy. There is good hope that something can be done for these dear souls, who are being lost by the thousands. Up to now I could find no way to save them! . . . Now I am happy and assured . . . I can commend to you my neglected Italians."[86]

Scalabrini's apostolic fervor was tempered, however, by practical necessity. Before allowing his missionaries to depart for America, he wanted the assurance of the Archbishop that his priests would be unhindered in their pastoral ministrations among the Italians, independent of other rectors, and provided with some type of house and independent church or chapel.[87] If these stipulations were met, Scalabrini promised to assume the entire Italian apostolate in New York, if Corrigan would so desire.[88]

The Reverend Marcellino Moroni had arrived in New York in October, 1887, having been commissioned by Scalabrini to report on the conditions of the Italian colony in the city, and to prepare for the arrival of his missionaries during the early months of spring, 1888.

Upon his arrival, Moroni was assigned by Corrigan as an assistant to the rector of Transfiguration Church, where he experienced firsthand the opposition of various New York rectors to independent Italian national churches and to the independent work of Italian priests. Those most strongly opposed to such independence were the Reverend Thomas Lynch, rector of Transfiguration Church, and the Reverend John F. Kearney, rector of Old Saint Patrick's Cathedral.[89] Regardless of this opposition, it was Corrigan's desire to establish a truly national church for the Italians in New York, especially since he had the assurance that Scalabrini's missionaries would staff it.[90]

By mid-April, 1888, Moroni had discussed with Corrigan the

possibility of purchasing an abandoned Protestant church within the boundaries of Transfiguration parish.[91] Corrigan decided against the proposal, since he deemed the property ill-situated and the asking price of $70,000 excessive.[92] Corrigan was also aware of Lynch's vehement objection to such an independent Italian church within his parish boundaries, and may have decided to avoid problems for the nascent Piacenzan institute that could develop because of Lynch's opposition. Besides, the rector of Old Saint Patrick's had offered Corrigan a chapel and house for the Italians within his parish territory.[93]

Moroni returned to Italy in June, 1888, after completing his task in New York. He was replaced by the Reverend Francesco Zaboglio who was charged by Scalabrini to continue the preparations begun by his predecessor. He was to establish an Italian patronage committee, to relay any additional information about the Italians and their needs to Piacenza, to deal with Corrigan, "in my name and as my special representative, and to . . . conclude definitively the planting of our Missionaries."[94]

By late June, 1888, Corrigan had secured a house and church for the Piacenzans. Scalabrini responded by sending two more priests and a lay catechist. He also wrote Corrigan, reflecting on the experience that Zaboglio had related to him in various letters while reiterating his own belief that the missionaries of the institute be totally united with the local bishop, and not bullied by local rectors. Scalabrini continued: "I intend that the Bishops and only the Bishops be the superiors of my priests. The most profound and scrupulous respect towards the hierarchical order is the force of the ministry and the pledge of sure victories."[95]

Scalabrini's restatement of his respect for the authority of the local bishops was prompted by Zaboglio's discovery that not all priests laboring among the Italians were so dedicated to such unity of action and obedience to the local bishop. Zaboglio learned that the independence of the Scalabrinian missionaries was threatened not only by various New York rectors, such as Lynch and Kearney, but also by an Italian priest, Gennaro DeConcilio, who himself desired to exercise a more prominent role in the direction of the future work of the missionaries in the United States.[96]

In his first report to Scalabrini, dated June 28, 1888, Zaboglio spoke of the various obstacles placed in the path of the missionaries by those who supposedly were assisting them.[97] Corrigan had assigned Kearney to the task of helping the missionaries establish themselves in New York City, unaware of Kearney's opposition. Kearney's unrevealed plan, according to Zaboglio, was to keep the missionaries dependent upon him by arranging that they remain in his rectory and under his control.

When Zaboglio revealed this to Corrigan, the Archbishop assured him that it was he who administered the Archdiocese and not his priests. However, since Kearney had been employed to arrange for the house and church for the arriving missionaries, he made sure that neither would be prepared for months, and that the property he had proposed for purchase by the missionaries was nowhere near the Italian colony in which they desired to work. The result of such a scheme would be Kearney's control of the Italian priests, who would live in Kearney's house, and the failure of the Italian mission itself, since the priests and their chapel would be too distant from their people to be of any effect. Zaboglio cabled Scalabrini, informing him not to send his missionaries, a fact which he kept from Corrigan. However, by the time Zaboglio sent his first report on June 29, Corrigan had obtained his own house and church, thus assuring the missionaries their required independence and foiling the plans for Kearney.

By July, 1888, Zaboglio reported that he also felt the pressure of DeConcilio's interference in the entire matter. Zaboglio was urged by DeConcilio to purchase property in the city, far removed from the Italian colony at Five Points. DeConcilio also insisted that the Italians themselves direct the entire transaction, not leaving it to be directed by the "Irish." Zaboglio concluded, "It appears to me that after escaping the slavery of the Irish, I was in danger of falling under DeConcilio."[98]

Zaboglio sought the advice of priests involved in the Italian apostolate. He spoke with the Pallotines at Our Lady of Mount Carmel in Harlem, with the Reverend Massi, S.J., and with the Reverend John Edwards, the rector of Immaculate Conception Church on East 14th Street, whom Zaboglio referred to as "my guardian angel." All cautioned Zaboglio to be wary of the various priests in the area, and advised him simply to rent rooms for the time being, instead of remaining dependent upon the hospitality of Kearney and others.[99] Zaboglio took the advice offered him and rented rooms on Grand

Street, sending Italians to collect money throughout the Five Points district, hoping to acquire a modicum of financial independence for the missionaries who were already on their way to New York.[100]

Fathers Vincenzo Astorri and Felice Morelli and Brother Pietro Pizzolotto arrived in New York on July 22, 1888.[101] They rented a store at 174 Centre Street and, on August 5, opened the provisional Chapel of the Resurrection.[102] Corrigan celebrated the opening Mass, and was so enthused by the Piacenzans' initial success that he wrote Scalabrini in early August, suggesting the opening of similar independent chapels throughout the city, staffed by Scalabrini's missionaries.[103] Corrigan continued to encourage Scalabrini and his missionaries in this their first success in New York, and requested more priests for the Italians.

The work of the Scalabrinians developed into three missions in New York: Saint Joachim Church, the Church of the Most Precious Blood, and the Church of Our Lady of Pompeii. However, as will be seen, the effectiveness of these missions in their early years was greatly inhibited by financial disasters, inept parochial administration, and by intense internal conflicts and congregational factions. It was not until the last years of the nineteenth century and the beginning of the twentieth that the Piacenzans became truly organized, and exercised an immensely positive influence upon the Italian colony in New York.

By early September, 1888, a parochial committee had been formed by the Reverend Felice Morelli for the newly founded mission of Saint Joachim. The committee was charged with the task of exploring the area to determine the needs of the Italians. Since a larger church was deemed necessary, an abandoned Presbyterian church on Roosevelt Street, the "Howard Mission," was rented on December 21, 1888, and solemnly opened for public worship on Christmas Day. The church was placed under the patronage of Saint Joachim, in honor of Pope Leo XIII, Gioacchino Pecci.[104] The Chapel of the Resurrection on Centre Street remained open under the direction of the Reverend Vincenzo Astorri, and eventually became the Scalabrinians' second New York Mission, the Church of the Most Precious Blood on Baxter Street.

These two facts — the splitting of the Resurrection Chapel into two church congregations, and the purchase of the "Howard Mission" by Morelli in April, 1889 — were not simply the fruits of a burgeoning apostolate, as Morelli's reports indicated. The founding of Saint Joachim's was undoubtedly necessitated by the size of the Italian congregation. The decision to divide the congregation, however, and the rapidity with which the second chapel was founded, were facilitated by the provincial tensions which were dividing the Italian colony itself.

Morelli did not help matters, since he favored the northern Italians from the areas of Pavia, Genoa, Piacenza, and Parma, often speaking out against the Italians from the southern provinces.[105] Morelli's regional propensities were made manifest in his dealings with Mr. Antonio Cuneo, a Genoese banker in New York who was the head of the parochial committee with which Morelli had met in November, 1888, to decide upon the future of the Scalabrinian mission and the purchase of land and a church.

Cuneo opened the subscriptions for the new church with a substantial offering and an interest-free loan to the priests for one year.[106] Cuneo received all the offerings and gave receipts to the donors. The money was held in the name of the donors and not in Morelli's, thus, so Morelli believed, relieving him of all financial responsibilities.[107] Morelli further complicated matters by entering into an agreement with four laymen of his congregation, named as trustees, who held the church's property in trust to be conveyed to a person or corporation, according to the wishes of the majority of the trustees.[108] None of these actions and agreements were entered into according to Archdiocesan regulations, since Morelli had not bothered to inform Corrigan of his financial arrangements or of his attempts to incorporate the property.

Corrigan had discussed the purchase of the church and land with Morelli, instructing the priest to wait until his agents could speak with the proprietor, since they would be able to acquire the property at a rate lower than the asking price.[109] Morelli did not heed Corrigan's advice, and purchased the property and building as arranged by Cuneo from a Mr. Mitchel A. C. Levy, at a cost of $82,000, with a mortgage for $53,500.[110]

Tensions grew between the Archbishop and Morelli, who was encouraged by the Italian societies of his church to demand the $5,000 from Corrigan collected by the Italians of New York a few years earlier.[111] Scalabrini wrote Corrigan, reporting that he had received a number of letters from the Italian colony and from his own priests, accusing the Archbishop of confiscating the money belonging to the Italian colony.[112] Corrigan defended himself, replying that the problem was with the intention of the contributors, who desired to build a church within their own quarter of the city to service only those Italians from their provinces and no others. Because of the radical exclusivity of this group, Corrigan had the account transferred to Morelli's name prior to the reception of Scalabrini's letter, in order to safeguard the funds from the self-serving machinations of the wily trustees.[113] It was during this first skirmish with the Archdiocesan authorities that Morelli requested Scalabrini's permission to return to Italy.

Morelli had a previous history of parochial financial mishaps while he was still in Italy. He had incurred large debts, was accused of and found guilty of forgery, and was sentenced to seven years imprisonment. He succeeded in escaping his imprisonment by assuming a false name, forging documents, and joining Scalabrini's institute, which conveniently sent him to New York in 1888.[114]

Morelli served as rector of Saint Joachim's from its founding in 1888 until 1890. Since the parish was somewhat of an intermediary stop for those missionaries assigned to South America, Morelli was assisted by no less than twenty-four priests, who resided with him for varying lengths of time during his rectorate.[115] It was also during Morelli's years at Saint Joachim that Mother Frances Xavier Cabrini and her sisters taught at the parish school, more of which will be said later in this work. The ministrations of the majority of these priests were exceptionally productive, bringing a number of Italians back to the Church and the sacraments. However, this spiritual betterment was limited primarily to the northern Italians, at least in the first years of the mission.

Zaboglio expressed this to Scalabrini in 1889, when he wrote, "I have observed a lacuna in New York. There is still the need of a Neapolitan priest among our missionaries."[116] Since the Neapolitan community was extremely large within the boundaries of Saint Joachim and Transfiguration around Mulberry Street, the need was immediate. However, once again the administrative inability and provincial sensibilities of Morelli interfered with any such provision.

By the end of 1890, Scalabrini decided to relieve Morelli of his rectorate by making him the provincial superior. He was replaced by the Reverend Domenico Vicentini,[117] who remained as rector of Saint Joachim until 1893.[118] Morelli had undertaken too many projects, and contracted debts too numerous and weighty for the newly established missionaries to bear. He purchased the Roosevelt Street property in April, 1889, for $82,000, with a mortgage of $53,500. Later in the year he purchased a house on Mulberry Street for $60,500, paying $3,000, and mortgaging the balance. The money that he paid at the closing and the money used to pay off the mortgage were provided by another loan. In November, 1890, he purchased property on Baxter Street, again on credit and mortgaged. Bolstered by the promises made to him by members of the Italian colony, he contracted for the construction of an enormous church that would cover the entire three-lot area he had purchased. Only the basement was completed, however, at a cost of $33,000. In order to pay his debts and mortgages, Morelli continued to borrow money at exorbitant interest rates, ineluctably drawing the Scalabrinian missions into the paralysis of further debt.[119]

Morelli's administrative ineptitude, which led to interference by various groups and societies within the church,[120] his prejudice toward the southern Italians, his unwillingness to follow the counsel of the Archbishop, the Archdiocesan officials, or even that of his own fellow missionaries, and his unfamiliarity with American finances and law, all made his removal from the parish imperative for the survival of the mission.[121]

The removal of Morelli, however, did not solve the problems of the mission, since Morelli, sustained by one of the Italian groups of the second Scalabrinian mission, Most Precious Blood, still considered himself to be the lawful rector[122] despite the objections of Vicentini and Zaboglio.[123] Morelli's response to the objections of his fellow missionaries was to submit his resignation from his newly acquired post as provincial superior. Scalabrini's immediate response was to beg him to remain in order to direct the entire Scalabrinian missionary effort.[124]

Morelli accepted, interpreting his superior's pleadings as tacit approval and permission to continue his parochial meddlings.[125] The inevitable result was the development of internal conflicts and divisions among the missionaries themselves, who broke into different camps of Morelli's supporters and opponents.[126]

Having weakened the administration of Vicentini as rector of

Saint Joachim, Morelli disobeyed the directives of his superiors to undertake no new projects until all debts were paid. He continued to buy land and to incur large debts, for which he decided to take personal responsibility.

Vicentini, meanwhile, attempted to resign his post at Saint Joachim, but was not allowed to leave until 1893, when Scalabrini asked him to do his best to save the Church of the Most Precious Blood, which was then threatened with public auction as a result of Morelli's continued interference and indebtedness.[127]

By 1893, the situation was totally intolerable, with all of the Piacenzan missions in New York threatened with public auction. Morelli, supported by a faction of Italians, continued to interfere with Saint Joachim and blocked the nomination of the Reverend Paolo Novati as rector.[128] Morelli justified this action by claiming sole responsibility for the church and its debts, professing that he could allow no one to interfere with the church's administration.[129]

Morelli agreed to leave the parish only on the condition that Corrigan personally assume responsibility for all the debts contracted by him. Corrigan refused and, left with no alternative, removed Morelli's spiritual, financial, and administrative faculties in regard to Saint Joachim, in November, 1893, appointing the Reverend Joseph Strumia the new rector.[130]

All Strumia's attempts to free the church of debt and to establish a school for abandoned Italian children were rendered useless due to the fact that the congregation had been entirely divided into factions either favoring or opposing Morelli.[131] Since the property was not yet incorporated as an archdiocesan holding, the finances were still in the hands of the various societies which, it was discovered, had not paid the interest on the mortgages, a sum amounting to $40,000 by 1893. The company holding the mortgages decided to auction the church. Strumia succeeded in obtaining an extension from the company and convinced the trustees to transfer the title to the Archbishop. However, Morelli once again interfered, convincing some of the Italians who had originally loaned money to the church to demand immediate restitution from Strumia, while retracting their consent to incorporate the church property.[132]

Corrigan, already mortified by the public auction of the Scalabrinian Church of the Most Precious Blood, offered to assist Strumia with Saint Joachim's if the church were incorporated in accord with Archdiocesan law.[133] Encouraged by Morelli, three of the lay trustees agreed to allow the incorporation of the church property on the condition that all the missionaries at Saint Joachim resign. Scalabrini consented, promising to effect the change as soon as new priests could arrive in the city. The trustees, therefore, reluctantly consented, and the church finally was incorporated and transferred to the Archdiocese on October 26, 1894, after the appointment of the Reverend Paolo Novati as the new temporary rector.[134] Both Novati and the Reverend Francesco Beccherini served briefly as rector of the church until late 1894, when Strumia was reappointed, remaining until 1898.[135]

Strumia succeeded in reuniting some of the factions and societies in the church, paid some of the debts left by Morelli, and began planning the construction of a school for abandoned Italian children.[136] However, his administration was not free of scandal or administrative problems.

In 1897, the rector decided to repair and redecorate the basement church of Saint Joachim, build a rectory and three additional houses on the adjacent property, thus raising the parish debt to $181,998.[137] Strumia had originally considered selling the property to pay off the debts, but reconsidered, deciding instead to build houses in order to collect the rents, even though Corrigan had opposed the plan. The construction of the houses was considered by the other missionaries to be the ruin of the parish.[138] Factions within Strumia's congregation and among his missionaries,[139] a lack of good priests,[140] and accusations of serious financial mismanagement marred his four years as rector of the church.[141] Strumia resigned on February 4, 1898 and returned to Italy. He was succeeded in March by the Reverend Oreste Alussi, who remained until April, 1902.[142]

By the time Alussi took control of Saint Joachim, the debt had risen to $185,000 with a required interest payment of $5,000 every six months.[143] Few Italian men went to church, as Alussi soon discovered, and Saint Joachim's acquired the title "Church of the women." There were twenty-four women teachers in the school, directed by two Christian Brothers, and a number of parish societies.[144] Within the first year of his administration, Alussi had improved the financial situation of the church by means of parish fairs, picnics, the sale of religious objects, increased society membership, collections, pew rentals, donations, and "magic lantern" shows.[145]

Alussi also made agreements and signed contracts with the various religious societies within the parish regulating their annual feast day celebrations, services for which the church would be remunerated, thus satisfying the various groups while increasing the parish revenue to pay off the church's delinquent debts.[146]

The parish did continue to grow despite intermittent provincial squabbles among the members of the congregation, as well as the interference of priests from other parishes, such as that by the Italian assistant at Transfiguration Church who began a price war with Saint Joachim, lowering his entrance fee at the church to "3 soldi" in order to steal Saint Joachim's people away.[147]

The final major battle endured by Alussi was with one faction within his parish who supported the nomination of the Reverend Lodovico Martinelli as rector of the church, making his appointment as rector a condition for the subsequent payment of the church's debts.[148] Martinelli finally became the rector in September, 1902, retaining the post until July, 1904.

Most Precious Blood, 113-117 Baxter Street, Sixth City Ward

The euphoria experienced by the Piacenzan missionaries, Corrigan, and Scalabrini as a result of the successful opening of the Chapel of the Resurrection in August, 1888, continued through the fall of that year and into the early months of 1889.[149] Corrigan requested more missionaries to staff additional Italian chapels, and Scalabrini promised the required men if churches and lodging could be found, no matter how crude.

Because of the growth of the congregation at the Resurrection Chapel, and the factional tensions between the northern and southern Italians who composed the congregation, the church was divided, and Saint Joachim's Church formed.[150]

Morelli had trusted the original enthusiastic promises made to him by the various Italian groups in Saint Joachim's Church, and was all too willing to enter naïvely into disastrous real estate and construction contracts, usually without consulting the officials of the Archdiocese, as seen earlier.

With the founding of Saint Joachim's, it was decided that the original Chapel of the Resurrection would be maintained for use by the southern Italians who lived in the immediate area around the chapel on Centre Street. They petitioned Corrigan for a larger church, since the northern Italians of Saint Joachim's did not welcome them, and since their own chapel was too small.[151]

Morelli met with influential members of the Italian community in November, 1888, purchased a house on Mulberry Street, and opened it for public worship on Christmas Day, 1889, under the patronage of Saint Michael. He concluded the transaction having only $3,000 in hand to pay toward the principal investment of $60,500, the balance of which was mortgaged. The $3,000 down payment was itself loaned to him to liquidate debts already incurred.[152] The new oratory soon proved too small for the growing southern community, and Morelli was forced to sell the Mulberry Street property, for which he received $3,500 after paying the balance of the mortgage and other debts.

In November, 1890, after having received the Archbishop's permission, Morelli bought property on Baxter Street, numbers 113, 114, and 117, at a cost of $82,500, again mortgaged, with down payments supplied by loans.[153] Morelli originally intended to build a church on two of the lots, and a house on the third, which he could rent in order to supply the parish with additional income. However, he was convinced by his fellow missionaries, and by members of the Italian community, that the church should be a splendid edifice, occupying all three lots. The faithful would be greatly impressed by its grandeur, the argument ran, and would contribute most generously, thus allowing for the payment of debts and an increase in capital. Morelli consulted with the Archbishop and, with his assistance, contracted a Mr. Deeves to begin construction of the basement church at a cost of $33,000.[154]

It was at this point that Morelli's unsound financial dealings became known, since he found himself unable to meet the interest payments on his various loans and contracts. Morelli finally approached the Archdiocesan officials, revealed his previous financial dealings, and requested financial assistance. In spite of the aid received, Morelli's situation worsened, and the chancery became very much aware of the extent of the missionaries' financial indebtedness resulting from Morelli's unfortunate land dealings, and requested his removal by Scalabrini.

The basement church was completed and opened on September

27, 1891, and named *Preziosissimo Sangue.* Within the first four months of the church's opening, 150 baptisms and thirty-eight weddings were performed. The entire population served by the new mission was estimated to have been approximately 20,000 persons of which an estimated 8,000 attended church with regularity.[155] Despite the promises of financial support made to Morelli by the Italians, the collections slowly dwindled.

The Reverend Domenico Vicentini was called upon in February, 1891, to replace Morelli at Most Precious Blood.[156] He succeeded in paying at least the interest on the enormous debts that had accrued under Morelli's administration: $115,000 on the Baxter Street property, and $15,000 in loans from members of the Italian community.[157] At the moment when improvement of the financial situation appeared to be at hand, the creditors demanded payment of the principal, no longer content with interest payments alone. Since the church could not meet their debts, the creditors began legal action to sell the church at public auction.[158]

Corrigan was displeased, to say the least. With the imminent sale of their newest church, as well as the financial and internecine troubles of Saint Joachim's, Corrigan lamented his having placed the entire Italian apostolate into the hands of the nascent Piacenzan institute, since they obviously were not yet well-organized. He expressed his views to Propaganda stating, ". . . and it is my impression that we should rely primarily upon the Regulars for our ever-increasing foreign population. No other Priests are permanent and stable."[159]

The public auction of a Catholic church was without precedent in the Archdiocese, and merited Corrigan strong criticism from members of the Italian community, both clerics and laymen alike, even though the legal proceedings against the church were begun by the lessors of the mortgages, and not by Corrigan. The Archbishop informed Scalabrini of the imminent sale of the church in late August, 1893. He calmly wrote that Morelli had been found guilty by a local judge of three separate charges dealing with his financial administration, and sentenced to pay some of the debts. The entire debt of the Most Precious Blood was $125,000, with only the basement church completed. Since Morelli could not possibly pay these sums, even though the Archdiocesan authorities had paid a sizable amount of money to assist the church, it was decided on August 29,

1893, that the church would be auctioned. In conclusion, Corrigan stated: "This will be the first time that such a disgrace has taken place during my episcopal life, that is the selling of a sacred place. It is all the fault of the Father who never wanted to do as the other diocesan Rectors do."[160]

Scalabrini responded in early September, 1893, reiterating his strong belief that his missionaries should be totally dependent upon the local bishop for everything. He wrote, "This is also one of the principal points of the Rule, and Morelli, who neither observed nor led, has brought all the penalty upon us."[161] Scalabrini concluded by requesting Corrigan to allow his missionaries the use of a small wooden chapel, or at least a room, in which to continue their work.

To complicate matters further, Morelli refused to obey his superiors' demands that he cease his meddlings in the parochial affairs of the Piacenzan churches, and announced his willingness to assume personal responsibility for all the debts incurred by him during his administration.

The matter did not remain within the confines of either the Archdiocese or the Scalabrinian institute, however. In May, 1893, the Reverend Pietro Bandini, a Piacenzan missionary in charge of the work of the Italian Saint Raphael Immigrant Society at the Port of New York, wrote to Cardinal Ledóchowski and to Archbishop Francesco Satolli, the first Apostolic Delegate in the United States, informing them of the threatened sale of the Italian church. In his letter, Bandini included brief, inflammatory reports on the condition of the southern Italian community in New York. Since the community was to be deprived of its church, Bandini wrote, its members would invariably turn to the numerous Protestant missions. Bandini alleged the debt of $6,000 to be the sole reason for the closure of the church, which could easily be liquidated by a diocesan collection or by a collection among the American congregations, neither of which the Archbishop would allow. The priest petitioned both Satolli and Propaganda to intervene with Corrigan and to send circular letters to the various parishes in the city, asking their assistance for the threatened Italian church.[162]

Satolli had written Corrigan concerning the Italian colony in his Archdiocese in late April, 1893. He was prompted by a not-too-complimentary report from the Reverend Gennaro DeConcilio, received earlier in the month, describing Corrigan as unsympathetic toward the Italians.[163] DeConcilio complained that Corrigan wanted only to subject Scalabrini's missionaries to Irish pastors as mere assistants, and refused to grant them independence of action. He condemned the Archbishop for his treatment of the Italians and praised the notion of independent Italian parishes, two shining and successful examples of which were Saint Joachim and Most Precious Blood, both in New York. Either DeConcilio was woefully misinformed, or his concept of parochial success included bankruptcy and congregational factions. Nonetheless, he condemned Corrigan and asked the Apostolic Delegate to intercede on behalf of his fellow countrymen.

In his letter to Corrigan, Satolli repeated the information supplied him by DeConcilio, without revealing his source, and requested Corrigan to submit a report on the condition of the Italian colony and the work of the Archdiocese in their regard.[164] Corrigan responded on the first of May, agreeing that the Italians were in a "rather deplorable" state, and promised to supply the desired report after he had gathered sufficient information from the rectors of the churches with large Italian constituencies.[165]

Satolli immediately wrote Propaganda, no doubt feeling his position secured by the letters received from such experts on immigration as DeConcilio and Bandini, and by the assurance of Corrigan himself that the religious state of the Italians in New York was pitiable. Satolli referred to Bandini's letter of May 3, emphasizing the work of the Protestant missions among the Italians, and parroted the priest's suggestion that a special collection be held throughout the Archdiocese to save the Italian church. He concluded his letter by requesting the Holy See to intervene in the matter, and that he be sent "instructions, suggestions and counsel" to help him in this crisis.[166]

Ledóchowski replied on May 30, lecturing Satolli on the responsibilities of the Apostolic Delegate, and commenting on the relationship that he should have with the American hierarchy. Satolli should refrain from interfering in diocesan affairs, the Prefect of Propaganda wrote, especially in the case of the Italians in New York, since that colony was numerous enough to support itself, or at least was able to produce some "beneficent personage" who could assist the church. Satolli should not be so ready with quick judgments, Ledóchowski continued, and should, instead, study the entire problem of Italian immigration, as he himself had suggested. Ledóchowski closed his letter by echoing the instructions Satolli received at the beginning of his mission as Apostolic Delegate in 1892, concerning the Church in America and the immigrants:

> According to my way of understanding the point, I believe that similar questions should be treated with extreme delicacy, since, while ample means of spiritual culture by which to preserve the faith should be provided the immigrants of various nations, yet one should avoid giving too national a direction and color to the various churches, which, as a result, could do not a little harm to the proper homogeneity and the good course of the Church in America, as experience has shown in other countries.[167]

Satolli's original instructions from the Vatican, given on the occasion of his appointment as the Apostolic Delegate in the United States in 1892, had been exceptionally clear concerning his dealings with immigrant groups and the hierarchy in the United States. He had been instructed about the strong animosities between the various immigrant groups, and cautioned to be wary of compromising the Church by championing the nationalistic fervor of any of these groups. The Vatican instruction continued:

> The principle that one should adopt in order to remove these animosities should be that whatever the origin of the immigrants in the United States, their new country is one for all, and politically all are American citizens; Catholics, therefore, should attempt to become politically and socially homogeneous with the nation; by this do they become a part.[168]

Corrigan sent his report on the Italians in New York City to Satolli on May 11, and described their sorry religious condition as well as his own deep sense of frustration regarding the seeming ineffectiveness of the means thus far employed on their behalf. He began, "I must state that the religious condition of the Italians in New York is rather deplorable, and confess frankly that I have lost, in great part, the hope to be able to provide sufficiently for the well-being of this people, which for many reasons, is dear to me."[169]

Corrigan believed the entire problem of supplying priests and independent churches for the Italians to have been solved with the arrival of Scalabrini's missionaries. The priests labored without salary, Corrigan explained, receiving only room and board. They built two churches, one of which, Saint Joachim, survived after many sacrifices, while the other, Most Precious Blood, was auctioned, since the creditors were impatient for the interest payments. A third chapel, next to the house of the Saint Raphael Society, was also administered by the missionaries and was also in financial difficulty, since that congregation too was incapable of meeting its debts.

The other two churches for the Italians were administered by religious communities and were doing well. The Church of Our Lady of Mount Carmel, a mixed congregation, was cared for by the Pallotines, while Our Lady of Loretto was under the care of the Jesuits. Corrigan expressed his belief that the Italians were incapable and unwilling to support an independent church, as evidenced by the then recent failure of the Scalabrinian mission, "which was in constant financial ruin, with rumors of people against their clergy, either because they were unable to pay the debts, or were accusing them of greed for money."

The Archbishop made four general observations concerning the Italian immigrants and their relationship with the Church: (1) the Italian colony was not suitably instructed in religion, many Italians having never made their first communion or confirmation; (2) Italians were not accustomed to supporting the Church, since, in Italy, the Church traditionally received state support. The work of the apostolate could not succeed, Corrigan observed, unless the laity contributed financially to the Church. This was a necessary condition of the Church in America, but "for the Italians, instead of sacrificing 5 cents, he [sic] prefers to sacrifice the right of a Christian." Corrigan made it quite clear that he was not referring to those poor immigrants who could not give to the Church: "I am sure that the Italian colony is relatively the most numerous in paying money to the banks: it is enough to state that in New York City alone there are more than one hundred exclusively Italian banks, and all live quite well." The religious education of Italian children was impossible, Corrigan believed, since they were forced to work in order to satisfy the family's need and desire to earn money; (3) the Italian population nurtured prejudices against the clergy. The result was that "it is impossible to find in the Italian colony that sentiment of faith and trust that is the prime factor of moral rapport between priest and faithful." This rapport was by no means improved by the numerous Italian priests of questionable character and morality, employed by American bishops because of necessity; (4) Italian immigration began with an element totally opposed to the ideas of religion, "fomenting hatred against throne and altar." These first immigrants, Corrigan commented, formed societies that influenced the later arrivals, instilling in them that selfsame hatred for the Church. Those who never saw the inside of a church in Italy cannot sympathize with religion in America. Before such a group of indifferent individuals, the priest, no matter how zealous, can accomplish little, able to build neither church nor congregation of believers. The poor, forced to emigrate from their homeland, often became the prey of "atheistic speculators," and were led further from the Church.

Corrigan then addressed the great fear of the Roman authorities that the Italians would become Protestants. The Archbishop assured Rome that the various Protestant missions were not overly successful in their efforts to convert the Italians, since the Italian had little interest in any religion. The efforts of the Church, Corrigan continued, were weakened, since the Italian government subsidized various Protestant missions and schools for the Italian immigrants in the United States.[170] American Catholics could not support the Italians, Corrigan added, because they had their own institutions to build, and because they held the Italians in contempt as a result of what they considered to be the Italians' irreligious life.

In regard to the Scalabrinian missions, the New York chancery paid $12,000 to save the Baxter Street church, but without effect. Corrigan himself paid $2,000 from his own pocket for the debts of the Italian Saint Raphael Society.

Corrigan's solution, in view of the apparent failure of the independent Italian churches, was not to abandon the Italians. Rather, he believed more should be done, since the apostolate had failed to bring the Italians back into the Church. Corrigan now believed that the Church's efforts on behalf of the Italians could not possibly take the traditional form of independent parishes, since the Italians were not able or willing to shoulder the enormous financial burden requisite for such structures. Parishes were the normal outgrowth of believing communities. Since the Italians were divided among themselves, and rarely possessed a Church-centered faith, they could not be expected to support those structures traditionally employed by the institutional Church. Faith and a love of the Church must first be developed, Corrigan stated, and then the establishment of traditional church structures naturally would follow and succeed. He concluded, "I would say it would be better to abandon the idea of instituting independent Italian parishes, and instead assign to American parishes one or more Italian priests; he [sic] would exercise the Sacred Ministry in the basement of the American church; in this way they will be able to overcome these serious financial disturbances, which, after all, cause very grave damage to the priesthood."

Satolli had been misled by some of the reports he had received, believing the Italian immigrants to have been deeply devoted to the institutional Church, that their attendant clergy were totally zealous for their salvation, and that simple solutions to the problems involved in assisting his conationals could be found with ease.[171] Satolli's response to Corrigan's report was to encourage the Archbishop of New York to seek out new ways to finance the Italian churches other than among the Italians. He thoroughly sympathized with the Piacenzan priests, and advised the missionaries to have recourse to Propaganda if they received no justice at the hands of the New York curia.[172]

Despite his support of the Italian colony and the missionaries, Satolli was awakened by Corrigan's reports to the reality of the apparent losing battle then being waged to assist the Italians religiously in the United States, at least with traditional ecclesial structures and institutions. The unfortunate failure of the Scalabrinian mission of the Most Precious Blood in New York rendered the reality even more jarring for the Delegate. Satolli had spoken with priests involved with the Italians in Baltimore, Philadelphia, and New York and was slowly coming to admit that the Italian immigrants "do very little for their church, and, while he [Satolli] naturally hopes that an effort be made for them, he does not consider it just that they should expect their fellow Catholics to build and maintain churches for them."[173]

The Church of the Most Precious Blood was sold at public auction in October, 1893, purchased by its original owner who had held the mortgage on the land for the Scalabrinians. By January, 1894, it was formally closed to public worship.[174]

As a result of the auction of the church, the Archdiocesan officials required a full financial report from Morelli, which revealed a deficit of $25,000. Morelli was suspected of gross mismanagement of funds and, unofficially, of embezzlement.[175] The missionaries were denied permission to open any new missions within the Archdiocese, no matter how small, nor were they to rent the auctioned church from the new owners, as they desired, since, in the eyes of the Archdiocese, they had shown themselves to be inept administratively.[176]

In the same month, Vicentini and Bandini began a campaign to save the church. They made house-to-house visitations throughout the Italian community previously served by Most Precious Blood, requesting subscriptions to reopen the church and signatures to a petition to be sent to Satolli and to Rome requesting the authorities to force the reopening of the church. The Scalabrinians began scare tactics with the Italian immigrants of the area telling them that unless the church reopened, the "Italians will be the SLAVES OF THE IRISH AS THEY HAVE BEEN BEFORE THE CHURCH IN BAXTER STREET EXISTED, and that they will always be slaves."[177]

Bandini held nightly meetings in the basement of the auctioned church, combining religious devotions with harangues against the New York curia. He claimed the Church of the Transfiguration was bankrupt and destined to close, thus forcing the reopening of the Piacenzans' church. According to the rector of Transfiguration Church, Bandini told the Italian gatherings, "You cannot conscientiously go to the Transfiguration. Therefore, Msgr. Satolli will see that you get your church back if the Archbishop of New York does not see to it. You have only to wait a just time and your wrongs will be redressed."[178]

The Piacenzans collected 11,000 signatures on their petition, which they sent to Satolli and to Rome, requesting direct intervention to save the church. Satolli responded to the petitioners in a very matter-of-fact manner, stating, "I will take the petition into consideration, provided that some of you 11,000 speakers give $1 in advance, in order to free the church."[179] The matter rested there, since the Italians made no response to the Apostolic Delegate.

The church did not remain closed for long. The Franciscans of New York, having become aware of the closure and of the straits of the Piacenzans, responded to overtures made to them by Satolli, quickly taking advantage of the situation, to the added embarrassment of the Scalabrinians. By the end of January, 1894, the Franciscans had applied to Corrigan and received his approval to take over the mission, with the understanding that the Franciscans would assume the responsibility for the parish debts.[180] The decision set off an explosion.

Scalabrini communicated his displeasure with the entire situation in a furious letter to Corrigan, dated February 5, 1894, accusing the Archbishop and his curial officials of falsifying charges and of forcing his missionaries to close their church.[181] Having received letters from Vicentini reporting his side of the affair, and after receiving counsel from various unnamed ecclesiastics, Scalabrini felt sure of Corrigan's guilt in having committed "an evil action and a grave injustice." Scalabrini was convinced of Corrigan's underhandedness: "The church is ordered closed, you damage the sacrosanct purchasing rights, you promise that all the debts would be paid, including those of the Italians, you induce the Superior [Morelli] with false promises, without means, to take upon himself the debts contracted by the church itself and, with that intention obtained, you send him from Herod to Pilate, the first makes a mockery of questions, the other washes his hands! But where are we, dear Monsignor? A Masonic lodge would not have done worse." Scalabrini concluded his letter threatening to refer the matter to Rome, and "to initiate a case *in forma.*"

Corrigan answered Scalabrini's letter on February 22, 1894, briefly responding to the Bishop's charges against him.[182] The missionaries' church, he stated, was closed by the New York municipal authorities after the usual legal procedures. Those responsible were Scalabrini's priests who abandoned their legal obligations and transgressed legitimate rights, forcing the lessors to their own legal recourse. The Archdiocese had paid $11,000 for the overdue interest on the mortgage, Corrigan claimed, since the missionaries had failed to meet the obligation: ". . . notwithstanding it [the Archdiocese] was constrained to tolerate a disgrace never before suffered in the history of the Diocese, which is the alienation of a Catholic church from divine cult."

The second disgrace was to be found in the near auction of the Church of Saint Joachim, which, again, was the result of the financial and administrative incompetence of Scalabrini's priests, Corrigan continued. The third establishment of the congregation, the house and chapel of the Saint Raphael Society, also would have been sold if Corrigan had not paid $2,000 of his own money to save it.

The question of debts of Most Precious Blood was then discussed. Corrigan asked how he could possibly be expected to obligate himself to pay the debts of the Baxter Street church, since they exceeded $120,000. Corrigan continued that he would not take responsibility for Morelli's personal debts, since there was an unexplained deficit of $25,000. He continued, "If Your Excellency believes that you should remove the Missionaries to send them elsewhere, where the financial difficulties are lesser, this may be the better solution. For the time being I have rented the Church of the Precious Blood to other priests, already experts in finances. . . . I have done more for the Italians than for any other people, and they repay me in this manner."

Scalabrini had been notified by his own men as well as by Corrigan numerous times before concerning the financial problems of his missionaries.[183] He had been notified of the fact that his missionaries did not comport themselves or their affairs in accord with the Archdiocesan authorities, even though Scalabrini himself had continually encouraged his priests to be obedient to the local ordinary in everything. Corrigan had even written Scalabrini late in 1893, "If the Missionaries would act as our priests in temporal affairs, and under the diocesan directives, all would go well."[184]

Scalabrini originally accepted the notification of the closure of the church with grace and docility, asking Corrigan to allow his missionaries to continue their work in New York despite their failure. He even expressed his thanks and esteem to Corrigan, especially because of the gentle manner in which the Archbishop had handled the "disgraceful Morelli affair." Scalabrini continued by asking Corrigan to watch Bandini, suspecting and fearing financial mismanagement in the Society of San Raffaele in New York.[185] His patience was entirely shattered, however, upon receiving news that his missionaries would not receive another church, and that the Baxter Street church would be given over to the Franciscans.

That Scalabrini might feel offended by the Franciscans coming to the rescue of the Italians in New York, at the expense of the Piacenzans, was logical, since the Piacenzans had done the exact thing a few years earlier in Boston, at the expense of the Franciscans. By coincidence, the Italian Franciscans in New York were then headed by the Reverend Anacleto da Roccagorga, O.F.M., who had been at Saint Leonard Church in Boston during the conflict with the Piacenzans and the Italian community there in 1888. Anacleto's letters to his Roman superiors concerning the auction of the Baxter Street church in New York, express his unchecked ebullience that this opportunity had fallen into the laps of the Franciscans, and that they had assumed the responsibility for the former Scalabrinian church.[186]

Ledóchowski wrote Scalabrini in late February, 1894, concerning notifications of the sale of the church, recently received by the Holy See, and concerning a petition bearing 11,000 signatures from the Italian colony in New York, also lately arrived, requesting the intervention of the Roman authorities to save their church.[187] He continued that the Franciscans had also made known their desire to take over the church and to assume the church debts incurred under the Piacenzan administration, minus the personal debts of Morelli.[188]

Scalabrini answered a few days later, sending documents prepared by Vicentini and other missionaries, supporting his claim that his priests had suffered an injustice. He wrote, "It was the Archbishop of New York who wanted the closure and he obtained it in a manner, to tell the truth, entirely other than upright."[189] Corrigan, in turn, supplied the Roman authorities with documentation by late April, supporting his position, along with notices concerning Saint Joachim's Church and its financial difficulties.[190]

Ledóchowski contacted both Scalabrini and Corrigan by May, 1894. The Prefect of Propaganda complimented Corrigan on his patience with his missionaries, "who have done nothing except moan," and stated that they had no right to the Church of the Most Precious Blood. It was the decision of Propaganda that the Franciscans remain in peaceful possession of the church. Ledóchowski was not so complimentary to Scalabrini. He simply asked the Bishop of Piacenza how he possibly could have suspected Corrigan of underhanded practices, or have expected him to pay the missionaries' debts, when his men had bungled the finances of all their New York missions to such an extent that they themselves could not even pay the interest on their contracts, or even secure enough money to block the sale of their own church.

Corrigan's secretary wrote Vicentini on May 4, informing him of the Archbishop's decision that Morelli's debts would be absorbed by the Archdiocese, thus freeing the missionaries of their final legal obligation in the matter of the Baxter Street church.[191] Corrigan wrote Vicentini, confirming his secretary's letter, and revealed the fact that Morelli's debts were to be covered by the generosity of a number of priests of the Archdiocese.[192] The church, however, remained in the hands of the Franciscans.

The first Franciscan rector of the Most Precious Blood Church was the Reverend Giulio d'Arpino, O.F.M., who administered the church until 1901, when he was succeeded by the Reverend Bernardino Polizzo, O.F.M., who constructed the main church, which was dedicated in 1904.[193]

Our Lady of Loretto, Elizabeth Street, Seventeenth City Ward

Corrigan wrote to the Superior General of the Society of Jesus in December, 1888, concerning the possibility of Jesuits working among the Italians in New York. He wrote, "It has occurred to me that the Religious Orders, already established here, might well depute one or two members, each, to supplement the work of the Secular Clergy."[194]

The Jesuits had been working in the area that became New York State since the time of Isaac Jogues in the mid-seventeenth century, and had, by the time of Corrigan's administration, become well established in the Archdiocese in both parochial ministry and Catholic education.[195] Corrigan was unable to grant the Jesuits either a church or residence in the city at the time of his request. The most he could do was to assure the general that expenses would not be heavy, since halls could be rented or church basements employed for worship.

Corrigan had spoken previously with the Reverend Thomas Campbell, provincial of the Maryland-New York Province, asking him to approach the general of the Society, Anthony M. Anderledy, on his behalf. Campbell wrote his superior in December, 1888, explaining that the work among the Italians in New York was not proceeding well. The Franciscans, he wrote, held exclusive claim to the work at Saint Anthony, but did nothing, while the Italian secular priests, who were of questionable moral caliber, usually left the Italians in a state worse than when they arrived. The Piacenzans were prohibited from making headway by the fact that they were northern Italians, while the majority of Italian immigrants hailed from Naples and the provinces further south.[196] All the Church's efforts in favor of the Italian immigrants, Campbell continued, were hampered by the ever-present Protestant Italian missions, staffed by apostate religious. Campbell expressed his greatest fear that the effects of the Italians' poor religious condition would be felt in the subsequent generations, which would be detached from, and hateful toward, Catholicism.

He petitioned his superior for five or six "truly apostolic men," who would restrict their efforts to the Italian community and who would not be given faculties for English confessions. He felt a knowledge of the English language by his priests could be dangerous and potentially damaging to the Italian apostolate, since it would tempt those priests involved away from exclusively Italian ministry.[197] He assured Anderledy that a church would not be necessary. Campbell preferred a school in which instructions could be given and Mass celebrated, that would serve as a base from which his men could go throughout the city teaching and administering the sacraments to the Italian immigrants.

Anderledy responded to Corrigan's request early in the New Year, asking for more detailed information and immigration statistics. Corrigan responded by January 14, 1889, once more revealing his plan to secure the assistance of the various religious orders already in the city for work in the Italian apostolate.[198]

Corrigan, however, had a change of heart sometime in late winter, 1889. He feared the further weakening of the entire Italian apostolate if the Jesuits were to arrive at that moment. The Piacenzans' work was seen to be progressing rapidly, so much so that more missionary priests and sisters had been sent for to assist the developing mission.

The general of the Society of Jesus was informed of this by Campbell in March, who explained Corrigan's fears that "difficulties, suspicions, jealousy, etc., etc., would spring up" if a new religious congregation were to enter the field of Italian work at that time. It was, therefore, felt to be more advisable and prudent to wait and see if the success of the Piacenzans would last, before sending any Jesuit priests to the Italian colony of New York.[199]

Within two years, it became quite apparent to those involved with the Italian apostolate in New York that the success of the Scalabrinian missionaries in the city had been short-lived.[200] Corrigan again contacted the Jesuits and continued to petition their assistance throughout the winter and spring of 1891 by means of Campbell, who interceded with the general in April and May of that year.[201]

The Italian priests in the city were far from happy when they heard of Corrigan's plans to employ the Jesuits in the Italian apostolate. Campbell informed his general of the fact, continuing, "Furthermore, there are some among them [Italian secular priests] who are seen to be scarcely orthodox. Therefore, . . . he [Corrigan] has turned to us again."[202]

Campbell reported to Corrigan in May that the Society had few available priests, but that an agreement might be reached: ". . . if he [Corrigan] would free us from the care of various religious houses. . . ," then Campbell would consider the matter.[203] Corrigan promised to name five diocesan priests immediately as chaplains to the religious houses then cared for by the Society, thus relieving the Jesuits to work with the Italians.[204]

The arrangements with the Jesuits now became muddled because of the intervention of the Prefect of Propaganda, Cardinal Simeoni, who received a letter from Corrigan explaining the planned Jesuit mission, petitioning Propaganda's permission. Simeoni wrote to Anderledy, describing Corrigan's mission proposal as a totally new mission, other than the one already agreed upon by Campbell and Corrigan.[205] Anderledy, totally confused by Simeoni and already short of available men, refused permission for the plan, believing Corrigan to have begun a new enterprise without consultation and requiring more priests than previously mentioned in his correspondence with Campbell.[206] He asked Simeoni to convey his refusal to Corrigan, which he did during the summer of 1891.[207] The correspondence continued between Corrigan and Anderledy by way of Simeoni for the remainder of the year. When all was finally clarified by Corrigan and Campbell, the general granted his approval to Corrigan's plan and Campbell was authorized to assign the Reverend Nicòla Russo to head the mission, assisted by the Reverend Aloysius Romano.[208]

The mission was to be directed toward the large southern Italian population, composed primarily of Neapolitans and Sicilians, who had been attended to by the Italian priests assigned to Old Saint Patrick's Cathedral on Mott Street. Since the response of the Italians in that area had been so poor, the Italian priests assigned to their care requested that Corrigan make other arrangements. Thereupon, the church basement was closed to the Italians.[209] Russo and Romano were assigned to attend to the southern Italians living in the area of the city from the Bowery to South Fifth Avenue, and from Bleecker to Broome Streets. An old barroom was rented and remodeled to serve as the church, and a sign hung outside, "Missione Italiana della Madonna di Loretto." The chapel was opened on August 6, 1891, with Campbell celebrating the opening Mass. Russo had anticipated a small congregation for the opening Mass, and, in order to entice more people to attend, he printed circulars announcing the Mass throughout the colony. He also arranged with the president of one of the local Italian mutual aid societies, the Association of San Rocco, to present the members formally in the church on opening day. At 11:00, on the morning of August 16, the Association processed down the street toward the church with banners, a full brass band, accompanied by a number of curious Italians who entered the chapel, filling it to capacity.[210] By means of home visitations, Russo and Romano were able to raise the number of those attending the four Sunday Masses to five hundred persons within a few weeks of the opening of the chapel.

The need for a larger chapel became apparent early in 1892. Russo purchased property and two tenement houses on Elizabeth Street, at a cost of $50,000. The contract was signed in the early months of 1892, Russo having paid $5,000 the day of the signing, and $10,000 to be paid in May, the balance being mortgaged. However, Russo quickly discovered that the Italians could pay only the interest on the mortgage and were unable to raise the needed money. He wrote, "That which is received from the Italians is enough for current expenses, if things are well administered, and if one lives like a poor religious. If you must give a salary to priests who administer the parish, it would be impossible to go forward, as it would have been impossible to build a church."[211]

By 1893, Campbell could report to his superiors that the previous year's expenses for the Italian mission totaled $75,000, of which the major portion had been paid, with only $30,000 remaining to be paid on the house.[212] By the end of 1894, the debt was reduced to $25,000.[213]

There were other problems threatening the financial stability of the mission. Corrigan had established the mission within the territory of Old Saint Patrick's Cathedral, much to the displeasure of the rector, the Reverend John Kearney, who demanded that the majority of Italian baptisms and weddings be performed by him within his parish boundaries, thus securing the attendant stipends for his church. As a result, Russo was unable to pay his rent during the first months following the mission's opening.[214]

Russo wrote Corrigan in March, 1892, expressing the difficulties of his new mission, and emphasized the lack of financial and moral assistance offered him by the local clergy. He wrote, "Remarks have reached me of late that are not flattering. The prospect is not encouraging. I feel that I am left alone."[215] Corrigan responded on March 15, informing Russo that he would pay the mission debt of $15,000, required at the legal closure for the buildings on May 6, 1892.[216]

A few weeks prior to the sale of the land to the Jesuits, the owner of the houses notified the tenants, the majority of whom were Italians, to vacate the building by May 3. Most left, but some were forcibly evicted on that day, unbeknown to Russo. The Italians, having no idea of the identity of the new proprietors, planned to avenge themselves on the owner for humiliating them. On the morning of May 7, 1892, a number of men entered the houses and destroyed the interiors with axes, until the police intervened just in time to save the walls. The Jesuits refused to prosecute when notified, and secured the Italians' release, thus gaining the immediate respect of the colony, with whose assistance they rebuilt the interiors within three months. The rooms on the ground and first floors of both tenements were gutted, and the structures were extended into the backyards in order to provide a suitable space for a chapel, which measured 40 feet by 100 feet. The two upper floors of the building were reserved for the residence of the priests.[217] The chapel was dedicated by Corrigan on September 27, 1892, and opened for public worship.

The congregation was composed primarily of "the roughest and dirtiest of Bassa Italia and Sicily, not caring much for the things of heaven."[218] Russo believed these people to be irreligious because of their indifference toward the Church and not necessarily because of their ignorance of religious doctrine. Since the Italians to whom he ministered were of the lowest social class, uneducated and knowledgeable of their local dialects alone, their answers concerning religion were unclear and "produce a very unfavorable impression. But if you know their dialect and HOW TO BE PLAIN WITH THEM, this impression is oftentimes removed."[219]

Russo believed the then present religious condition of the southern Italians in New York could have been improved if the Church had begun work when the Italians first began to migrate. Their poor religious condition, resulting from a lack of religious instruction given them in Italy as well as by their extreme poverty, was aggravated by their lack of education and schools in the United States. Russo wrote, "I have heard it from their own lips: They were inclined to believe that this is [sic] a land of freedom with regard to religion as well as everything else."[220]

Russo began his project for a parish school by dividing the church basement into six temporary classrooms to accommodate approximately two hundred children. This arrangement did not prove very suitable, since many of the parents complained that the unventilated gas-illuminated basement was unhealthy. The provincial, having received complaints concerning the school's location, inspected the site himself and ordered a more commodious building purchased, if possible.[221]

Two houses adjoining the church were purchased by 1895, costing $35,000, in which Russo hoped to open a school for boys and one for girls.[222] Problems arose, however, with the city building authorities who threatened to condemn the houses as unsuitable for Russo's projected schools unless major renovations were effected. Russo legally protested the city's decision and a board of inspectors was appointed by the city, with representatives of the building department and from the church who reinspected the site, and judged only minor renovations as necessary, costing $1,500. By mid-October, 1895, the schools were opened. The student body grew steadily, so that by 1896 there were nearly five hundred children in attendance.[223]

When the mission opened in 1891, Russo estimated the local Italian population to have been 12,000 persons, of which only 100 frequented church with any regularity. By 1895, he boasted that the number had risen to nearly 3,000 persons frequently attending the mission on Sundays.[224]

The only problem that seems to have affected the mission during

these years was one of maintaining proper living quarters and conditions for the priests. In September, 1891, a report was sent to the
general of the Society complaining about the condition in the parish
house, and the fact that two of the four priests then working in the
mission were not from the Sicilian Province of the Society. Russo
was accused of allowing abuses in the house to continue, the most
serious of which being the fact that the priests were forced to take
their meals in public restaurants because of the alleged household
mismanagement.[225]

Russo died on April 1, 1902, in New York City. So commendable
was his work among the Italians that even the *New York Times*, not
renowned for its favorable reports concerning the Church, published
the following about Russo:

> At the cost of great privations, and in spite of continued ill-health,
> he [Russo] lived in absolute poverty in a part of the tenement house
> which he had converted into a church, and by the help of donations
> from a few devout friends succeeded in establishing not only a
> flourishing congregation, but also a school in which several
> hundred Italian children are being educated.[226]

Romano wrote the general of the Society in June, 1902, submitting his suggestions for a successor as rector of the Italian mission.
He recommended that the man chosen be able to speak English in
order to assist the second generation of Italians in New York. He also
mentioned that an Irish or an American priest would not adapt as
readily as would an Italian to the "incommodious straitened circumstances" of the small parish house, which he described as being
unlike any other Jesuit house in the province.[227] Romano was appointed to administer the mission until the Reverend William H.
Walsh was appointed on July 1, 1903.

Our Lady of Pompeii, Bleecker Street and Sixth Avenue, Ninth City Ward

The perils to which the European immigrants were subjected
during their journey to America were well known to the Holy See,
especially through the work of Peter Paul Cahensly and Bishop
Giovanni Scalabrini. Both men established Catholic immigrant
societies to assist their Catholic conationals in the crossing to the
New World. Cahensly assisted the German Catholic immigrants

while Scalabrini attended to the Italian Catholic immigrants, both societies under the patronage of Saint Raphael.

Various immigrant societies had begun work among the arriving immigrants at Castle Garden in New York City by the middle of the 1880's, the most significant of which were the German Saint Raphael Society and the Mission of Our Lady of the Rosary, established to assist Irish Catholics. Propaganda authorities had attempted to initiate various committees in Italy and in America to assist the Italians at the point of their European departure and at the port of their entry in America. Unfortunately, all attempts proved to be either ineffectual or impractical.

In June, 1888, Scalabrini assigned the secretary general of his missionary institute, the Reverend Francesco Zaboglio, to visit New York, in order to meet with Corrigan to establish the missionaries in the city, and to study the possibility of establishing committees of patronage for Italian immigrants, similar to the German and Irish committees already at work there.[228]

As a result of Corrigan's petitions to Scalabrini for assistance with the Italians in New York, the Società San Raffaele for Catholic Italian immigrants was established in New York in June, 1891. Corrigan was named its first active president, and the Reverend Pietro Bandini of Forlì, the first executive secretary.[229] Bandini actually headed the port mission and took charge of the daily administration of the institution.[230]

The aim of the Society was to assist and protect the Italian immigrants landing in New York. The Society would find housing for the poor immigrants and children until they could contact family or friends. It would assist in the permanent settlement of immigrants in the city and help find employment, as well as provide religious assistance when needed.[231]

To ensure the effectiveness of Bandini's work, Scalabrini insisted upon his full liberty of action at the Port of New York. This was an extremely important demand, as Cahensly earlier had discovered regarding the German chaplain. Some of the "Irish" clergy of the city believed the German and Italian chaplains at the port should be appointed as their assistants, under their administration, and balked at the idea of independent chaplains.[232]

Bandini proved himself to be an extremely efficient and forceful worker at the port. He set about assisting the new arrivals, many of whom were detained until their families could assure the authorities that they would be cared for. Many were seriously ill upon arrival, without money or family, and it fell to Bandini to assist his helpless conationals, caring for them as best he could. In 1893, cholera was detected on board one of the ships recently arrived in New York. Nine Italians were suspected of having contracted the disease and were detained. Since they could speak no English Bandini felt obliged to help them. He wrote Corrigan, "I guess it is my right and duty to go among them and I beg Your Grace to appoint me for the temporal and spiritual relieve [*sic*] of my people. . . . There is no other priest who may claim the rights I have on the Italian immigrants."[233]

Bandini also instituted a labor bureau at the port. It was to assist the Italian immigrants by pressing government officials to accept them into the country, aiding in their settlement, and securing employment for them.[234] He defended the immigrants, protecting their rights, forcing the various employers to fulfill their obligations of salary, transportation, and the supplying of letters of reference for the Italian laborers. Bandini's ministry in the port was of extreme importance. Within the first year of the opening of the Society in New York, he assisted over 20,000 Italian immigrants.[235]

A house was purchased at 113 Waverly Place, and solemnly blessed by Corrigan on September 24, 1892. A small chapel attached to the house had been opened on May 8, 1892. This chapel was the origin of the Church of Our Lady of Pompeii, the early history of which is inseparably linked with that of the Società San Raffaele and Bandini's work in New York. The chapel was intended from the beginning to serve not only the immigrants in transit but also those Italians living in the surrounding neighborhood.[236]

The question of immigrant chapels near the New York Port, and the possible granting of parochial status and rights to such chapels, was an extremely tender subject in the Archdiocese. Various rectors whose parochial boundaries included the area around Castle Garden felt such a concession to the various national groups to be a violation of their parochial rights.[237]

Bandini wrote Satolli in April, 1893, describing the sorry condition of the Italians arriving at the port. He told the Apostolic Delegate that the Germans and Irish had been granted parochial rights for their port chapels, and, as a result, received funding from special collections held throughout the Archdiocese. The Italian house and chapel of the Società San Raffaele alone had to fend for itself. He complained that the chapel on Waverly Place required money in order to maintain two priests, needed a larger school, and would be greatly assisted if granted parochial status and rights.[238]

With or without parochial status, the chapel's schedule was similar to the other churches in the city. There were four Sunday Masses, beginning at 5:30 a.m., each with a sermon. Baptisms, blessings, and house calls followed lunch. Catechism classes occupied the afternoon with over two hundred children in attendance, the number being limited only by the lack of available space. There was Benediction of the Blessed Sacrament for the children following the classes, and then meetings of the various societies, followed by vespers, preaching, and Benediction for the entire congregation. Once a month Benediction would be followed by a conference for the parents of families who attended the church.[239]

Scalabrini had some suspicions as to the security of the San Raffaele house and about Bandini's administrative honesty, despite the complimentary reports of his pastoral successes sent by the priest to Piacenza. Fearful that Bandini might be abusing the precept of strict dependence upon the local ordinary, employing it as a pretext for not submitting accurate reports concerning the mission, Scalabrini wrote Corrigan in September, 1893, requesting that the Archbishop secure an accounting of the financial status of the mission from Bandini.[240] Corrigan instructed Bandini to prepare an account, and received it by early October.[241]

The account revealed that the income from the Society's immigrant house and chapel was not substantial enough to afford any progress whatsoever, nor was it sufficient to pay the debts of nearly $20,000 and a promissory note for $5,000 with its interest. Corrigan himself paid the interest for the previous six months, but the balance and the annual interest were still due. Regardless of the apparently good attendance at the chapel services, the contributions were not generous enough to maintain the mission and the immigrant house.[242] Both the house and chapel were threatened with legal foreclosure resulting from Bandini's failure to pay the interest due on the mortgage.[243] Faced with the recent sale of the Church of the Most Precious Blood, and the opening of legal proceedings against Bandini's mission, stayed only by Corrigan's payment of

$2,000, the Archbishop was intent that the Piacenzans concentrate their efforts on their one semi-stable mission of Saint Joachim.[244]

Scalabrini wrote Corrigan immediately, asking him to postpone "his grave measures" of closing the immigrant house. He promised to assist the mission, to convince Bandini of the necessity of reducing expenses, and, if need be, of replacing administrators.[245]

Corrigan apparently agreed, seeing the necessity of the port mission for the Italians, for it was decided in 1894 to consider a new site for a larger church. The Archbishop favored the idea only if funds could be raised, thus preventing further financial catastrophes for the missionaries.[246] The proposal was presented by the Archbishop to the council of vicars of the Archdiocese, who approved it at a meeting of the Archdiocesan consultors with the stipulation that the property desired should be rented for the first year, with the option to purchase the site after the expiration of the year's lease.[247]

The property was located at 214 Sullivan Street, which was an abandoned Protestant church, known as the "Bethel Methodist Colored Church."[248] The church was a two-story structure. Bandini hoped to use the first floor for children's Masses, a catechetical school, and meeting hall for the parish societies. The second floor would be used as the church proper.

Financing the project was the major obstacle. Bandini had promised Scalabrini to collect offerings only, and not to accept individual loans, as had other members of the missionary institute, thus creating enormous financial problems.[249] Bandini also applied to Satolli, and to priests in the Archdiocese of New York, requesting financial assistance for his venture.[250] Satolli employed his influence by personally contacting clerics in New York in an attempt to secure funds for Bandini's church project.[251] Priests from throughout the Archdiocese contributed generously, as did Miss Annie Leary, one of the most influential and generous donors to the Archdiocese. She intended to establish an association called the Auxiliary Ladies of Saint Raphael, composed of various wealthy matrons who would give monthly contributions so that the Society could provide training in "women's work" for poor Italian girls.[252] Despite the efforts, the response was not overwhelming, but at least resulted in sufficient funds to pay the required rent, and to better the financial state of the Society's immigrant house.

Bandini received permission to proceed with his project, and on

March 6, 1895, signed the contract to rent the vacated Protestant church, with the option to buy the property, along with two attached small houses after the expiration of the one-year lease. He planned to take possession of the property on May 1 but was forced to delay, since his financial problems were not ended. Despite the delay, and the uncertainty of the mission's future, Bandini was determined to make a great show of the Italian church dedication by securing Satolli's presence at the opening ceremonies,[253] an invitation forcefully declined by the Apostolic Delegate over and over again.[254]

The church was finally dedicated by Corrigan on April 28, 1895. The Apostolic Delegate, absent for the actual dedication, was present at the evening vespers service and delivered the sermon, exhorting the Italian congregation to be faithful to the Church of their fathers: "Here you have every incentive in the example set by Catholics of other nationalities, and in the kind care, protection and interest of your beloved Archbishop. You should remember that other nationalities look to you in a special manner for examples of Christian faith and fervor, being, as you are, the representatives of the nation in which Christ has located His visible representative on earth."[255]

Despite his seemingly successful beginnings, Bandini did not succeed in ingratiating himself either with the local clergy or with the priests of his own congregation. While the Church of the Most Precious Blood was being auctioned, Bandini spoke out at public meetings against the "Irish" clergy and the injustices he alleged had been inflicted upon the Italian colony by Archbishop Corrigan. Bandini infuriated his own colleagues by employing the assistance of various clerics of questionable rectitude, by not administering his house according to the rule of the congregation, and by incurring additional substantial debts.[256] Bandini had been warned continuously by the Archdiocese against defaulting his loans. Nonetheless, the lessors of the Waverly Place property reported to Corrigan that Bandini had failed to make his interest payment of December 1, 1895. The chancery wrote Bandini concerning this, especially since the owners threatened legal proceedings against the priest: "If this has to be done, and the mortgage foreclosed, then His Grace will take such measures as will ensure the reputation of all those who have acted rightly in the matter, and will adopt such means as will protect the Diocese from a repetition of a similar occurrence in any of the other churches which are in charge of Italian Priests, and which have been the first to bring discredit, in the financial sense, to this Diocese."[257]

Bandini was accused of various offenses. He allowed the Reverend Felice Sandri to preach at the mission's Christmas novena in 1895, even though Sandri had been suspended earlier by Corrigan.[258] Members of Scalabrini's institute had left the mission house in New York because of the trying living conditions, and because of the various people Bandini allowed to live there who were neither members of the institute nor clerics.[259]

Bandini's response to all accusations and threats of legal action was to announce his assignment to an Italian agricultural colony in Arkansas by Satolli, who wanted to see "if the colony would be a fact or a fiasco."[260] The plan for such an agricultural colony was the idea of Austin Corbin, a wealthy New York industrialist and owner of the Corbin Banking Company and the Long Island Railroad. The settlement was to be called "Sunnyside," and Corbin hoped to interest Italian families to move west in order to raise cotton. He requested Satolli's approval of Bandini as the chaplain of the colony which he had begun to settle late in 1895.[261] Zaboglio wrote Satolli twice in early January, 1896, apologizing that he could not accommodate Bandini in his plans to go to Arkansas, since Bandini was needed in his own New York mission.[262] In the second letter to the Apostolic Delegate, Zaboglio went on to point out that he had received a letter from Bandini on January 6, 1896 from Baltimore, reporting that Satolli had instructed him to leave for the colony immediately. Nothing had been heard on the subject from Scalabrini concerning any permission for Bandini's departure from his New York post. Because of this, Zaboglio was left totally without guidance. He concluded his letter to Satolli by asking him not to allow Bandini to leave his church on Sullivan Street, overburdened as it was with a debt disproportionate to the size and generosity of the church congregation.[263] Zaboglio was convinced of Satolli's responsibility for Bandini's proposed move to Arkansas. He also believed firmly that Bandini was little more than a scoundrel, totally unworthy of belief or trust.[264]

Whether Satolli officially supported Bandini in this is unclear. Bandini had told Satolli of his intention not to renew his vows for Scalabrini's congregation, thus providing a convenient escape from the irate members of the institute.[265] Certainly, the delegate personally encouraged Bandini and approved of his actions, promising assistance and support whenever possible, even though he knew that Bandini was working against the express wishes of his superior and was aware of the need of the New York Italian mission.[266]

With Bandini's departure, the Piacenzans were faced with their third financial failure in New York. Waverly Place was sold almost immediately by the Archdiocese, at a personal loss of $3,000 to Corrigan, who had involved his personal finances in an attempt to save the institution.[267] Bandini tried to clear his name of the charges leveled against him soon after his departure. He wrote to the Archdiocesan officials, and to Corrigan himself, expressing astonishment at the accusations blaming him for the New York mission's financial failure. He felt a good deal of fine work had been accomplished among the Italians, which was true, but continued, "Of course it may not be so if you look only in the financial sense. . . . I find it very painful after having worked very hard for five years with all my strength, to be considered a burden and a discredit to the diocese."[268]

Bandini resigned from the Piacenzan institute, absolving himself of all responsibility for the financial disasters left in his wake: "Whatever I did in these five years I did it as a member of a Congregation, to the Congregation then belongs everything I have done . . . supposed [sic] I am dead and the Congregation of Msgr. Scalabrini has to take care of everything I left behind me."[269]

The future of the Sullivan Street church, however, was uncertain. The Archbishop hoped it would remain open if it could operate with a debt. It was quickly discovered that the church could not continue without incurring additional debts, since the missionaries were incapable of even paying their rent. Moreover, since the church was located so close to the Franciscan church on Sullivan Street, the hope of financial solvency was dim.[270]

Zaboglio wrote Scalabrini in April, 1896, explaining all that had transpired during the past months. The Piacenzans refused to take responsibility for the church and its debts, informing both Corrigan and Bandini of that fact. Satolli and Farley, the vicar general and auxiliary bishop of New York, both insisted upon continued maintenance of the church by the Scalabrinians. Zaboglio visited Satolli in Washington in order to explain the situation of the missionaries to him, but to no avail; Satolli continued in his insistence. Upon his return to New York, Zaboglio was summoned to Farley's office, only to discover that Satolli had officially intervened with the Archdiocese, reiterating his insistence that the Piacenzans retain the administration of the church.

The missionaries persisted in their refusal, forcing the Archdiocesan authorities and Satolli to offer the mission to other congregations, but without success. Faced with the choice of supporting the missionaries if they would accept the mission, or closing the mission entirely, the authorities decided to consider an able successor for Bandini from among the Scalabrinians, with the intention of assisting him.[271]

The major obstacle to the missionaries' acceptance of the responsibility of the church was the debt left by Bandini. This was removed by the intervention of Annie Leary, the wealthy Catholic New York philanthropist who promised to pay all the debts and to financially support the mission.[272] She not only supplied the mission with large sums of money to cover the various debts, but also assumed responsibility for the daily expenses of the mission which she paid in smaller installments.[273] As a result of the generosity of Annie Leary, Zaboglio agreed to accept the administrative responsibility of the mission.

Zaboglio described the extent of Annie Leary's generosity and interest for the Italian mission in a letter to Scalabrini: "If it had not been for her, our church of the Madonna of the Rosary of Pompeii would have been closed. She gave her own money, had a concert for the church, last Sunday she had another entertainment, she had the façade repaired, mended the stairs in the church and in the house, ordered a painting of the Madonna of Pompeii from Italy, she is repairing and furnishing all the rooms and maintaining the work school for the Italian children, but what is most important, she has the intention to found industrial schools even for the young men and to acquire new sites."[274]

The missionaries were entrusted with the church, but were allowed only to renew the contract to rent the church, and not to buy it, at least not until the mission was finally secure.

Zaboglio met with Corrigan and with the two vicars general of the Archdiocese on April 9, 1896 to discuss the future of the mission. The owners of the Sullivan Street church had expressed their willingness to renew the missionaries' lease, due to expire in 1898. The Archdiocese was prepared to give the missionaries a church originally built for a Black Protestant congregation, and later purchased by Black Catholics, under the title of Saint Benedict the Moor.[275] The Piacenzans would be obliged to assume the responsibility of paying the interest on the mortgage for the church property, valued at $70,000.

The missionaries could not comply, since they were unable even to meet the interest payments on Bandini's church, valued at $52,000. It was decided, therefore, to close the Sullivan Street church, and to give the Church of Saint Benedict the Moor on Bleecker Street to the missionaries, with the stipulation that they were responsible at least for the remainder of Bandini's debts.[276]

On July 14, 1897, an explosion occurred in the Sullivan Street church, causing severe damage, and killing the sacristan, Samuel Vincentini, while seriously injuring Zaboglio.[277] With the near destruction of the Sullivan Street church, there was no option but to move the mission. Corrigan gave Zaboglio permission to raise funds necessary for the church. He raised nearly $70,000 in two mortgages and temporary loans, and the new church opened on May 1, 1899. Zaboglio resigned as rector in the same month, still suffering from injuries incurred during the explosion of the previous year.[278]

Zaboglio was succeeded by the Reverend Antonio Demo, who had been the curate under Zaboglio at Our Lady of Pompeii. He was assisted by the Reverend Riccardo Lorenzoni, Carlo Delbecchi, and the Reverend Pio Parolin.[279] Demo began to reorganize the mission by establishing various societies and groups, and by transforming the basement of the new church for meetings.[280] He organized a Sunday school with the Christian Brothers, a catechetical school with Mother Frances Xavier Cabrini and her Missionary Sisters of the Sacred Heart, as well as an arts and crafts school to train young Italian girls in skilled trades.[281]

The church's Mass schedule was reorganized to resemble those of other American churches, as opposed to those of southern Italy.[282] The result of this regularization of parish activities, and the stabilization of the administration, was a slow yet perceptible development of the mission. Religious education classes were held every Sunday afternoon for two hours. After the first hour, the priest would speak to the children, and then celebrate Benediction. The afternoon was usually occupied with baptisms, weddings, hospital calls, family visitation, and sick calls. The day ended with sung vespers.[283]

During the summer of 1901, Scalabrini visited his missions in New York as part of a visitation of all his missions in North and South America.[284] He arrived in New York on August 3, 1901 and was met at the dock by his missionaries and the local authorities of the Italian colony, who accompanied him to the Church of Saint Joachim. Scalabrini visited Ellis Island and various national branches of the Saint Raphael Society. On August 9, he blessed the new Casa San Raffaele on Bleecker Street, which would serve for the reception of Italian immigrants.[285] Corrigan commented on Scalabrini's visit, "He [Scalabrini] has been very active and his visit will have good results. Amongst other things, he is re-organizing the St. Raphael's Emigrant Society for the Italians on a better and longer basis."[286]

Years before, Scalabrini had confessed to his missionaries the reason for the many problems of his missionaries in New York. He wrote in 1896 that "our fault was to spread ourselves too far."[287] Nearly six years later, Scalabrini saw the work of his men. On August 11, he stopped at Our Lady of Pompeii Church. Greatly encouraged, he approved the work of his missionaries and the good already accomplished among the Italians of the mission, the evident result of organization and a unity of action among the missionaries.

Church of the Transfiguration, Mott and Park Streets, Sixth City Ward

Since the time of the 1883 Roman preparatory meetings for the Third Baltimore Council, the Salesians of Don Bosco had been considered able priests who would work well among the Italians in the United States.[288]

The Archbishop of New York, John McCloskey, was among those hoping to secure the assistance of these priests for the Italian immigrants. He instructed his coadjutor, Archbishop Corrigan, to contact them during his time in Rome for the preparatory meetings, and "to make all necessary arrangements with them if you can secure them."[289]

Corrigan contacted Don Bosco while in Rome in December, 1883, requested the assistance of his priests, and reminded him that "the Sacred Congregation of Propaganda Fide has shown much care that an Italian mission be established in New York City."[290] The Archbishop requested a meeting with Don Bosco, offering to alter his own departure date to accommodate the priest. The meeting was not successful, Corrigan being unable to secure any priests, since the Salesians had recently opened a new mission and would not be in a position to send priests to New York until 1886.

The coadjutor again contacted Don Bosco in March, 1884, informing him that Italian immigrants were being taken from the Catholic Church and confirmed by Protestant ministers. Because of the dearth of good Italian priests in New York, the Italians were confused and attended Protestant services, since an adapted form of the Roman ritual had been translated into Italian, transplanted, and employed by various Protestant missions to the Italians. Some Protestant missions, often run by apostate Italian priests, designed such services, Corrigan continued, in order to secure the Italians' membership, since the Italians would think the Protestant church to be the American version of the Catholic Church.[291]

In February, 1888, Corrigan again petitioned the Salesians for assistance, this time by means of the Reverend Edward M. Parocco, who wrote: "The Archbishop of New York City, Corrigan, a prelate of virtue, zeal, prudence and of *words*, has repeated to me more than once, if he could obtain your Priests, he would provide them with whatever they desire. I don't believe that there is any other city in the world where our Church would be prepared by better means. . . . If they [the priests] were not to have any lodging or means, just like another S. Charles Borromeo, and other sacred Bishops, he would open to them his own house. For the good of your Congregation, I greatly desire you not to allow this opportunity to vanish to establish yourself in this great city of New York, in which a bright future for our holy Church is destined by Divine Providence."[292]

In October, 1897, Corrigan again wrote the Salesians, informing them of his decision to build new churches for the exclusive use of the Italian colony in the city. In order to provide for the success of these new churches, the Archbishop had decided to offer them to various religious institutes, one of which was the Salesian.[293] The Archbishop explained the high property and construction costs in the city, as well as the American system of paying church debts only with the contributions of the faithful, instead of depending upon any state or ecclesiastical subsidies. The Italians, he continued, were not generous to the Church in the United States. Because of this, missions usually began in rented stores or rooms until a congregation was formed. He concluded his letter reflecting that "One spirited priest, of true zeal, will find immense work in the midst of the Italian colony."

The Salesians were unwilling to commit themselves to such projects without firm assurances from the ordinary that a definite parish, or location for the priests, would be assigned and provided.[294]

Corrigan received a response dated November 8, 1897. He answered immediately, expressing his delight at the Salesian acceptance. He told the general that there were no problems of location for their work, only of immediate construction of a church, assuring him that there would be ample work and means for his priests.[295]

The priests did not arrive as planned, so that by late February, 1898, Corrigan wrote to the Salesian general, the Reverend Michele Rua, asking that the priests be sent immediately, "since the spiritual necessity of the faithful does not allow postponement. . . ," and since "this gravest of obligations weighs upon my conscience to provide for the salvation of souls."[296] Despite the continued requests and petitions, the Salesians were unable to provide priests for New York until late 1898.[297]

The first Salesians sent to New York were the Reverends Ernesto Coppo and Marcellino Scagliola, along with two laymen, one of whom was Faustino Squassone.[298] They arrived in New York on November 12, 1898, and were met by Monsignor John Edwards, rector of the Church of the Immaculate Conception, whom Corrigan had assigned to assist the arriving priests as they began their mission.[299]

Edwards had been of assistance to the Italian missions previously, when he cautioned the Piacenzan missionaries upon their arrival in the city in 1888 about their dealings with the various city rectors. He now continued to help the Italian colony by cooperating in the establishment of a new mission. Edwards helped them rent two floors of a house located at 315 East 12th Street,[300] which was furnished by Corrigan.[301] The Archbishop assigned Coppo and Scagliola as chaplains to the Christian Brothers' La Salle Institute on 59th Street, for which they received monthly stipends to pay expenses until an Italian congregation could be formed.[302] Their Italian mission was to begin in the basement of Saint Brigid's Church, located at 119 Avenue B, until circumstances would allow them to build a church.[303] The rector of Saint Brigid's was the Reverend Patrick McSweeney, who had occupied that position since 1877, and would continue until his death in 1907.[304]

During the 1880's and 1890's, the ethnic composition of the parish rapidly changed, the Irish being replaced by Poles, Russians, Hungarians, and Italians. The Poles had their own church, dedicated to Saint Stanislaus, while the Hungarians were relatively few and, therefore, unable to support an independent church. They worshipped in the basement of Saint Brigid's, as did the Italians, who posed the greatest pastoral challenge for McSweeney. By 1896, McSweeney reported that the number of Italian families in his parish totaled about sixty, mainly Sicilian and Neapolitan, of which twenty "still seem to have the faith, but have little love of the church."[305]

By 1893, McSweeney had employed the Italian priest to attend to the Italians in the basement church. However, the rector was not pleased with the priest's work, since he had his mother, sister, and nephew living with him, and was opposed to any attempt to Americanize his conationals.[306]

McSweeney's attempts to aid the Italians were not overly successful until the arrival of the Salesians in the fall of 1898. McSweeney reported to Propaganda, in 1898, that the Italian population within the boundaries of his church had risen sharply to about 1,000 persons within the previous few years. Few of this multitude frequented church. He did his best to induce the Italians to attend, McSweeney went on, by assigning them free seats and by street preaching.[307]

The Salesian mission at Saint Brigid's opened on Christmas Day, 1898, with a Mass attended by twelve people.[308] The attendance at Mass and other functions slowly increased, so that by Easter, 1899, there were six hundred persons at Mass at the close of the first Italian parish mission.

Even though some stable parish structures and societies were being established for the Italians, the numbers in attendance began to diminish, necessitating the continual transformation of the basement church into a theater in order to support the new mission by means of various entertainments.[309]

McSweeney described the sad state of affairs in a letter to Corrigan in October, 1899: "Fr. Cirigione got almost nothing in the baskets last Sunday, except $100 which [Reverend] Dr. [Richard] Burtsell put into it. The Italians returned the compliment by stealing his new overcoat worth $50 and his new breviary. One of the Italian priests told me that Fr. Cirigione has only received $800 in two months from them."[310]

On August 17, 1899, Corrigan offered Coppo the mission among the Italians in the northeast section of the city, between 14th and 16th Streets.[311] Coppo accepted, and began a mission on 11th Street, preaching to the Italians of the area in one of the local theaters, encouraging them to support his efforts to build a church.[312]

The entire area around Saint Brigid's Church on East 8th Street and Avenue B — including the parishes of Saint Ann on East 12th Street, Immaculate Conception on East 14th Street, Nativity on 2nd Avenue, and Saint Rose on Cannon Street — was the home of approximately 10,000 Italians, of which an estimated 2,000 attended the basement church of Saint Brigid as a result of the Salesians' work. McSweeney wrote Corrigan that the Salesians had "succeeded in gathering quite a congregation of them [the Italians], having four masses on Sunday, and I feel that if they left, it would cause their [the Italians'] dispersion. The secular Italian priests don't seem to draw them as well."[313]

The Salesians opened their Italian mission in the basement of the Church of the Epiphany, on Second Avenue, occupying the property between 21st and 22nd Streets, in November, 1900.[314]

Regardless of their success among the Italians, the Salesians still had neither a steady, substantial income with which to support their missions, nor the church promised them by Corrigan when they first arrived in the city. The problem was such that Coppo wrote to Corrigan in December, 1900. He requested that the English-speaking parishioners of the Churches of Saint Brigid, Saint Ann, and Nativity be divided in such a way that they would be under the jurisdiction of the first two churches, thus freeing the Church and house of the Nativity for the Salesians and their Italian mission. Coppo continued, "The very difficult problem of a convenient and permanent settlement for them [the Salesians] in this neighborhood and diocese, from which to continue and advance their mission for the benefit of the Italians, would then be solved."[315]

In response to Coppo's request, Corrigan promised the Salesians the independent administration of the Church of the Transfiguration, which he would give over to the Italian colony of the area.[316]

The English-speaking members of Transfiguration Church continued to move away as the Italians moved into the neighborhood, thus making an Italian national church imperative for that section of the city. Corrigan's plans to grant the church to the Salesians, however, were delayed by a fire that seriously damaged the church in 1901.

The financial instability of the church, resulting from the lack of contributions exacted from the growing Italian constituency of the parish, was very evident by early 1894, when the rector, the Reverend Thomas Lynch, was transferred to the Church of Saint Theresa, and succeeded by the Reverend Thomas McLoughlin.

Corrigan and McLoughlin had discussed at least two plans for the financially weak parish, which included the Salesians once they had arrived in the city. The first plan was to consign the entire parish to the Salesians. The second plan, suggested by McLoughlin, was to assign two Salesian priests to replace the Italian priest already at the church. The plan was an objectionable one, since the Salesians would then be assistants to the rector, while independent in their work among the Italians, thus "the question of *finance* and pastoral rights would become even more muddled."[317] The attendance at Sunday Masses now totaled only seven hundred adults, who donated an average of $90 per week from all sources. McLoughlin wrote the Archbishop, "Eventually (perhaps in five years) this must become an Italian parish or else be sold out, for today we have *one-half* the number attending Mass that we had four years ago. . . . The younger generation here would have not (alas!) the sentimental notions of their fathers and mothers regarding the old church, and are quite prepared for the change, and speak of it as a fact that must come to pass very soon."

As the financial stability of the parish worsened, and the insistence of the Salesians continued for their own parish, Transfiguration was finally transferred to their administration in May, 1902.[318]

McLoughlin had formulated another plan, without the assistance of Corrigan, by which he would move uptown, gathering the old Irish-American members of his congregation into a new parish, which would retain the title of their Mott Street church. Knowing that the Salesians were not to own the church or the property, and that "the Italian people will take possession of their [Irish-Americans'] well-beloved church,"[319] McLoughlin's party of loyal supporters demanded financial restitution be made to their rector by the Italians for his years of hard work on their behalf. According to McLoughlin, the lay trustees were very insistent that the sum of $24,000 be given to him and his proposed exiled congregation, who had been forced to leave their beloved parish by the waves of incoming Italians. This money would be the equivalent of the amount paid by McLoughlin on the parish debt during his years of administration. He felt it would be just that the Italians receive the parish with the same debt of $70,000 he had received when he was first appointed to Transfiguration in 1894. The rationale behind this demand was the belief that the Salesians were backed by a "rich corporation," and by the belief that they would receive more money in stipends from the Italians than McLoughlin had received from all church sources combined.[320] McLoughlin's request for full reimbursement — and especially for permission to retain the parish title — was denied by Corrigan.[321]

On May 1, 1902, the Salesians left their house on East 12th Street and took possession of the Church of the Transfiguration, along with the rectory, on Mott Street. They rented an apartment on the first floor of number 299 8th Street, from which an Italian priest, funded by the Salesians, administered the sacraments and celebrated daily Mass for the Italians in the area. A Salesian from Mott Street also celebrated two Masses there every Sunday.[322] Additionally, the Salesians continued to maintain their Italian mission in the basement of Saint Brigid's Church until 1911.[323]

Conclusions

The establishment in the United States of national churches, distinct from territorial churches because of language and nationality, was an extremely delicate task, in spite of Propaganda's decision of 1887. That decision judged such establishments to be necessary, albeit temporary, concessions to the pastoral exigencies caused by the numerous Catholic European immigrants in America at that time.

The difficulties were multiplied in regard to the founding of independent Italian churches throughout the country. New York City was no exception. Coming from the Kingdom that had conquered the Papal States, the Italians were judged unfairly by many Americans to be totally anticlerical. The majority of the Italian immigrants were desperately poor, and unaccustomed to the American practice of financially supporting their church. Most were poorly educated religiously, having received only the barest essentials of the faith while in Italy. In America their faith was practiced as it was in their homeland, often with celebrations and rituals judged unorthodox or superstitious by many an American cleric and layperson. Because of this, the Italians were judged to be irreligious by many American-born Catholics and by those of other nationalities. Moreover, strong regional prejudices and linguistic differences divided the immigrants of northern Italy from those of the southern provinces of the peninsula, making the establishment of any united parish community a near impossibility.

The wretched religious condition of the Italians in New York was aggravated by a lack of suitable and zealous Italian priests, both diocesan and religious, by little or no organization among those who did work among the Italians, by conflicts among the Italian clergy themselves, and by squabbles between American rectors over territorial jurisdiction and rights.

Pastoral work among the Italians was not easy. The first attempts to establish independent Italian churches in New York City met with enormous difficulties resulting from these problems, despite the eventual moral and financial support granted them by the Archdiocese.

The question, therefore, seems not to have been how to supply independent ecclesiastical institutions for the Italians in New York, but rather how to attend to the multifaceted needs of these immigrants, since the traditional parochial structures affected only a small portion of the Italian community then resident within the city.[324] The prime motivation dominating Corrigan's actions and decisions was the salvation of these people. The enormous difficulties encountered in the founding of the various parishes during these early years of the Italian apostolate in New York, as seen earlier, pointed clearly to the fact that means other than those traditionally employed by the Church in America at that time were necessary to assist the Italian immigrants.

171

CHAPTER FIVE

Mother Cabrini: Early Years in New York

From Rome to New York

The year 1887 marked the jubilee celebrating the fiftieth anniversary of the priestly ordination of Pope Leo XIII.

Archbishop Corrigan assigned his secretary, the Reverend Charles McDonnell, the task of representing him at the Roman festivities marking the occasion. He was also to represent the Archbishop in dealing with various ecclesiastics on behalf of the Italian immigrants in New York City, requesting financial support, zealous priests, and capable women religious.

Corrigan wrote McDonnell on January 7, 1888, instructing him to speak to Archbishop Domenico Jacobini, the secretary general of Propaganda, concerning a plan for an Italian orphan asylum, proposed by the Countess Palma DiCesnola.[1] He was to present a letter Corrigan had enclosed to Jacobini while expressing Corrigan's own reservations about the possible success of, or need for, such an institution in New York City.[2]

Madame DiCesnola had informed Corrigan of the nature of her philanthropy as early as the winter of 1885.[3] She planned to found an Italian orphanage and industrial school in the city, to be staffed by Italian nuns who would instruct the young wards in the "usual school education, fine needlework and fine laundry-work."[4] Corrigan gave at least tentative approbation to the plans, since Madame DiCesnola entered upon a program of fund-raising in order to procure $5,000 that she and Corrigan had agreed upon as a sufficiently sizable sum with which to begin the enterprise.

The Countess was far from practical in her approach to the legal, religious, and financial requirements involved in the establishment of a Catholic charitable institution, regardless of the nobility of her intentions. Her charity, in which she involved her daughters and society friends, was of a social nature.[5] It was an elite charitable enterprise, typical of the period, and was intended by her to be entirely under her direction.[6] Neither Corrigan, who as Archbishop of New York viewed the ministry to the Italians as much more than a social hobby, nor Frances Xavier Cabrini, the very independent foundress of the Missionary Sisters of the Sacred Heart, would find dealing with Mary DiCesnola an easy task.[7]

The relationship between the wealthy and the working poor of the city during this period was a source of consternation among the city's cultural elite. The dilemma of their relationship with the economically deprived, poorly educated yet enfranchised classes posed serious questions to the well-educated. They were not simply questions of morality and economics, but, and more importantly, questions of the authority of culture and intellect in a democratic society in which both the cultivated and illiterate held equal rights, at least in theory, before the law. Social charities, therefore, served two ends for the intellectual and cultural elite. They were a means of alleviating the sufferings pursuant to the economic inequalities of capitalism, as well as instruments by which the members of the upper classes could exercise the authority over society they felt derived from their cultured lives.[8]

The Countess's orphanage project was conceived during the period when her husband's position among the New York intelligentsia was threatened from all sides. Luigi Palma DiCesnola was then the director of the fledgling Metropolitan Museum of Art in New York City. His fame was based upon the large collection of antiquities unearthed during his archaeological excavations in Cyprus. The collection was sold to the museum by DiCesnola, who was soon after appointed its first director. Immediately, charges of fraud were leveled against him by art dealers and critics. DiCesnola was accused of having created statues by assembling fragments from various antique works with the use of an adhesive composed of lime dust and honey.

A flurry of accusations, news stories, political cartoons, and editorials continued the attack, pointing to the galleries of the museum as containing the proof of the forgeries, since, on humid days, swarms of flies could be seen shrouding the nude statues, attracted by the honey-based cement that held the compositions together. Further accusations and rebuttals, public examinations and trials followed, bringing the entire controversy before New York's cultivated elite during the early 1880's, placing a cloud over the authenticity of the collection and questioning the honesty and credibility of DiCesnola's scholarship for years to follow.[9]

Finally vindicated after an array of investigations which left more confusion than answers concerning the collection, DiCesnola was again in the public eye by early 1887. This time the controversy centered upon the proposed Sunday opening of the museum, which would allow the working classes to visit during their only free day of the week. Despite the support for Sunday opening expressed by the press and the public, DiCesnola steadfastly refused, citing excessive operating costs and his disdain for the members of the uneducated working classes, who, he claimed, if allowed within the museum, could be expected to eat their lunches, peel bananas, and even expectorate within his sanctuary of culture.[10]

The DiCesnola orphanage project was a means of securing the social status of the Countess and her husband following these turbulent years of controversy while exercising the social influence, through charitable works, alleged to be theirs as members of the cultivated elite of the city. This is borne out in the numerous letters sent to Corrigan by the Countess during this period concerning the projected orphanage. The limited purpose, small scale of the planned orphanage, and continuous demands and instructions concerning the women religious to be employed by her, clearly suggest that her project, while providing a small number of Italian children with a home and a vaguely religious training, was of the nature of other elite charities of the period, and was designed to enhance the status of the patroness and of her beleaguered husband.[11]

Corrigan was very much aware of the problems involved in the DiCesnola plan. He could only counsel Rome that the Countess's plans were unsound. That was the extent of his ability to determine any decisions or plans concerning the religious sisters of Mother Cabrini, since the Roman authorities were canonically in control of the Italian apostolate in the United States, America being still a mission territory at the time. Propaganda authorities took the advice of Bishop Scalabrini. As will be seen, the flaw in Scalabrini's counsel was the erroneous information sent him by his missionaries in New York, resulting in Rome's support of the DiCesnola plan and the sending of Mother Cabrini and her sisters, contrary to Corrigan's advice.

Corrigan had written to Scalabrini in early February, 1888, praising the Bishop's then newly approved missionary institute, and requested that Italian priests be sent to New York. This request was supported by McDonnell's visit to Piacenza, at which time the Archdiocese's need for Italian women religious was also revealed to Scalabrini. McDonnell's plea elicited the Bishop's immediate promise of assistance.[12]

Scalabrini was in Rome in the summer of 1887 where he first met Mother Cabrini, who desired to open a new religious house within the borders of his Diocese. Scalabrini blessed her new house of Castel San Giovanni on September 4, 1888, at which time he mentioned to Mother Cabrini his desire "to have her Sisters as collaborators in the work begun by him in favor of the Italian emigrants in New York."[13]

Mother Cabrini's missionary interests were not directed toward New York at all, but rather toward China. Besides having little interest in missionary work in the United States, she was fearful lest her newly approved missionary congregation lose its independence and be subsumed into Scalabrini's own missionary work.[14]

Regardless of this, Scalabrini continued to suggest to her the needs of the Italians in New York, presenting her with the concrete plan of Madame DiCesnola's orphan asylum and the offer of a school affiliated with the Church of Saint Joachim, cared for by his missionaries. Scalabrini received information from his missionaries already in New York who were then involved in the establishment of Saint Joachim's Church. Both Zaboglio and Morelli met with DiCesnola in October, 1888. They wrote their superior and insisted upon his swift action to provide Italian sisters in order to realize the Countess's project. Morelli wrote, "Here is a massacre! Unless the Church builds schools and orphanages, then the future of the Colony, whether in respect to faith or nationality, is well gone! In the new church that we are building [Saint Joachim] we hope to make room for these things. If we could have two or three nuns, besides teachers, we could be sure to free the children from the Protestants, and avert a great evil to faith and country."[15]

The weak link in the entire plan was the erroneous, often exaggerated information concerning the orphanage, the sisters, the Countess, and the Archbishop, relayed by the missionaries to Scalabrini.[16] The priests wrote that three sisters were needed who could meet DiCesnola's requirements. They counseled Scalabrini to send the sisters immediately, "and without too many conditions," since Madame DiCesnola and Corrigan would serve as the sisters' protectors. They continued, "In particular, concerning that which regards means, it is well known that here there is no lack of public charity to generously assist pious works, when they are promoted and patronized by influential personages distinguished for their virtue and dignity."[17]

This was far from the truth, since neither the federal nor the New York State governments granted funds to similar Catholic projects. Corrigan had made this quite clear in letters to Propaganda and to Scalabrini, in which he expressed his own reservations regarding Madame DiCesnola's plans and concerning the slim probability of the success of such a financially insecure project. He wrote this to McDonnell in 1888, prior to the priest's visit to Scalabrini, instructing him to convey his thoughts to the Bishop of Piacenza and to show his letter to Archbishop Domenico Jacobini, the secretary general of Propaganda: "My impression is that there would be very great difficulty in establishing an Italian Orphan Asylum; difficulties almost insuperable, unless we obtain aid from the government, which is not giving to our other orphanages."[18]

Corrigan reiterated his objection to Madame DiCesnola's plan in a letter to the Prefect of Propaganda Fide, Cardinal Giovanni Simeoni, clearly explaining the impossibility of the project because of a lack of financial means. He wrote, "It is only a question of moral and material means. If Your Eminence would give me a Colony of Religious women: if you would give me 100,000 lire [$20,000] from the funds of Propaganda although that is only one-fifth of the necessary cost, I guarantee you, within six months, an Italian orphanage built and complete."[19]

Corrigan sent the series of letters he had received from Madame DiCesnola concerning the asylum project to Simeoni, hopeful that their content would convince the Prefect that the project was unsound. He informed Simeoni that the work of Reverend Giorgio Lagana and the Sisters of Charity with Italian children in the city already met the need for such an asylum.[20] The Archbishop continued that all institutions of the Archdiocese were open to the Italians and that the cathedral alone had paid $100,000 that year in order to establish a school for the Italians. Corrigan wrote Scalabrini, providing him with the same information, in February, 1889: ". . . but I confess to Your Most Reverend Excellency that I do not see clearly the means to have the necessary and suitable assistance [for the orphanage and the sisters]. . . . We must rely solely upon our own money, and not expect any subsidy from the Government, because the civil law actually prohibits the granting of funds to any sectarian Institutes . . . which means to Catholic Institutes. . . . The nuns can always earn their own living in some manner; but how, precisely, I would not know."[21] His warnings went unheeded.

Corrigan himself preferred to train American sisters for the work as a much more practical solution than the importing of Italian religious. He expressed this to Scalabrini in April, 1888, when he wrote that it would be an invaluable boon to take advantage of "the ability to avail ourselves of the resources of one of our very numerous Communities, rather than some Sisters coming from Italy for hard work, rather than doing battle with their ignorance of the language, of our customs and their inability to face the many difficulties that probably will arise."[22]

Madame DiCesnola was obdurate in the matter of employing only Italian sisters.[23] Corrigan, accordingly, requested Scalabrini to secure some of the Sisters of Saint Anne to teach and to perform various charitable works among the Italians of the city.[24] Unbeknown to Corrigan, Scalabrini's hopes for expanding his missionary work in New York with the help of Mother Cabrini had been excited further by a telegram sent him by Madame DiCesnola on January 3, 1889, stating "The nuns' house is ready."[25] Believing the DiCesnola cable and his priests' reports, Scalabrini insisted upon the sisters' immediate departure.

In December, 1888, Mother Cabrini went to Rome to consult with Propaganda authorities about the proposals made to her concerning her missionary work among the Italian immigrants in New York. Scalabrini had spoken already with Cardinals Parocchi and Jacobini, both of whom encouraged Mother Cabrini to accept the New York mission. Pope Leo XIII himself personally encouraged her to go, "Not to the East, but to the West. . . . The Institute is still young, and in need of financial means; go to the United States where you will find them along with an enormous field for work."[26]

Propaganda notified Corrigan in the early fall of 1888 that some Italian sisters would be arriving around October 15, 1888.[27] No sisters appeared, but Madame DiCesnola took the opportunity to rent a small house uptown for a monthly rent of $100.[28] By late January, 1889, Scalabrini informed Corrigan of his plans and the decision to send Mother Cabrini and her missionary sisters to New York.[29] In spite of Corrigan's continued objections to the importation of Italian women religious, and his misgivings as to the probable failure of the orphanage, Mother Cabrini and her missionary sisters were assigned to attend to the orphanage and to the Italians of New York by Propaganda in January, 1889.

Scalabrini cabled Morelli concerning the sisters' departure, instructing him to announce to Corrigan their projected arrival toward the end of March, 1889. Faced with a *fait accompli*, Corrigan wrote Mother Cabrini, welcoming her and her sisters to New York, promising to do all in his power to ensure the success of their mission.[30] He assured her that there would be no lack of means in New York for the sisters, who were very much needed to teach. He advised the sisters concerning the insecurity of Madame DiCesnola's orphanage plans, and revealed his own preference for a school for the Italians: "We have a great need of Italian schools and religious teachers, so that I am sure that with the blessing of God all will go well. There will be difficulties, and serious difficulties for the Orphan Asylum, but we must at least make an attempt, and if we do not succeed, the sisters will always be useful and well employed in the schools."[31]

Corrigan concluded the letter by requesting the sisters to remain in Italy for the time being until all had been readied in New York. Mother Cabrini did not receive the letter, since she and her sisters left Codogno, Italy, to begin their journey to New York on March 18, 1889.

Mother Cabrini and her six missionary sisters — Serafina Tommasi, Umilia Capietti, Margherita Ramelli, Saveria Rizzi, Albina Gentili, and Concetta Arnaboldi — sailed from Le Havre on March 23, aboard the steamer *Bourgogne*.[32] They arrived in New York Harbor about 7:00 on the rainy evening of March 31, and were met by Scalabrini's missionaries.[33]

There are two versions describing the rest of the evening. The *Memorie*, or convent diary, recalls the sisters dining with the priests at the Piacenzan house on "American fruit and wine," after which they were brought to "what seemed to us to be a first-class hotel."[34] The other version, composed by one of the sisters years after the event, describes a radically different reception by the Piacenzans. After having eaten, the sisters requested to be brought to the house which the missionaries had said was prepared for them. "But after having had some embarrassed and evasive sentences as a response, they [the Piacenzans] told us that at least for the night, it would be necessary to sleep in a hotel." The sisters were led in the pouring rain through the Italo-Chinese quarter of the city, "in which no American woman, at that time, would ever have set foot," and were put in a dirty, rundown hotel for the night.[35]

The Countess, the Piacenzans, and Mother Cabrini

The sisters met with Corrigan and Madame DiCesnola the following morning, at which time Mother Cabrini received her first view of the mounting tensions between the Archbishop and the Countess over the orphanage project. Faced with Italian religious women whom he had not expected until later in the year, and a project he did not support, Corrigan instructed Mother Cabrini and her sisters to return to Italy. Exhausted, and deathly afraid of ocean voyages, Mother Cabrini's response was immediate: the sisters had come to New York by order of the Holy See, and therefore, they would remain. Taken aback and impressed by the strength and determination of this woman, and aware that he had no real authority to countermand the decisions of Propaganda, Corrigan agreed that they might remain and begin work among the Italians, but on his terms.[36] Corrigan reiterated that which he had written to Mother Cabrini in his letter of March 8, which she had not received, explaining his fears concerning the DiCesnola plan.

The Countess expressed her readiness to care for the sisters, since she had rented a house uptown in a fashionable district, "so that her sheltered orphans could be nearer the ladies of high society from whom she [DiCesnola] hoped for subsidies for her orphans."[37] The house was located at 43 East 59th Street, far from the Italian colonies and too small to be of any real usefulness, since it could accommodate only six children.[38] The sisters were somewhat confused, since the close of the meeting was marked by DiCesnola's demanding the obedience of the sisters to her will and their total dependence upon her largesse. She is recorded as having said, "My nuns must come from me and they will come!" Mother Cabrini understood quickly that she and her sisters had been placed in the awkward position of having to please both the Countess and the Archbishop, a near impossible task, since their views of the orphanage varied radically.[39]

The unpreparedness and instability of the plan became apparent to Mother Cabrini, who had been led to believe that all the necessary preparations for her sisters and the proposed orphanage had been completed. The Scalabrinians in New York had wrongly informed their superior, as the sisters soon discovered. Sister Bernardina recorded the admission of one of Scalabrini's missionaries that the superior of the New York mission, the Reverend Felice Morelli, had knowingly misinformed his superior concerning the state of preparations for the sisters' arrival and the orphanage project. The priest was reported to have replied to the sister's blunt demand for an explanation for the unpreparedness of the sisters' house: "I wrote the lie myself, but I wrote at the order of the Superior [Morelli]. I knew nothing. I acted in obedience and nothing else, truly believing that all was in order."[40]

The final outcome of the meeting between the sisters, the Countess, and the Archbishop was the decision to begin an Italian school until a house could be found and purchased that would prove suitable for an orphanage, and which could be paid for by the Italian colony itself. All agreed to the plan, except the Countess.[41] Following the meeting, the sisters were brought by the Archbishop to live with the Sisters of Charity, who directed an orphan asylum next to the cathedral.[42]

Mother Cabrini met with Archbishop Corrigan the following day. He again insisted that the location for the orphanage chosen by Madame DiCesnola was unsuitable and impractical. The Archbishop added that he would not oppose the project if the house were in the lower city, near the Italian schools, where he thought a residence might be purchased for about $9,000. Corrigan finally instructed the sisters to learn English and to familiarize themselves with American customs in regard to the administration of American schools.[43]

The Countess would approve no plan allowing the sisters to live in two separate locations — at her orphanage and at Corrigan's school. She required all the sisters to be "at her disposition alone."[44] She demanded the total separation of the work of the proposed school from that of her orphanage, since she could never permit the sisters destined for the orphanage to help at any other house or in-

stitution. She also believed the sisters capable of supporting themselves if they sought outside employment. If the sisters were ambitious, so the Countess reasoned, their wages might also supply the
funds necessary for the maintenance of the orphanage.

Madame DiCesnola instructed her lawyers to draw up a legal
document of incorporation for her orphanage, unbeknown to Corrigan, who had told the nuns that such an instrument would not be
necessary for the orphan asylum, at least not at the present time.
The document, as recorded in the *Memorie*, makes no mention whatsoever of the supposed affiliation of the orphanage with the
Archdiocese of New York. The asylum was conceived of as an independent corporation, one that would retain the legal title to the
property, and elect its own trustees. The document fails to make any
reference to the Archbishop of New York or to the Missionary Sisters
of the Sacred Heart as individuals having any relationship with the
institution essential to its existence. The position assigned to the
Archbishop by Madame DiCesnola was that of an inessential col-
laborator, while the sisters were no more than a source of inexpen-
sive labor required to maintain the institution and to attend to the
children, rather than a group of Catholic missionaries brought to
America to assist in the religious and educational development of
poor Italian children. The institution outlined by the document of incorporation was far from keeping with the intentions of either Corrigan or Mother Cabrini.

There are seven paragraphs in the "Instrument" of incorporation,[45] as it is called:

1 ● Objects of the corporation: To receive female orphans of
Italian parentage and to provide legally for their support, education,
and training. Other Italian girls desiring to perfect their education
and training would also be accepted.

2 ● The corporation is to be known as "St. Zita's Female Orphan
Asylum and Industrial School."

3 ● The corporation will acquire the lawful care and custody of
the girls of Italian parentage, or those having one Italian parent. Any
judge, police officer, or other magistrate or officer is authorized to
commit any Italian orphan under twenty-one years of age who is
without the means of support.

4 ● The corporation can adopt a corporate seal, have the power
to sue and to be sued. It can hold, accept, and sell property which

was for the benefit of the corporation. The real estate held at any one time by the corporation is not to exceed $2,000,000, and the annual income of its personal estate is not to exceed $200,000.

5 ● The age of the girls given by the parents, guardian, or magistrates is to be regarded as true.

6 ● Any other legal charitable institution, corporate authority, asylum, or school could assign custody of any girl under twenty-one to this corporation with the corporation's approval.

7 ● The real and personal property of the corporation is non-taxable so long as it is a charitable institution. The trustees have the power to adopt a constitution and to prescribe rules and regulations not inconsistent with the Constitution of the United States or of the State of New York for the election of officers. All debts and contracts are to be signed by the president and the director, with the corporate seal affixed. The trustees will remain in office so long as they are efficient. Their successors are to be elected by the corporation or by their successors.

Because of this, and because Mother Cabrini realized the futility of any mission for her sisters in New York without the assistance of both the Countess and the Archbishop, she convinced Madame Di-Cesnola of the necessity of submitting to the Archbishop's plans if she expected the sisters' assistance and the success of the orphanage.[46]

The final meeting between the Archbishop, the Countess, and Mother Cabrini concerning the orphanage was held on April 10, 1889. The nuns had spent the previous week visiting various Catholic charitable institutions throughout the city in the company of the superior of the Sisters of Charity, whom Corrigan had appointed to the task.[47] As Mother Cabrini wrote to Scalabrini, "It is not rare that the Archbishop accompanies us with his goodness and fully fraternal benignity."[48] Corrigan had contacted various religious superiors during the week, asking their advice. They had suggested an industrial school as having the greater chance of success than an orphan asylum.[49]

The project for a Catholic asylum was finally approved, with the *proviso* that a house in the lower portion of the city would be found and purchased. The funds thus far collected, totaling $4,900, were to be entrusted by Madame DiCesnola to Mother Cabrini. It was also decided to limit the solicitation for financial assistance to Italian churches and benefactors. This last condition was not the result of any alleged "Irish" anti-Italian sentiment on the Archbishop's part, but simply the result of the practical necessities of providing for numerous groups of immigrants and American-born Catholics by the Archdiocese. By 1891, the Archdiocese had a debt of $20,000,000, brought about by the building of schools, churches, charitable institutions, and other projects aimed at assisting the general Catholic population. According to the Third Plenary Council of Baltimore, every parish was required by law to build a school, and every diocese a seminary. The clergy of New York recently had requested Corrigan not to allow any special collections for religious or national groups unless for extreme emergencies, since the parishes were strapped for funds as a result of the above-mentioned legislated building programs.[50] The one exception to Corrigan's limitation on special collections concerned those of Christmas and Easter sent to the various orphanages in the city, including the Italian.[51]

Besides the orphanage, which opened on April 21, 1889, the sisters were also required to begin a school near Saint Joachim Church in order to assist the Scalabrinian missionaries. They began their work on Sunday, April 7, 1889, gathering the children at both Saint Joachim and at the Chapel of the Resurrection for classes in Catholic doctrine.

The classes were very primitive, since there were no school furnishings or equipment of any kind provided the sisters by the missionaries. The children who met in Saint Joachim Church, numbering one hundred in the day school by the eighth day of inscription, met in three "classes," located in the church choir loft, below the loft, and in a small room next to the sacristy.[52]

Problems arose between the sisters and the Piacenzans, since Mother Cabrini required some form of guaranteed security for her sisters from the priests. She spoke with Corrigan concerning the school and a needed residence. The Archbishop proposed that, in accord with New York custom, the rector of the parish within which the school was located be required to pay an annual salary of $300 to each teaching sister. Mother Cabrini was immediately taken with the idea and, bolstered by a letter written to Morelli by Corrigan, spoke with Morelli the following day.[53]

Morelli refused to agree to such a proposal, stating that the Italian colony would willingly give over some land near the church for the sisters to build a house, school, orphanage, and college complex instead of accepting Corrigan's skimpy plan. Madame Di-Cesnola balked at the proposal, and the sisters were left without their hoped-for security.[54] The house provided them by the Piacenzans on Roosevelt Street was uninhabitable, and Mother Cabrini resolutely refused to accept it. She visited the Archbishop, complaining against the Scalabrinians. Corrigan gave her a check for $1,237, which had been deposited for the orphanage, and promised that he would fix both house and school if the priests were unwilling to accommodate the sisters.[55]

Corrigan wrote Scalabrini on May 8, 1889, reporting on the missionaries and the sisters and the difficulties that had arisen recently between them. He conveyed the sisters' dissatisfaction, since they were without a decent house or fixed salary, and had received from the missionaries "only the promise that they would not be wanting for anything."[56]

Mother Cabrini and her sisters remained with the Sisters of Charity until Morelli could give them decent lodgings, on the property recently purchased by the missionaries, which he hoped to complete by May 1. After showing Mother Cabrini some rooms and promising to renovate them, he promptly rented them out, giving the sisters instead "two small holes, lowly, filthy and very tiny, barely large enough for two nuns let alone five."[57] Mother Cabrini refused even to enter them, whereupon, according to Corrigan, Morelli promised his own rooms, until he could build the sisters two or three of more suitable quality.

Continuing, the Archbishop related to Scalabrini the fears of Mother Cabrini concerning the success of her mission, threatened by the impracticality of Morelli's plans. He wrote, "It is necessary to give the nuns at least a healthy place to live, that is clean and sufficiently comfortable. Besides, I would like to give them a fixed pension, as is the custom with the other nuns in the Diocese. I will try to settle this. It seems to me to be better to follow the extant customs of this country in this matter. I do not tell you this in order to complain, but merely to show you the actual situation."

The house was finally completed, but the nuns were fearful that they would not receive it as promised, even though Corrigan himself had come to inspect the renovations. Mother Cabrini had become very much aware of the growing financial problems within the

Piacenzan mission, and of the resulting internal conflicts among the missionaries, who now looked upon the sisters as an added expense.[58]

The sisters received confirmation of their fears on May 31, when the Piacenzans informed them that they had decided to occupy the house intended for the sisters, who were promptly shown another hovel. It was at this point that Mother Cabrini decided that all her sisters would live together. Frustrated in her attempts to placate Madame DiCesnola by bowing to her demands that the school sisters not reside with her orphanage sisters, and enraged by Morelli's empty promises, she demanded that a house be provided for the sisters by the missionaries near the Roosevelt Street church. While the newly acquired shanty was being prepared, the sisters moved into a temporary residence on White Street.[59]

These temporary quarters were "discreet but filthy," without beds, sheets, or any other basic amenities, according to the sisters.[60] Things promised by the missionaries never arrived, with the excuse that since the sisters were moving in a few days to their new residence, the provision of furniture for their temporary residence was a useless and extravagant expense.[61] Beds, some small kitchen utensils, and a butcher's block were finally provided nearly a week after the sisters' arrival in their temporary quarters.[62] By June 8, 1889, the new house was finally ready for occupancy by the sisters. However, upon their arrival they found the house infested with insects and the stove broken, forcing the sisters to eat cold food for a number of days.[63]

Morelli wrote Scalabrini on June 9, giving his version of the situation.[64] He portrayed the sisters as troublesome and never content with his efforts on their behalf, since in Italy they were accustomed to "their convents and their vast Italian gardens." He reported that the nuns lived in a "luxurious apartment" provided them by Madame DiCesnola at great expense. He claimed he had provided a house for them at an exorbitant rent, but Mother Cabrini, dissatisfied, decided to surrender it in favor of another next to the church which was in need of restoration. Such restoration was costly, and was delayed, not by any laxity on the Piacenzans' part, as alleged by the sisters, but because of the city's delay in sending building officials to inspect the house and approve the proposed renovations. Morelli concluded his letter by complaining that he had spent

$1,000 for the sisters in less than two months' time, and had bought furniture for them at the additional cost of $370, which was much more than he had spent on his own missionaries.

Mother Cabrini rendered her point of view to Scalabrini in a letter dated June 10, in which she emphasized the need to organize the school.[65] She asked Scalabrini to insist upon the immediate provision of the school and the sisters' house with the basic necessities by his priests. Concerning Morelli she wrote, "This Father [Morelli] is very good, full of the best qualities for which we truly esteem him, but when one tries to deal with the school and the nuns, one must content oneself with good desires and promises, he always tells me yes, but finishes nothing." She continued to narrate the chain of events similar to that recounted in Corrigan's letter to Scalabrini, pleading with Scalabrini to instruct his missionaries to put all in order so that she might begin "doing that which you brought me here to do."

Scalabrini wrote his priests in mid-June, informing them that they were bound in conscience to provide for the sisters. As a result, a house was finally readied near the church.[66]

The school opened in May, 1889.[67] Even with the eventual provision of a residence, the relationship between the sisters and the Piacenzans did not entirely improve, thereby continuing to block the effective beginning of the sisters' apostolate. Morelli decided that, since the sisters desired a salary for their teaching, they could exact it from the Italian children attending the school. Because the children were required to pay fifty cents per month to attend the school, the sisters could collect a suitable wage from them.[68] The arrangement was not a satisfactory one, and the question of salaries needed to support the sisters would continue.

The sisters taught the Italian children in a day and a night school at Saint Joachim Church, with more than two hundred students, both boys and girls, in attendance by late July, 1890. They continued to teach catechism each Sunday, with daily classes in preparation for the reception of the sacraments. The sisters also had a direct effect upon parish life in areas other than education, organizing various societies for young girls and women, and beginning an apostolate of visitations throughout the area.[69] Mother Cabrini's sisters continued to teach at Saint Joachim's until August, 1892, when the Piacenzans could no longer pay the sisters' stipends as a result of their own financial problems in their other missions in the city.

Manresa at West Park

By early April, 1889, when Mother Cabrini and the Countess Di-Cesnola met with Corrigan concerning the proposed orphanage, the sisters already had four Italian orphans in their care, residing with them at 43 East 59th Street.[70] After wading through the conflicts between the Archbishop and the Countess, Mother Cabrini was faced with the problem of legal incorporation of the new orphanage in accord with the laws of the State of New York. A meeting of Mother Cabrini, two of her sisters, Monsignor Donnelly (one of the vicars general of the Archdiocese), and Josephine Shaw Lowell (the Commissioner of the State Board of Charities) had been arranged by Donnelly on June 15, 1889, at the rectory of Saint Michael Church, to discuss the state's requirements for the incorporation of the orphanage.

Mother Cabrini was opposed to any idea of legally incorporating the asylum or of naming trustees. According to the *Memorie*, she requested information concerning the commitment of children to the asylum by the courts. She believed there could be no legal obstacles, since the vicar general of the Archdiocese of New York was involved, and could clear up any complications by the mere exercise of his authority. She and the sisters were dismayed to find the legal requirements of the state, as recited by Commissioner Lowell, to be "the same ideas of the Archbishop."[71]

The difficulties put forth by Mrs. Lowell were three: (1) the city already had a number of such institutions with a total of 15,000 orphans and derelicts cared for as wards of the state; (2) the children of various nationalities should be brought up as Americans, being taught by Americans in English; (3) in order to receive government funding, a charter was required and, according to some, administration by laypersons. Other opinions, the commissioner continued, held that women religious could also be administrators, but they must appear as laywomen before the government. In her report of July 11, Mrs. Lowell recorded her meeting, "I explained to them [the sisters] and to the vicar general that I thought it necessary to be very careful in acting in this matter; that it would be a dangerous precedent to grant a charter to foreigners coming here for the purpose of opening an asylum for foreign children, to be supported by money raised by taxation. I said that it seemed to me to be necessary to secure responsible residents of New York City as incorporators and to have very strict limits as to age, length of residence in the United States, and in New York State and City, ability of parents to pay, numbers to be supported, length of time for which supported, and probably as to the other points, in order to avoid the establishment of such an asylum acting as a temptation to poor Italians to immigrate."[72]

Determined to establish her orphanage on a firm basis, despite any legal obstacles or requirements, Mother Cabrini began casting about for suitable property and a larger house to accommodate her wards. She was interested in new property for a number of reasons. The location the sisters then occupied was unsuitable, being far from the Italian colonies. The house rented by Madame DiCesnola, originally intended for six children, was crammed with twenty-four orphans by 1890. The unpleasant dependence of the sisters upon the Piacenzan missionaries for everything added an extra emotional burden on the sisters as well. The rent and living expenses required to live within the city were extremely high, and the relationship between the Countess and the Archbishop, as well as between the Countess and the nuns, continued to be strained.[73]

When the Franciscan sisters put their house on 109th Street on the market, Mother Cabrini first considered purchasing it for $55,000. While considering the purchase, and the feasibility of the transaction, Mother Cabrini returned to Italy in July, in order to attend to matters at the motherhouse in Codogno, and to bring other sisters back to New York. During her absence the Jesuits decided to sell their novitiate property at West Park. The sisters wrote to Mother Cabrini, informing her of the availability of the property. After her return to New York the following April, she visited the proposed site.

Manresa, as the property was known, was in the Catskills on the Hudson River, a two-hour ride from New York City. Mother Cabrini had visited the property once with Corrigan while inspecting the various charitable institutions of the Archdiocese. The property and partly furnished houses were offered at a relatively low price, the ostensible reason for the sale having been a paucity of fresh water.[74] The property was purchased in June, 1890,[75] and became the site of the Sacred Heart Orphan Asylum and the novitiate for the Missionary Sisters of the Sacred Heart.[76] The DiCesnola house continued to serve the sisters, but only as a house of admission for the orphans.[77]

The project received no public funding for the first years of its existence.[78] Nonetheless, the church authorities saw the orphanage as an opportunity, not only for sheltering Italian children, but for educating them in a truly Christian manner. Cardinal Simeoni wrote Mother Cabrini soon after the purchase of Manresa: ". . . your field of action is not restricted only to this [providing housing for orphans]. The civil and religious education of numerous Italian boys and girls is given you, and the fruit that they [the children] gather from your efforts will be very satisfying."[79]

Columbus Hospital

As the Italian immigrants became more numerous in New York City, the need for a specifically Italian hospital was felt. A small dispensary and hospital had been begun by the mid-1880's. Originally called the Garibaldi Hospital, it was later reorganized and known as the Italian Hospital,[80] located at 117 Second Street, in which the Piacenzan missionaries served as chaplains.[81]

Scalabrini's missionaries drew up a plan for a Catholic hospital which was approved by Scalabrini and the Archdiocesan consultors by December, 1890. Corrigan expressed his desire that the proposed hospital be administered by a congregation of women religious, and that Morelli meet with the Archdiocesan officials in order to receive further instructions regarding the congregation to be employed, as well as the means of soliciting funds for the project.[82]

The missionaries believed sufficient funds could be collected by the Italian sisters themselves, who could go about the city soliciting financial assistance for the hospital from local merchants and Catholics. As one of the Piacenzans in New York wrote, "It is enough that a nun (they enjoying great respect) present herself at a store, warehouse, factory; she obtains that which she desires, even more if she is working for the sick or for orphans: one can find charity in every class of people, and all beings."[83] The Piacenzans managed to collect $10,000 in one week of solicitation, which they used as a down payment on ten lots, located at 109th Street, at a cost of $50,000.[84] This was the beginning of Columbus Hospital.[85]

Scalabrini engaged the Sisters of Saint Anne to work in the new Italian hospital, six of whom left Piacenza on March 18, 1891, accompanied by the Reverend Pietro Bandini, and arrived in New York by early April. Since the sisters were prohibited by their foundress from collecting for the hospital, they were unable to continue their work, thus necessitating the engagement of another congregation of women religious by the Scalabrinians.[86]

Mother Cabrini was apprehensive when first approached by Scalabrini to accept the hospital work. She had already warned her sisters in New York following Morelli's invitation to take over the hospital, telling them: ". . . go slowly and do not bind yourselves; go slowly and speak to Morelli."[87] After Cardinal Simeoni voiced his thoughts, supporting Scalabrini's insistence, Mother Cabrini became convinced of the necessity of the hospital work in New York.[88] Simeoni wrote Corrigan in July, 1891,[89] as did the Cardinal Vicar of Rome, Cardinal Parocchi, commending Mother Cabrini and her work in the hospital to the care and protection of the Archbishop.[90]

There were conditions insisted upon by Mother Cabrini if her sisters were to assume responsibility for the hospital project. She required the sisters to live separated from the patients; Mass was to be celebrated daily in the hospital; the doctors and nurses were to be chosen by the sisters according to need, but the bulk of the work was to be carried out by the sisters themselves in order to keep the number of doctors low; the sisters were to receive one-half of the total money collected for the hospital; no families were allowed to live inside the hospital at all. These conditions were not to be agreed upon verbally. Mother Cabrini insisted that they be written and signed by the commission dealing with the legal incorporation of the institution and by Corrigan himself.[91]

Mother Cabrini returned to New York in September, 1891, accompanied by ten sisters destined for the new hospital. She remained in the city only long enough to organize the sisters and their hospital work, and then, on October 10, she departed for Nicaragua, where she opened a house and school in Granada, thus beginning the missionary efforts of her institute in Central America. From Nicaragua, in response to an invitation extended her by Archbishop Janssens, she traveled to New Orleans, where she established a house and school for Italian children.[92]

During her absence from New York, the hospital and the sisters' relations with the Piacenzan missionaries took a decided turn for the worse, compelling Mother Cabrini to return on April 27, 1892. Having incurred debts to supply the hospital, Morelli found he could not meet his financial obligations, and attempted to relieve himself of his liabilities by shifting the burden of both the debt and accumulated interest for the various loans to the nuns.[93]

Supported by Corrigan, Mother Cabrini decided to quit the Piacenzan hospital, which by August was threatened with public auction, and to begin her own Italian hospital. Armed with a total of $550, the fruit of donations from Corrigan and from four wealthy Italians whom the Archbishop had recommended, Mother Cabrini rented two apartments at 41 East 12th Street, costing $300 per month, thus beginning Columbus Hospital anew on September 17, 1892.[94] On December 17, 1894, Mother Cabrini purchased additional property for the hospital at numbers 224, 226, 228, and 230 East 20th Street.[95]

Conclusions

Mother Cabrini and her sisters continued to expand their work in New York, embracing other activities among the Italian immigrants. By 1902, the Missionary Sisters of the Sacred Heart were involved in school and catechetical work at Transfiguration and Saint Roch Churches. They taught at and administered an industrial school at Our Lady of Pompeii Church, conducted both the Sacred Heart Orphan Asylum at Manresa and the Columbus Hospital. They visited Bellevue and City Hospitals, the city almshouses, as well as the Tombs and Sing Sing prisons in search of their needy fellow countrymen.[96]

The major obstacles to the progress of Mother Cabrini's work in these her early years in New York were a lack of funds and a lack of united effort on the part of those involved in the Italian apostolate. Restricted by Corrigan from collecting outside the Italian colony, so as to minimize the frictions between the national groups in the city, and faced with an Italian colony that was neither generous, wealthy, nor accustomed to contributing to the Church, the Missionary Sisters had recourse only to Propaganda Fide, which had supported their work morally from the beginning. Propaganda, in financial straits itself and bound to support other missions throughout the world, supported Mother Cabrini's efforts as best it could.

As the result of her independent spirit and strong faith, Mother Cabrini proved to be quite capable of maintaining the unity of purpose and action among her sisters, and thus overcoming most obstacles and opposition to her work in New York. Once she had convinced Corrigan of the strength of her purpose and of her dedication to the salvation of her conationals, the Archbishop granted her financial and moral support, as well as the authorization necessary to embark upon her numerous works.

Mother Cabrini wrote Cardinal Ledóchowski in 1894, concerning the religious condition of the Italians in the United States and of the great threat to their salvation she believed existed in America at the time. She reflected that every individual and institution "flourishes . . . in regards human industries, and are equally wretched to the eyes of the faith in this country in which heresy triumphs, and the Catholic participates in that apathy, in that religious indifference, in that worldly spirit."[97]

She discovered in New York that variety of religious indifference and ignorance among the Italians she would find common among her conationals elsewhere in the country. She went on to point out that "among the majority of Italian immigrants nothing more is known than that Religion exists." The Italians, she continued, rarely frequented church or received the sacraments, and would simply tell her, "We will go to church when we return to Italy."[98] The Italians, she concluded, were affected by their poverty and the materialistic spirit of the United States, leading them to a state of indifference toward the institutional Church.

The Catholic faith of the majority of Italian immigrants, populated by saints, angels, spirits, and demons, was more a homespun folk religion that reflected their limited world than an expression of credence in the Church's dogmatic formulations. Since the religious faith and practice of the Italian immigrants was not always liturgically correct, or orthodox, according to American Church standards, it was seen as irreligion by those who actively supported the institutional Church. Propaganda was convinced that deep within every Italian peasant was the seed of a Catholic dedicated to the institutional Church. All that was necessary to nurture that seed of orthodox faith and practice was a number of clergy and religious who, with zeal and charity, would save the Italians.[99] For the Vatican, Corrigan, and Mother Cabrini, the institutional Church was the center of one's Catholic life. For most Italian immigrants, it was only a small and sometimes dispensable part of their religious life.

Mother Cabrini saw one of the necessary solutions to the problem as being Catholic schools for the Italians, in which they could be instructed in their religion, while also being prepared to join the culture and society of their new homeland as Americans. She was opposed to Scalabrini's idea of purely Italian schools for Italian immigrants in America. Mother Cabrini believed this to be senseless, feeling such schools to be counterproductive to the real interests of the Italians, since it was imperative that they learn English and the customs of their adopted country.[100]

In her opinion, a broad education steeped in the customs and language of America, bolstered by life within the Church, would protect the Italians from the numerous missions supported by the various Protestant churches, and from the religious indifference and materialism of the American culture, seen by Mother Cabrini as posing a serious threat to the already tenuous relationship many Italians of New York had with the Catholic Church.[101]

CHAPTER SIX

Aspects of Italian Parish Life in New York

The churches and chapels that provided for the spiritual needs of the Italian colonies in the Archdiocese of New York numbered twenty-two at the time of Corrigan's death in May, 1902.[1]

The Congregation of Propaganda Fide had determined as necessary the provision of national churches — either as quasi-parishes, or succursal chapels. Such churches were judged by Propaganda to be temporary concessions to the Catholic national groups in America. However, their development and establishment was not looked upon as temporary by those Catholic immigrants who formed their congregations and supported them financially.

Conscious of the tensions and animosities existing between the national groups then in the United States, the Holy See felt that too strong an emphasis upon the national spirit of the individual groups by the Church was unnecessary, if not harmful, to the faith of the immigrants. The Church felt it necessary to do all in its power to remove the obstacles standing in the way of the immigrants joining with their coreligionists from other nations and with American-born Catholics to form a united Catholic Church in the United States.[2] Many Catholic immigrants in the United States were not overly affected by these Roman decisions concerning their national churches, for in spite of the limitations and directives of the local ordinaries and pastors, the immigrants expressed their Catholic faith in ways familiar to their European homeland. The Italians were no exception.[3]

Their newly united nation had no official connection with the Church, yet the Italians desired that their own churches be similar to those established throughout the country for other immigrant groups, whose patriotism usually was linked to their faith. When these churches were granted the Italians, either as independent or annex congregations, the Italian immigrants quite naturally expressed their faith by means of religious ceremonies and customs brought with them from Italy, which were not always looked upon favorably by American Catholics.

One of the major difficulties encountered in providing pastoral care for the Italians in the United States was the provision for the differences of dialect and custom, as well as the problems brought about by the regional rivalries of the northern and southern Italians, which often led to open conflict within congregations. These factors all contributed to confirming the erroneous view generally held by Americans that the Italian immigrants were irreligious and barbarous.

With no link between nationalism and Church, divided by provincial loyalties and dialects, and practicing their own traditional religious customs, the relationship of most Italian immigrants with the Church in America had to begin in very practical terms. For the Italians, whose relationship with God and the saints was a very practical and utilitarian one, the Church, the instrument of that same God, had also to be found practical and useful to the Italian immigrant by helping to protect and assist him in the New World. It was necessary for the Church to show itself as truly Catholic, rising above national differences, preferring no one group over another, and interested in the welfare of all its members. It also had to prove itself to be concerned for the salvation of the Italians, and not interested in their exploitation for monetary gain or political power, as was feared by many Italian immigrants. The pope, then so recently without land or temporal power, was required to show himself to be God's man, interested enough in the well-being of his expatriate conationals and coreligionists that he would make manifest his earnest pastoral solicitude by means of the local bishops, priests, and churches dedicated to the welfare of the Italians in America.

The Italian priest felt the tension of ministering to his conationals. He was called upon to attend to his people in a manner to which they were accustomed in Italy, employing familiar dialects, symbols, and ceremonies, while at the same time being sensitive to the need to slowly harmonize the Catholic practices of his congregation with those of the Church in America.

Officially, the Church was not interested in making the Italians into Americans, nor was it dedicated to preserving their Italian identity *per se*. Rather, the Church desired to preserve the Catholic faith of its people by ensuring that their religious observances and traditions, so often bearing a nationalistic air, were not destructive to their unity with other Catholics in the United States.

Since the vast majority of Italians in New York City did not frequent church services or receive the sacraments with regularity, the Church attempted to attract them by meeting the extraordinary needs of the expatriate Catholic Italians that were other than sacramental. This was done especially by means of priestly assistance, religious education, mutual aid societies, and the celebrations of feast days familiar to the immigrants.

Priestly Assistance

As a result of the political tensions between the Church and the State of Italy, many Italian immigrants in New York were decidedly anticlerical. Corrigan saw one of the major problems in the Italian apostolate to be a lack of "that sentiment of faith and trust which is the prime factor of the moral rapport between the priest and the faithful."[4]

The development of this necessary rapport was aided by the fact that those Italians who did frequent church required that there be at least a good priest capable of speaking Italian as a prerequisite for their attendance.[5] This was the wedge necessary for the slow improvement of relations between the Italian immigrant and his Church. The response to the Church by the first-generation Italians in New York was slow, but it continued to improve because of the efforts of zealous priests who were faithful and devoted to their spiritual charges. An example of this was seen in the ministry of the Reverend Nicòla Russo, S.J., at the Church of Our Lady of Loretto. Within a few weeks after beginning his work, he brought 1,000 Italians back to the Church and the sacraments.[6] In time, he succeeded in bringing more than 5,000 back to the Church, mainly immigrants from southern Italy.[7]

The work of dedicated priests was not limited to the sacramental ministry alone, for as the Italian colony in New York grew, so too did their needs. Since few city or government officials spoke Italian, the only individuals to whom the Italians could turn in time of need were the labor bosses and the priest. The priest was obviously the only one of the two formally associated with an institution, and usually the only one not interested in personal gain. Quite naturally, then, did he begin to fulfill some of the functions of the *padroni*, if not always as effectively, at least with less costly requirements to those he assisted.

The priests within the Italian colonies came to assist children without homes or family; they watched over and aided young men and women released from correctional or charitable institutions; they attended to the needs of the Italians arrested and convicted of various crimes; they counseled those unjustly convicted or in need of legal advice; they visited the sick and provided for their assistance in the various city hospitals; they secured jobs for arriving Italian immigrants and strove to protect their legal rights regarding work, salaries, and contracts; they protected and guided the arriving Italians at the city port; they assisted the immigrants in the parish itself, helping them to adapt and adjust to their new surroundings; and they tried to better the lives of the immigrants by educating them and their children.

Education

The need for education among the Italian immigrants in New York was strongly felt by Corrigan and by some of the priests and religious involved in the Italian apostolate. However, by the end of the Archbishop's life, there were only six parish schools within the Archdiocese specifically for Italian children.

There were two reasons for this lack of distinctly Italian Catholic schools. The first was the constant lack of sufficient funds on the part of the individual churches and of the Archdiocese to construct, operate, and maintain individual Italian parochial schools. The second reason was that many of the Italian immigrants took the education of their children for granted, and, since many suffered extreme poverty, required their children to work rather than to study or attend school.

The majority of the Italians arriving in New York were also found to be without a rudimentary knowledge of their Catholic faith, oftentimes coming to the churches to be married without ever having prepared for or received their first confession or communion, and rarely being confirmed.[8]

The Archdiocese was faced with the problem of providing facilities at least for the religious education of these children. However, the obstacles were similar to those encountered by the parochial schools, especially the problem of a lack of parental cooperation.[9] Most parishes had catechism classes, which did affect a large number of Italian children, especially in classes preparatory to the reception of the sacraments. These programs, and the early efforts to educate the Italian immigrants, were not so fruitful as was hoped during the beginning years of the organization of the Italian apostolate in New York. Much more effective in the life of the Italian colonies were the various parish societies.

Parish Societies

Each parish, whether national or territorial, had its religious societies. These attracted members of the congregation — men, women, adolescents, and children — who were drawn together for devotional, social, and charitable reasons. The religious society served as a social forum while performing various parochial functions and usually led the members to a regularized sacramental and spiritual practice. Such societies were the "soul of the parish,"[10] and offered their members a dignity and a society oftentimes prohibited them in the larger American society because of linguistic differences and racial and economic prejudices. In the parish societies the members felt a sense of importance and could rise to positions of leadership often denied them outside the Church.

The Italians expanded upon this basic social and religious structure of the parish by creating societies offering assistance to the members in time of need, death, illness, disaster, and, sometimes by serving as labor organizations or forms of what might today be considered banking and credit unions. Such societies were known as mutual aid societies. The official purpose of such societies was, of course, religious in nature, usually involving the assistance of the members by the strengthening of their Catholic faith.[11]

The societies were bound to the church by their respective constitutions, clearly describing their obligations and rights in relationship to their parish, pastor, and members. Each member was bound to pay a membership dues or tax, the larger portion of which went for the support of the parish church, while the balance was retained by the societies for social functions, patronal celebrations, and the assistance of needy members. Each society had its own elected officers, usually watched over by one of the parish priests, and always subject to the rector.

The more practical reason for the existence of such organizations was the moral and financial support offered to the members and their families in time of need and tragedy. The members could receive loans, legal assistance, limited hospital and medical aid, the assurance of a Christian burial with honors, as well as temporary financial assistance for the surviving family members of one of the society associates.

By means of such societies the Church provided religious, charitable, and social services to members of the Italian community who most likely would not otherwise have had recourse to the Church or its ministers.

Feast Days and Patron Saints

The annual celebrations in honor of the patron saints of the parish and of the Italian societies marked the liturgical and social high points in the life of the Italian colonies.[12] They were also the source of great embarrassment for many American Catholics, ever mindful of the foreign appearance of their Church before the American Protestant majority. Such celebrations were pointed to by American Protestants as confirming their suspicions concerning the Church as superstitious. To the Italian immigrants these celebrations were essential expressions of their faith as well as links to their culture and homeland, even though considered unorthodox by many American Catholic clerics and laypersons.

In the parish church, each society had its own shrine with a statue or image of its patron, jealously guarded over by the society members, and maintained and decorated by their financial support. In some churches the competition grew so fierce between societies formed by members from different Italian towns, or by northern and southern Italians, that contracts were entered into between the individual societies and the church's rector. These contracts clearly established the equal rights of each society, the societies' financial obligations toward the parish church, and the church's obligation to provide ceremonies of equal elaborateness and solemnity for each society on their respective feast days.[13]

The religious celebrations usually began three nights before the actual feast day with a triduum in honor of the patron, composed of nightly sung vespers, a panegyric extolling the wonders and virtues of the patron saint, and Benediction of the Blessed Sacrament. The vigil of the feast was celebrated with solemn sung vespers.[14] The feast day itself was observed in the most elaborate fashion possible with the church societies all in attendance at the high Mass, followed by a procession with the statue or image of the patron through the streets of the colony.

The streets forming the route of the procession were usually decorated with lights, draperies, and garlands, the elaborateness of which was limited solely by the funds collected by the society from members of the colony. An altar would usually be erected in the street and decorated with candles, flowers, tinsel, and the image of the patron saint. Those in attendance would be expected to make an offering to the saint, in order to defray expenses. If the statue or image were newly purchased, individuals could gain the honor of being the patron's godmother or godfather for a slight offering to the society.[15]

Parochial Life[16]

The entire parochial life of the Italian churches and congregations in New York was usually composed of a blending of cultures, customs, ceremonies, and beliefs, as well as provincial and familial allegiances. These latter were not always harmonious, but were brought together in the local parish church by practical necessity. The volatility of such allegiances and provincial prejudices was unexpected and unimagined by Church officials prior to the phenomenon of mass immigration to America.

The Italian immigrants could not be expected, and did not themselves expect, to be forced to forget their own culture and traditional loyalties upon arrival in the United States. The Church provided the vehicle — the national parish — by which the Italians could gather for worship and social exchange in a manner familiar to them, while at the same time slowly changing and adapting to the American culture around them naturally and without coercion. Constant requests for devotional books, relics, religious objects, and images were sent to Propaganda officials, local Italian bishops, and fellow priests in Italy from Italian priests working among their fellow countrymen in New York.[17]

The liturgical year was a continuous celebration of various major feast days of the Universal Church, the local devotional feast days, and commemorations valued by individual members of the Italian congregations reminiscent of their Italian village life. Such celebrations would be prefaced by novenas and Benediction lasting three to seven days, oftentimes offered by an individual member of the parish for the intention of a deceased relative or friend. On such occasions, invitations would be extended by the donor and the parish to all friends and relatives of the deceased that they might attend the church function. By such means and ceremonies, the Church slowly became a center of life for the Italian colony, uniting the Italians' sense of loyalty to family and friends with religious observance, while identifying the Church as the protector of that which was sacred to the Italian immigrants in their new homeland.[18]

Since the Italian immigrants in New York were more willing to attend such functions than Mass, ceremonies such as novenas, Benediction, and other non-sacramental rites became very important in the life of the national parish and were celebrated with great frequency during the liturgical year. The attendance being very good at such functions, they proved to be occasions during which religious instruction could be given the people by means of a sermon, explaining doctrine, encouraging more frequent reception of the sacraments, and full participation in parish life. Loyalty to the pope as a religious leader was also stressed during these ceremonies. The Italians in attendance were reminded of the pope's concern for them. Concrete proof of his pastoral solicitude for them was provided by offering the Italian immigrants present his papal blessing or small religious articles blessed by him especially for the members of the parish. The anticlerical prejudices of many were thereby weakened, or at least called into question, since most parochial references to the pope avoided political controversy and were made in the context of actions or occasions expressing the pope's personal generosity to the Italian immigrants as his far-off children.[19]

The Church officially wanted no exclusive affiliation with any one national group, and forbade the consecration of any one cultural form or Catholic national group in the life of the national parishes, fearful that exaggerated nationalism on the part of the Catholic immigrants could seriously damage the unity of Catholicism in the United States. However, on the practical level of day-to-day parish life, the cultural expression of the faith was inevitable, and could not be easily banned without possible harm to the faith of the immigrants themselves.

The subtle Americanization that naturally took place among the

Italian immigrants in the United States can be seen in most aspects of the immigrants' life, including the liturgical practice of the parish. Such things as a call for uniformity in worship on the part of the congregation, the revamping of certain ceremonies, and even the reorganization of Mass schedules and aspects of parish life to follow American practice, attests to the slow, natural yet persistent Americanization of the Italians in response to the new culture around them.

However persistent the pressures of the American society might have been upon the Italian colony to adapt quickly to their new surrounding culture, the Italians tenaciously clung to the values and traditions brought with them from Italy, since they were the mainstay of their lives as expatriates. Preeminent among these was a strong sense of family unity and loyalty. All else paled before the Italians' sense of family. This sense of familial loyalty and obligation served as another source of unity between the Italian immigrants and the Church in America, since the Church also insisted upon the sacredness of the family and strove to uphold and preserve its importance among its members.[20]

The Italian parish in New York City proved itself to be an institution truly concerned for the welfare of the Italian immigrants, interested only in their salvation, and willing to employ the customs and language of the Italians in order to protect them and to strengthen their faith. The parochial ministrations, the religious and social programs of the various churches may not have been so successful as originally desired and hoped, but the Church proved to be loyal to its constituents, even in the face of the religious indifference and anticlericalism of many of its Italian members. By preserving the cultural forms and expressions of the faith so familiar to the Italians, and by assisting them socially in the difficult transition to their new American life, the Church invited the Italian immigrants to abandon the prejudices so prevalent in the nation recently left behind, and to embrace the Church of their fathers, so deeply rooted in the traditions of their homeland, while they were seeking a new life in a land offering unlimited opportunities for all.

Conclusions

The United States had been the ultimate destination for Catholic European immigrants since colonial times. With Catholics from different nations gathered together in one country, the Roman authorities prudently decided that the Church could not favor any one national group or any one culture. It was imperative that the Church disengage nationalism as much as possible from the faith of the immigrants, allowing for the individual cultural expressions of the faith as necessary for the salvation of souls, so long as such expressions presented no obstacle to the faith or unity of the Church in the United States.

It was during the final twenty years of the last century that Propaganda authorities were made very much aware of the pastoral need for the Church to assist the thousands of Italians who were then emigrating to America. Since the Italian government did little of value in favor of the Italian immigrants, the Church was granted a clear opportunity to assist its members which could not be ignored.

The Vatican, still smarting from the wounds inflicted by the government of the *Risorgimento*, saw this pastoral necessity as also affording the Church an opportunity to defend itself against the anticlericalism of the new united Italian state while regaining the respect and trust of the Italians themselves by extending to those expatriate conationals of the pope the pastoral solicitude of their Holy Father. The plan of action, developed primarily by Scalabrini and taking the form of his Missionary Institute of Saint Charles Borromeo and the Società San Raffaele, was, on paper, the ideal solution. However, the project was not so immediately effective as intended, since adequate preparations were not made to train the priests or to formulate the actual work of the society in detail.

By late 1887, Propaganda Fide itself decided to guide the pastoral efforts in favor of the Italians emigrating to the Americas, sending priests and religious, funds and ecclesiastical goods, while instructing the American bishops how best to cooperate. The American hierarchy had already expressed its unwillingness to grant special attention to the Italian immigrants, or to any individual immigrant group, by way of the letter authored by Bishop Thomas Becker in the name of the fathers of the Third Baltimore Council. America felt the problem to exist in Italy; Rome informed America that the problem had moved to America, and it was there that the solution would be found under the guidance of Propaganda.

The American hierarchy was very much aware of the foreign image of the Catholic Church before Protestant America, and, therefore, became divided over the whole question of pastoral care of Catholic immigrants in a Church striving to be loyal to its European heritage while adapting to its American surroundings and institutions. This division became more pronounced, since it touched upon the entire question of Catholic education. It contributed to the formation of a liberal party within the American hierarchy, favoring the rapid Americanization of the Catholic immigrants and of the Church itself, led by Archbishop John Ireland of Saint Paul; and a conservative party, favoring the natural Americanization of the Catholic immigrants while striving to protect their faith, led by Archbishop Michael Augustine Corrigan of New York.

Corrigan, as coadjutor Archbishop to Cardinal John McCloskey, had spoken out against special provisions for the Italian immigrants in America, preferring a more concerted effort in favor of all Catholic immigrants. However, as the ordinary of the Archdiocese of New York, faced with so many thousands of needy Italians within the confines of his Archdiocese who appeared indifferent to the Church, and confronted by Rome's insistence that special care be given them, Corrigan did his utmost, outstripping all other American bishops in his efforts in favor of the Catholic Italian immigrants.

Seeking Italian priests by petitioning various religious congregations and Italian bishops, Corrigan attempted to secure the manpower necessary to embark upon what would become his own personal project. He gave moral and financial support — both personal and Archdiocesan — to the project of establishing Italian national parishes, schools, and other facilities required for the salvation of souls.

Unfortunately, during these early years of the establishment of the Italian apostolate in New York, the practical problems and obstacles to the success of any plan for the Italians were never-ending. Among these were a lack of sufficient funds and priests, the disunity of effort among the priests and religious involved in the work, nationalistic prejudices, the uncooperative spirit of many city rectors — American and immigrant-born alike — who jealously guarded their own parochial rights, the lack of enthusiasm toward the Church among the majority of Italian immigrants, who had little desire to frequent or support any Catholic institution, the provincial rivalries among the Italians themselves, the problem of providing for numerous local dialects and customs, and their grinding poverty.

Corrigan was more than willing and generous to provide the traditional Catholic structures and institutions in abundance to assist the Italians. But when faced with the vast numbers of Catholics who cared little for the Church, and who desired no assistance from any traditional Catholic institutions or agencies, Corrigan was left helpless and frustrated.

The Italian immigrants in New York were faced with very difficult lives, filled with practical and emotional problems unimaginable to either the Vatican's officials or to America's ecclesiastics. Added to the enormous difficulties involved in such a radical change of life as experienced by the Italian immigrants, was the frustration of fitting their Old World beliefs into their New World lives. For many of the Italian immigrants in New York, the Church would not exert any profound effect upon them during these early years of the Italian apostolate, since the means provided to instill and nourish that faith had been rejected by so many of them even before they set out on their self-imposed exile from their homeland. For a great number of the Italian immigrants, when they left Italy, they left the Church with it as part and parcel of a world offering nothing but hardship. The mere fact that the same Church existed across the ocean in a new land was not sufficient to instill faith within the immigrants' hearts or a desire to actively participate in it.

The sincere efforts made by Archbishop Corrigan and by the priests and religious of the Archdiocese working with him on behalf of the Italians did not cure the indifference to the Church so pervasive among the members of the Italian colonies in New York. They did, however, succeed in breaking down some of the anticlerical sentiments held by many of the Italians, by means of the practical assistance and concern shown them in the various parishes and Catholic institutions established for their welfare.

The pastoral efforts initiated by Pope Leo XIII and Propaganda Fide — and put into place in the Archdiocese of New York by Archbishop Michael Augustine Corrigan — succeeded in manifesting the Church's sincere concern for the Italian immigrants in America when no other institution cared about their welfare. The response to those efforts depended upon the immigrants themselves. Once freed from their degrading poverty, provincial prejudices, anticlerical sentiments, and distrust for the Church, they did respond positively, and took their place as important members of the Catholic Church in the United States.

Appendix

Our Lady of Pompeii Church Announcements, 1894-1895[1]

Sunday, December 2 [1st Sunday of Advent]

♦ Friday is the first Friday of the month and a day of general communion for the Society of the Sacred Heart. The exposition of the Blessed Sacrament of the first Mass begins at 6:00 a.m. precisely and closes at 9:00 a.m. The honor guard (of the society), which receives communion, will be given a memento of the Sacred Heart blessed by the pope.

♦ A reminder that the parish has begun the celebration of the novena in preparation for the Immaculate Conception.

♦ Children in catechism class will begin school on Sunday at 2:00 p.m. All children who are to receive their first communion must attend catechism classes every weekday after school.

♦ Sunday evening the papal blessing will be given.

♦ The church is in need of oil for the Blessed Sacrament lamp.

Sunday, December 9

♦ Following catechism class today there will be a general meeting of the Society of the Sacred Heart.

♦ After vespers tonight there will be a panegyric delivered in honor of the Immaculate Conception, followed by the papal blessing.

♦ Friday begins the novena of Christmas, which will include Benediction and a sermon every night.

♦ Next Sunday is the third Sunday of the month, and general communion and meeting of the Society of Our Lady of Pompeii.

♦ We wish to thank those who supplied the oil for the sanctuary lamp.

♦ There are some members of the congregation who say the Rosary without holding it in their hands. To correct this abuse, there will be a number of Rosaries which have been blessed by the pope, provided at the doors of the church.

♦ Remember to kneel during the consecration of the Mass, from the beginning of Mass, "in order to be uniform [in worship]." Also, (1) kneel from the beginning of Mass until the priest goes up to the altar; (2) stand until the end of the oration; (3) sit for the epistle; (4)

stand for the gospel; (5) sit for the announcements; (6) stand while the priest recites the creed.

Sunday, December 23

♦ Tomorrow is the vigil of Christmas and a day of fast and abstinence.

♦ Tuesday is the solemnity of Christmas. The church will be open to the public before 4:00 a.m. The Mass schedule for Christmas day is: 4, 6, 7, 8, 9, 10, and 11 (solemn sung Mass) in the morning.

Wednesday, December 26

♦ Today is the feast of Saint Stephen. Vespers and a panegyric will be celebrated tonight at 8:00.

♦ There will be Benediction every night during the octave of Christmas.

♦ Please return the envelopes distributed for the special Christmas collection between today and Tuesday.

Sunday, December 30

♦ Tomorrow is the last day of the year. There will be a sermon and solemn Benediction to thank the Lord for blessings received during the past year.

♦ Tuesday is the first day of the year and the Feast of the Circumcision of the Lord. It is an obligatory feast and all must attend Mass and abstain from servile work, as is the custom in this country. Masses will be celebrated at 6:00, 8:00, 9:00, and 10:00 a.m. Evening services are the same as on Sunday.

♦ Friday is the first Friday of the month and a day of general communion for the honor guard. There will be exposition of the Blessed Sacrament at the Masses until 8:30 a.m. There will be exposition and Benediction at night. (Repeated monthly.)

♦ Next Sunday there will be meetings for the honor guard and for the Society of Saint Joseph. These will be important meetings, so invite all the men of the parish who are interested in the Church and the missions.

♦ Tuesday at 3:00 p.m. will be the Christmas celebration for the children of the catechism classes with a Christmas tree and the distribution of gifts. A reminder to the parents: please have your children on time and "well cleaned."

♦ Next Sunday is the feast of the Epiphany and will be the closing of the *presepio*. "It is the last time that you can give a kiss to the *bambino* after Mass and the blessing."

1895
Sunday, January 6
♦ Friday evening at 7:30 will be the *Via Crucis* and Benediction. (This announcement is repeated weekly.) Reminders for the first Sunday of the year: (a) be punctual for all church services, especially for funerals; (b) silence in church, especially from the young people; talking in church shows a lack of respect for the Lord and is a sign of great impoliteness toward those who wish to pray. "Speaking in church also indicates a thoughtless, empty head (like drunkards) who know neither what they say nor do"; (c) show proper respect in church. "In church do not spit on the floor"; (d) at the door of the church are found the church collectors who accept offerings for the maintenance of the church, parish house, etc. "There are those who have too short memories: they do not remember to put money in their pockets for church and that it is a precept and commandment of the Church for the faithful to cover the costs of cult and the maintenance of the priests"; (e) parents must be vigilant that their children come to catechism classes. Those parents with children who are altar boys: make sure the children are at the church on time for Mass and vespers.

♦ "At the entrance of the chapel you will find a book for the registering of names of those who, for an offering of one dollar, desire that the 7:00 a.m. Saturday Mass to the Immaculate Heart of Mary, offered for the conversion of sinners and the needs of families, be offered for their intentions." (Repeated weekly.)

Sunday, January 13
♦ The 7:00 a.m. Mass today is offered for the intention of those who gave $1 at least one time during the year. The Mass register is at the church door. (Repeated weekly.)

♦ Next Sunday is the third Sunday of the month and general communion and a conference for the Society of Our Lady of Pompeii.

♦ One of the Masses on Monday will be offered for those who gave $1 (five *soldi*) at the Masses on Sunday. (Repeated weekly.)

♦ Each night of this week there will be Benediction in continuation of the novena of Our Lady of Pompeii, ordered by a cable received from Lourdes.

♦ A reminder that the 9:00 a.m. Sunday Mass is primarily for children. All seats in front of the altar are needed. Adults please take the back seats.

Sunday, January 20

♦ Today is the feast of the Holy Name of Jesus. There will be a panegyric tonight.

♦ Wednesday is the feast of the Marriage of the Virgin. This is a devotional feast. Tonight there will be Benediction.

♦ Friday is the commemoration of the Conversion of Saint Paul. There will be Benediction in the evening.

♦ Monday catechism classes resume for those children preparing to receive their first communion and confirmation. The classes begin immediately after school. The parents are obliged to send their children.

♦ Next Sunday is the fourth Sunday of the month and is a day of general communion for the Children of the Immaculate and for all young men belonging to the Società di San Luigi. In the afternoon, immediately after catechism, there will be a meeting for both societies.

Sunday, January 27

♦ Wednesday, Thursday, and Friday will be the triduum in preparation for the feast of the Purification of Mary. There will be Benediction at the triduum.

♦ Saturday, February 2, is the feast of the Purification of Mary. Masses will be at 6:00, 8:00, and 9:00 a.m. Blessing of the candles will take place at the 8:00 a.m. Mass. There will be Benediction and a sermon in the evening.

Sunday, February 3

♦ Today is the beginning of the novena to Our Lady of the Rosary of Pompeii, with Benediction every night, by order of a cable received from Lourdes.

Sunday, February 17

♦ Next Sunday, precisely at 10:30 a.m., the Office for the Dead will be sung along with the sung Mass for the soul of Caterina (Grilla) Rivata. The Office is ordered by her husband, who invites all friends to attend.

Saturday, February 24

♦ Tuesday is the last day of *carnevale*. There will be Benediction in the evening.

♦ Wednesday is Ash Wednesday and the first day of Lent. The chapel is open at 5:30 a.m. Masses and the distribution of ashes will be at 6:00, 8:00, and 9:00 a.m. Lent begins in the evening. Meat may be eaten for lunch on Mondays, Tuesdays, Thursdays, and Saturdays of Lent, except Ember Saturday and Holy Saturday. Sunday is not a fast day; "however, it is never permitted to eat fish and meat in the same pasta during Lent."

♦ The Easter duty may be fulfilled from the first Sunday of Lent until Trinity Sunday. There will be Benediction each night during Lent. Friday and Tuesday evenings there will be the *Via Crucis*. Wednesday and Thursday there will be different guest preachers, who will deliver sermons during Lent. "A reminder to all of the obligation that we have to listen to the Word of God especially during Holy Lent, and the obligation which the parents have to send their children to catechism classes, especially during the week for the children preparing to receive the sacraments."

♦ The month of March is devoted to Saint Joseph.

Sunday, March 3

♦ Wednesday, Friday, and Saturday are Ember days, which are days of fast and abstinence.

♦ Friday is the commemoration of the Crown of Thorns of Our Lord.

♦ Benediction will be celebrated each night during Lent.

♦ Tomorrow morning at 6:00 is the anniversary of the death of Luigi Malaspina; family and friends are invited to attend the Mass.

Sunday, March 10

♦ Reminder: (1) everyone is obliged to listen to the Word of God, especially during Lent; (2) Easter duty may be fulfilled any time from the first week of Lent until Trinity Sunday.

♦ Last Wednesday (March 6) the (Scalabrinian) missionaries purchased the property of a "Negro church" on Sullivan Street. Please prepare to contribute money to the collectors who will come around to each house.

♦ There is a need for additional collectors, singers, and altar boys, since we have a new church. The Saint Joseph Society has promised to supply the collectors. You must help by volunteering as singers and altar boys.

Sunday, March 17

♦ Tomorrow is the devotional feast of Saint Gabriel the Archangel.

♦ Tuesday is the feast of "the most glorious Saint Joseph." The solemn feast will be celebrated on Sunday.

♦ Friday is the commemoration of the Five Wounds of Our Lord.

♦ Please make a contribution for the new church as soon as possible. Thanks to those who have already contributed: ". . . your names will be inscribed in the books of the church, but that which is most important is that they will be written in the Book of Paradise."

♦ Please begin thinking about offering oil, candles, and flowers needed for the Holy Sepulcher on Holy Thursday.

Sunday, March 24

♦ Today we solemnly celebrate the feast of the patron Saint Joseph. There will be vespers and a panegyric tonight.

♦ Tomorrow is the Annunciation of the Blessed Virgin Mary. Masses will be at 6:00 and 8:00 a.m. with Benediction in the evening.

♦ Friday is the commemoration of the Most Holy Blood of Our Lord.

♦ Sunday is Passion Sunday, which is dedicated to the Holy Souls in Purgatory. Following vespers there will be a sermon for the relief of the Holy Souls. The *De profundis* will be sung, and a generous collection expected.

♦ At the sung Mass the total collection for the new church will be read out.

Sunday, March 31

♦ Today is dedicated to the Souls in Purgatory. The money collected today will be applied to the relief of the Holy Souls. There will be a sermon this evening.

♦ Friday is the feast of the *Madonna Addolorata* and is the first Friday (of the month).

♦ Sunday is Palm Sunday. Palms will be blessed before the sung Mass and distributed during the Mass. Please prepare oil, candles, and flowers for the Holy Sepulcher and for the altar at Easter.

Sunday, April 7

♦ Today is Palm Sunday. "There is no room during the ceremonies to explain the gospel." So, tonight there will be a homily and Benediction at vespers. Benediction is to be celebrated tonight according to the intention of a sick member of the parish.

♦ Wednesday at 7:30 p.m. begins the Office of Tenebrae. The sung Mass on Holy Thursday will be at 8:00 a.m. followed by adoration and visits to the Holy Sepulcher until 7:30 p.m., when the Office of Tenebrae will be celebrated.

♦ Friday: the Office of Tenebrae will be celebrated at precisely 6:00 a.m. with a sermon on the Passion of Christ followed by adoration of the Cross. Tenebrae will be celebrated again at 7:30 p.m. followed by the *Funzione della Desolata*.

♦ Sung Mass on Saturday will be at 7:00 a.m.

♦ Easter Sunday Masses will be at 6, 7, 8, 9, and 10:30 in the morning. Vespers will be in the evening with Benediction and a sermon.

♦ Remember your Easter duty. During Holy Week, confessions will be heard at all hours.

♦ Those who want to be altar boys must give their names to the priest and report for the necessary instructions during Holy Week.

♦ There will be a special collection today to pay for the palm.

Sunday, April 14

♦ Tomorrow and the following day will be the second and third celebrations of Easter respectively. There will be Benediction each evening.

♦ Benediction tonight will be according to the intention of Andrea Saberia, who requested it.

♦ We will be in our new church by the 28th of this month, which is a Sunday. The ceremonies will begin at precisely 10:00 a.m. with the Apostolic Delegate presiding and Archbishop Corrigan, who will solemnly bless the church, followed by solemn Mass. The delegate will preach at vespers in the evening.

Sunday, April 21
♦ Catechism class is canceled because of the altar boy meeting.

♦ Tonight there will be meetings of the Societies of Our Lady of Pompeii and Saint Joseph and the parish collectors.

♦ This is the last Sunday during which we will gather in this chapel. Next week there will be a quick Mass celebrated without a sermon in the basement of the new church at 7:00 a.m. The solemn blessing of the church and Mass will be at 10:00 a.m. The entrance fee will be 25 cents. The Apostolic Delegate will preach at vespers in the evening.

♦ The *Mese di Maggio* begins Tuesday night. Sunday night there will be a parish mission with two excellent preachers.

Sunday, April 28
♦ "Today the Church of Our Lady of the Rosary of Pompeii was opened on Sullivan Street."

Sunday, May 5
♦ "How are we to maintain this new church?" There are seven new benches and seven new confessionals and other furnishings that must be paid for.

Sunday, May 12
♦ Sunday is the closing of the parish mission with general communion. There will be exposition and Benediction in the evening.

♦ There will be a special collection during all the Masses after the Elevation to pay for the new confessionals.

Sunday, May 19
♦ Monday, Tuesday, and Wednesday are Rogation Days. Mass, the Litany of the Saints, and the blessing of grapevines will begin at 6:00 a.m.

♦ Thursday is the Ascension, a feast of great devotion. Masses will be at 6:00, 7:00, 8:00, and 9:00 a.m. Sunday, June 9, is Trinity Sunday, the day on which first communion will be given.

♦ Society banners will be blessed today at the sung Mass.

◆ The parish mission closes today with the papal blessing and a procession of the parish societies.

◆ Tomorrow's Mass will be offered for the souls in Purgatory.

Sunday, May 26

◆ Today is the beginning of a new parish society: the Society of the Altar, composed of women of good will to clean the church on a regular basis.

◆ First communion will take place today at 3:00 p.m.

◆ Next Sunday is Pentecost and the end of the *Mese di Maggio.* "There will be general communion in the morning for all who love Mary." Solemn vespers and Benediction followed by the procession of the societies will be in the evening.

◆ Today at 3:00 p.m. is the final opportunity to make the Easter duty. (A long talk on the importance of industrial schools for Italian girls and the evils of Protestant schools followed.)

Sunday, June 2

◆ Monday and Tuesday are the first and second devotional feasts of Pentecost.

◆ Wednesday, Thursday, Friday, and Saturday will be a parish retreat.

◆ According to the desire of the Holy Father and the Archbishop, during the Octave of Pentecost there will be nightly Benediction with special prayers for the peace and concord of all.

◆ Tonight is the solemn closing of the *Mese di Maggio* and the consecration of our hearts to Mary.

◆ There will be a benefit concert for the new church on June 20th.

Sunday, June 9

◆ Tonight following vespers will be the renewal of baptismal vows for the first communion children and their consecration to Mary.

◆ Tuesday is the devotional feast of Saint Barnabas.

◆ Wednesday begins the novena to the Sacred Heart of Jesus. There will be nightly Benediction.

◆ Thursday is the solemnity of *Corpus Domini,* which is a great feast, and will be celebrated next Sunday with a procession.

Sunday, June 16

♦ Tonight will be exposition and Benediction, solemn vespers, a panegyric on the Blessed Sacrament, and a procession by the Societies of San Luigi, the Children of Mary, the Guard of the Sacred Heart of Jesus, the Madonna of Pompeii, and Saint Joseph.

♦ Friday is the solemnity of the Sacred Heart of Jesus. It is a solemn feast of the Honor Guard. The solemn celebration will take place on Sunday. Exposition will be from 6 in the morning until evening.

♦ The societies will guard the Blessed Sacrament during the following hours: the Children of Mary from 6:00 a.m. until 9:00 a.m.; the Guard of the Sacred Heart from 9:00 a.m. until 12:00 p.m.; the Madonna of Pompeii from 12:00 p.m. until 3:00 p.m.; the Society of Saint Joseph from 3:00 p.m. until 6:00 p.m. The Honor Guard of the Sacred Heart will be consecrated to the Sacred Heart with full ceremonies following the panegyric on Sunday.

Sunday, June 23

♦ Today is the feast of the Sacred Heart. All societies are requested to be present tonight to assist at the ceremonies.

♦ Tomorrow is the feast of Saint John the Baptist, who is the patron of the *Genovesi.* The 7:00 a.m. Mass will be for the deceased members of the parish. Benediction will be in the evening.

♦ Saturday is the Feast of Saints Peter and Paul. Masses will be celebrated at 5:30, 7:00, and 8:00 a.m., with Benediction in the evening.

Sunday, June 30

♦ Tomorrow begins the triduum to the Madonna of Pompeii for the intention of Maria Alpi, who has requested it. There will be Benediction every night.

♦ Tuesday is the feast of the Visitation of the Blessed Virgin Mary.

♦ There will be no catechism classes after lunch during the months of July and August. They will be held after the 9:00 a.m. Mass on Sundays.

Sunday, July 7

♦ The Feast of Our Lady of Mount Carmel will be solemnly

celebrated this year on the Sunday following July 16th. All should wear their scapulars that day.

Sunday, July 14

♦ There will be Benediction tonight, tomorrow night, and Tuesday night for the triduum in honor of the feast of Mount Carmel.

♦ Tuesday is the feast of Mount Carmel. The distribution of the "little habits of Mt. Carmel" will take place on Tuesday and Sunday for those who wish to receive them.

Sunday, July 21

♦ Thursday is the feast of Saint James, and Friday that of Saint Ann. There will be Benediction each night.

Sunday, July 28

♦ The 7:00 a.m. Mass tomorrow is for the souls in Purgatory. "We remember our beloved dead at least once a month."

♦ A lady brought a pair of little gold earrings *in voto* for the Madonna of Pompeii in thanksgiving for an instantaneous recovery following prayer.

♦ There will be a second collection every fourth Sunday of each month to pay the rent which is due on the church the first of every month.

♦ The first Monday of September is "il Laborday" and there will be a church picnic. It is hoped that many will come for two reasons: (1) profit to the church should be as large as possible; (2) the more people who attend, the more good spoken about the church.

♦ Evening catechetical classes will begin next Sunday.

Sunday, August 4

♦ Monday is the feast of Our Lady of the Snows.

♦ Tuesday is the feast of the Transfiguration. Tomorrow evening is the beginning of the novena in preparation for the feast of the Assumption. There will be Benediction and the Rosary each night.

♦ Saturday is the feast of San Lorenzo.

Sunday, August 11

♦ Next Sunday is the celebration for Our Lady of Guadalupe, preceded by a triduum of prayer and Benediction. The solemn Mass will be celebrated next Sunday at 10:30 a.m. with a panegyric. This feast is especially important to the *Genovese* women of San Stefano, who will help to defray the expenses of the feast. "Remember, the more who are generous, the greater the feast."

♦ Wednesday is the vigil of the Assumption and a day of fast and abstinence. This is an obligatory day of observance. Masses will be according to the August schedule: 6, 7, 8, 9:30, and 11:00 in the morning. There will be Benediction, vespers, and a panegyric in the evening.

♦ Benediction on the Assumption is to be given for the intentions of a pious person.

♦ Friday is the feast of San Rocco. Masses will be at 6:00, 8:00, and 11:00 a.m., which will be a sung Mass with orchestra.

Sunday, August 18
♦ Benediction next Sunday will be according to the intention of a pious person and for the relief of the suffering in Purgatory of a soul of one of the deceased members of the parish.

♦ Today's Benediction is given for the intention of those who promoted this feast of Guadalupe.

♦ Saturday is the feast of Saint Bartholomew.

Sunday, August 25
♦ Friday is the beginning of the novena for the feast of the Nativity of the Virgin.

Sunday, September 1
♦ Sunday begins the autumn schedule of Masses. The sung Mass with homily will be celebrated at 10:30 a.m. The other Masses will have only a brief explanation of the gospel. There will be catechism class at 2:00 p.m.

Sunday, September 8
♦ Today is the feast of the Nativity of the Virgin. Masses will be celebrated at 6, 7, 8, 9:30, and 10:30 in the morning, which will be a sung Mass. There will be a panegyric on the birth of the Virgin by a guest preacher this evening: the pastor of the Italian church in Cincinnati.

♦ Catechism class will be at 2:00 p.m.

◆ Next Sunday will be the feast of the Holy Name of Mary.

◆ The church picnic was a success; thanks to the various committees.

◆ A beautiful cloth has been given, which you can see on the altar rail. We would like to thank the pious person, and fervently pray that "the sacramental Jesus be good enough to repay the donor. . . . We hope this example will stimulate others to give a little something to the church and to the altar where the sacramental Jesus dwells."

Sunday, September 15

◆ Today is the feast of the Most Holy Name of Mary.

◆ Wednesday, Friday, and Saturday are Ember days, and are days of fast and abstinence. However, there is an indult received for Wednesday and Saturday.

◆ Saturday is the feast of Saint Matthew.

◆ By order of the Archbishop the 18th, 19th, and 20th will be a triduum of prayer and Benediction "to implore the necessary graces for the Sovereign Pontiff and the perfect liberty required for the exercise of his exalted functions." (The year 1895 marked the twenty-fifth anniversary of the seizure of Rome by the Italian forces.)

Sunday, September 22

◆ Today is the feast of the Sorrowful Mother. There will be a panegyric tonight.

◆ There will be spiritual exercises given on Friday evening.

◆ Sunday begins the solemn novena of prayer for the Daughters of the Rosary. A sermon will be delivered nightly.

◆ The normal door offering is 50 cents. However, it has been decided that free access to the church be granted to those who cannot afford to donate that amount.

Sunday, September 29

◆ Tonight begins the octave in preparation for the feast of the Madonna of Pompeii.

◆ The Rosary will be recited, in conformance with the wishes of the pope, every morning during the octave and during the month of October at the 7:00 a.m. Mass.

◆ Next Sunday will be the solemnity of the Madonna of the

Rosary, the principal feast of this church. General communion will be at the 8:00 a.m. Mass with all the societies present.

Sunday, October 6

♦ All societies are to assist at the sung Mass today in honor of the church's patronal feast.

♦ Daily catechism classes begin tomorrow.

Sunday, October 13

♦ Friday is the feast of Saint Luke.

♦ The church windows and doors need to be repaired before the cold weather. We need $33 (for the repairs). There will be a second collection at all Masses and Benediction in an attempt to raise the sum.

Sunday, October 20

♦ Thursday will be the feast of Saint Raphael, the protector of immigrants and travelers. The feast will be transferred to next Sunday, with a triduum beginning Monday evening.

♦ Friday is the beginning of the triduum in honor of All Saints' Day.

♦ The second collection today is to pay for the windows and doors.

♦ Saturday is All Souls' Day. Envelopes and paper will be distributed to write the names of the dead and to include offerings for them; "if they could be [written] in Italian it would be more intelligible for all." The feast will be solemnly observed with very good visiting preachers.

♦ There will be Benediction tonight, tomorrow, and Tuesday for the intention of a pious person and in thanksgiving to the Madonna of Pompeii for graces received.

Sunday, October 27

♦ Tomorrow is the feast of Saints Simon and Jude.

♦ Thursday is the vigil of All Saints' Day. It is a day of fasting.

♦ Friday is the first Friday (of the month) and All Saints' Day. Masses will be at 6:00, 7:00, 8:00, 9:30, and 10:30 a.m. The beginning of the octave of the dead begins in the evening.

♦ Those desiring candles for All Souls' Day may find them at the entrance to the church.

♦ Saturday is All Souls' Day. The Office and Mass of the Dead begins at 5:30 a.m., continuing at the same time throughout the octave.

♦ The Office and Mass on Monday of the octave is for the special intentions of the Society of Saint Joseph. Tuesday will be for those of the Society of the Madonna of the Rosary. Wednesday for those of the Honor Guard of the Sacred Heart. Thursday for the Daughters of the Immaculate and the Society of San Luigi Gonzaga. Three members from each society are to be present and receive communion at their respective Mass.

♦ Those who would want the funeral Office and Mass sung during the octave or during the entire month of November must make their intentions known in time.

♦ Tonight there will be a reading of a letter from the pope addressed to members of the parish.

♦ Tonight will also be a panegyric in honor of Saint Raphael.

♦ The triduum in thanksgiving to Our Lady of the Rosary of Pompeii for graces received begins tonight.

♦ Tuesday morning at 7:00 will be the solemn funeral Office and sung Mass for the third anniversary of the death of Giorgo Livellana.

Friday, November 1 [All Saints]

♦ Tomorrow at 7:30 p.m. will be the recitation of the Rosary for the souls in Purgatory.

♦ Reminder for the Honor Guard of the Sacred Heart that the communion for today and Sunday is for the soul of their member Oresti Bianchi, "who has passed to a better life."

Sunday, November 3 [All Souls]

♦ The octave of the dead will be until next Sunday and will end with a solemn closure.

Abbreviations Used in Notes

AABo * Archives of the Archdiocese of Boston, Brighton, Massachusetts.

ACMS * Archives of the Center for Migration Studies, Staten Island, New York.
SRSR * Records of the St. Raphael Society.

ACS * Archives of the Society of the Salesians of St. John Bosco, Rome, Italy.

AGS * Archives of the Generalate of the Congregation of the Missionaries of St. Charles (Scalabrinians), Rome, Italy.

AMSH * Archives of the Generalate of the Missionary Sisters of the Sacred Heart, Rome, Italy.

ANAC * Archives of the North American College, Vatican City State.

AANY * Archives of the Archdiocese of New York, Dunwoodie, Yonkers, New York.

AOFM * Archives of the Generalate of the Franciscan Friars Minor, Rome, Italy.

APall * Archives of the Pious Society of the Missions (Pallotines), Rome, Italy.
SACante * Archives of the Sacred Congregation per given year.

APF * Archives of the Sacred Congregation for the Evangelization of Peoples, or "de Propaganda Fide," Rome, Italy.
ACTA * The "Acta" of the General and Particular Congregations of the Sacred Congregation "de Propaganda Fide."
APNS * The "New Series," 1893-1922.
Lett. Occid. * Fondo "Lettere."
S.C. Amer. Cent. * "Scritture Riferite nei Congressi. America Centrale dal Canada all'Istmo di Panama."

APF (continued)

    S.O.C.G. * "Scritture Originali Riferite nelle Congregazioni Generali, 1622-1892."

    Coll. d'Italia * "Collegi d'Italia."

ARSI * Archives of the Roman Curia of the Society of Jesus.

ASV * Secret Vatican Archives.

    SdiS * Archives of the Secretary of State.

    DelApUSA * Archives of the Apostolic Delegate in the United States.

AUND * Archives of the University of Notre Dame.

WIA * Archives of the Diocese of Wilmington.

n.d. * No date given in a document referred to.

n.p. * No place of origin given in a document referred to.

Notes

Introduction

1. APF, ACTA 1873, vol. 239, f98r-126v, "Sulle Elezioni dei Vescovi per le vacanti diocesi di Vancouver, di Savannah e di Newark, Gennaio 1873."
2. William Henry Thorne, "Michael Augustine Corrigan," *The Globe*, XII (1902), 142.
3. Robert E. Curran, *Michael Augustine Corrigan and the Shaping of Conservative Catholicism in America, 1878-1902* (New York: 1978), 45-46.
4. John A. Mooney, "A Biographical Sketch. The Most Rev. Michael Augustine Corrigan, D.D.," *Memorial of the Most Rev. Michael Augustine Corrigan, D.D., Third Archbishop of New York City* (New York: 1902), 21.
5. Mooney, "A Biographical Sketch," 21.
6. Giovanni Schiavo, *Italian-American History* (New York: 1949), 708.

Chapter 1 / The Huddled Masses

1. Emma Lazarus, "The New Colossus," *The Annals of America* (Chicago: 1968), XI, 107.
2. Gerald Shaunessy, *Has the Immigrant Kept the Faith?* (New York: 1925), 77.
3. Ibid., 166-172. The Catholic statistics include Catholic immigrants, natural increases, and conversions.
4. *N.Y. Times*, April 14, 1880: The *Times* periodically gave statistics of the various churches in the United States. In an article entitled "A friendly warning," the statistics show Catholic (identified with the Irish) growth over the previous one hundred years, along with the caustic remark that so long as the Church was controlled by Jesuits, and there was a Syllabus of Errors, the Church would be a constant menace to freedom. *N.Y. Times*, October 18, 1879: An editorial entitled "A Note of Warning" on the rising number of Irish Catholics in America stated, "It is equally true that the Romish Church . . . is hostile to free institutions." The editor continued that the Church would not triumph in America because "American Protestant Freedom" is stronger.
5. Ray Allen Billington, *The Protestant Crusade, 1800-1860; A Study in the Origins of American Nativism* (Chicago: 1964), 279-280.
6. *N.Y. Times*, December 15, 1884.
7. Bernard Lynch, "The Italians in New York," in *The Catholic World*, XLVII (1888), 67-68. Most of the problems commonly associated with large cities and industrialization, such as poverty, slums, political corruption, and class conflict were seen by many as due to the influx of these new immigrants who could not adapt to American society. Cf. Vincent DeSantis, "The American Historian Looks at the Catholic Im-

migrant," in Thomas McAvoy (ed.), *Roman Catholicism and the American Way of Life* (Notre Dame: 1960), 226.

8. *N.Y. Herald*, September 15, 1870. *N.Y. Sun*, August 4, 1870.

9. *N.Y. Times*, December 5, 1878: Italy was the most heavily taxed country in Europe. The paper claimed that Italian advocates of the system "declare, however, that, although it renders the means of subsistence among the peasants much more difficult, it is the only method of cementing the unity of the nation."

10. Robert Foerster, *The Italian Emigration in Our Times* (Cambridge, Mass.: 1919), 63.

11. U.S. Bureau of the Census, *Historical Statistics of the United States; Colonial Times to 1957* (Washington, D.C.: 1960), 56-57.

12. Edward Claude Stibili, *The St. Raphael Society for the Protection of the Italian Immigrants, 1887-1923* (South Bend: 1977), 5 (unpub. dissert.).

13. Childe Cromwell, "The Arrival of the Immigrant," *N.Y. Times Illustrated Magazine Supplement*, August 14, 1898.

14. Foerster, op. cit., 327.

15. Edward Stibili, op. cit., pp. 118-119. By the end of the nineteenth century, two-thirds of the Italian laborers in New York City were controlled by *padroni*. Cf. Luciano Iorizzo, "The Padrone and Immigrant Distribution," Silvano Tomasi, Madeline Engel, *The Italian Experience in the United States* (New York: 1970), 52-58.

16. APF, S.C. Amer. Cent., vol. 46, f532r, Abp. Corrigan to Giovanni Card. Simeoni, New York, March 29, 1887.

17. AANY, C-6, Louis Bergamini to Abp. Corrigan, New York, April 2, 1884. The Banco Bergamini of New York City informed Corrigan that they had sent nearly 1,500,000 francs from Italian immigrants to Italy, to support their families and to prepay their passage to America. Italians generally were hard workers, as can be seen in New York City, where, by 1901, Italians owned 1,300 delicatessens, 250 butcher shops, 2,750 barbershops, 2,300 shoe repair shops, and 10,000 other shops. There were over two hundred Italian banking and industrial companies with assets over $50,000. There were nearly two hundred Italian societies, mutual aid and fraternal societies, and ethnic labor unions. Cf. Silvano Tomasi, *Piety and Power* (New York: 1975), 26.

18. ACMS, St. Joachim Marriage Registers, 1892-1894, Box 1, Registers. This provincial identity of the Italian immigrants was very strong, binding them into small provincial communities, relationships, and even marriages. In St. Joachim Church in New York, from July through December of 1893, there were forty-five marriages recorded. In thirty of these, both husband and wife were from the same town or province. Of the 101 marriages registered from January through December, 1894, sixty-four of the couples came from the same town or province.

19. Charlotte Gower Chapman, *Milocca: A Sicilian Village* (Cambridge, Mass.: 1971), 27.

20. Foerster, op. cit., 30.

21. Leonard Covello, *The Social Background of the Italo-American School Child: A Study of the Southern Italian Family Mores and their Effect on the School Situation in Italy and America* (Leiden: 1967), 106.

22. Gianfausto Rosoli, "Chiesa e Comunitá Italiane negli Stati Uniti (1880-1940)," *Studium* (Roma: 1979), 28.

23. Nicholas J. Russo, *The Religious Acculturation of the Italian in New York* (New York: 1968), 69 (unpub. dissert.).

24. Lawrence Pisani, *The Italians in America* (New York: 1957), 164.

25. Roger Aubert (ed.), *The Church in A Secular Society* (New York: 1979), 84.

26. Covello, op. cit., 137.

27. Phyllis Williams, *South Italian Folkways in Europe and America* (New York: 1966), 146 ff.

28. In an interview with Mrs. Anthony Gabriele of Bridgeport, Connecticut, the author was given the ritual against the *malocchio*, or evil eye, which she had received as a child from her mother who had immigrated to America from the Abruzzo region of Italy at the turn of the century. To determine the actual effect of the evil eye upon a child who might be ill, olive oil is poured from a spoon over the thumb and allowed to drip into a basin of water. If the oil forms individual drops in the water, the child is in no danger. If, however, the oil spreads over the water without beading, the following ritual is observed to free the child from evil: the woman performing the rite traces a cross on the child's forehead reciting, "Malocch', malocch', dichiarà che solo la malocch' far l'andar." The rite closes with the recitation of one Our Father and one Hail Mary. The water was then thrown into the street, in hopes that the evil would be removed from the child and contracted by the first unsuspecting passerby who would carry it away.

29. Ella Edes, an American and a clerk at Propaganda Fide, while also serving as the Roman agent of Cardinal McCloskey, Archbishop Corrigan of New York, and Bishop Bernard McQuaid of Rochester, believed Rome's information to be generally useless, or erroneous at best. AUND, X-2-h, Edes to Rev. Daniel E. Hudson, Rome, September 6, 1881: ". . . but here America is of no account — unless they need to get money thence, and there exists a most blissful state of ignorance, relative to 'The Land of the Free and the Home of the Brave.' Fancy Leo XIII actually asking an American prelate who repeated it to me, if the United States were not the same with MEXICO. . . ."

30. APF, Lett. Occid., 1883, vol. 379, f27r, Simeoni to the American Archbishops, Rome, May 22, 1883.

31. APF, ACTA 1883, vol. 252, f1097r-1099v.

32. APF, Lett. Occid., 1883, vol. 379, f121r, Simeoni to Gibbons, Rome, March 6, 1883.

33. APF, S.O.C.G. 1887, vol. 1018, f1079r-1091r, Spalding to Propaganda, Peoria, September, 1883.

34. APF, ACTA 1883, vol. 252, f1241r, Spalding to Propaganda, Peoria, September, 1883.

35. APF, ACTA 1883, vol. 252, f1112r. This was approved by the pope on October 22, 1883.

36. *Relatio collationum quas Romae coram S.C. de P.F. praefecto habuerunt archiepiscopi pluresque episcopi Statuum Foederatorum Americae, 1883.* This contains the minutes of the Roman meetings along with the views and interventions of the participating prelates. An English translation is found in *The Jurist*, XI, January, 1951, pp. 121-132; April, 1951, pp. 302-312; July, 1951, pp. 417-424; October, 1951, pp. 538-541. The eighth session dealing with immigrant care is found in the October, 1951, number, pp. 538-539.

37. For a more detailed account of the Roman meetings, cf. John Tracy Ellis, *The Life of James Cardinal Gibbons* (Milwaukee: 1952), I, 210-217.

38. Gibbons to Elder, Baltimore, May 8, 1884, quoted in Ellis, *Gibbons*, I, 232.

39. ACMS, SRSR, #005, Box 1, Simeoni to McCloskey, Rome, March 6, 1884.

40. APF, S.C. Amer. Cent., 1884, vol. 40, f497rv, Gibbons to Simeoni, Baltimore, April 4, 1884.

41. APF, S.C. Amer. Cent., 1884, vol. 40, f493r-496r, Simeoni to Gibbons (draft), Rome, April 29, 1884.

42. APF, S.C. Amer. Cent., 1884, vol. 40, f303r, Corrigan to Simeoni, New York, January 25, 1884.

43. APF, Lett. Occid., 1884, vol. 380, f93r, Simeoni to Corrigan, Rome, February 15, 1884.

44. APF, S.C. Amer. Cent., 1884, vol. 40, f501r-523r, Corrigan to Simeoni, New York, March 28, 1884.

45. APF, S.C. Amer. Cent., 1884, vol. 40, f505r, Rev. Francis McSweeney to Corrigan, New York, n.d., 1884.

46. The three reports were written by priests in New York City: the Rev. Francis McSweeney, a diocesan priest, who, due to illness, resided with his brother, the Rev. Patrick McSweeney, rector of St. Brigid Church, which had a growing Italian population; Rev. Anacleto da Roccagorga, O.F.M., rector of St. Anthony of Padua Italian Church for seven years; Rev. Giulio d'Arpino, O.F.M., assistant at St. Anthony's for ten years.

47. APF, Coll. d'Italia, vol. 43, f1442r-1444v, Corrigan to Simeoni, New York, August 4, 1884. Ibid., f1445r-1446v, Lynch to Corrigan, New York, n.d., 1884. ACMS, SRSR, #005, Box 1, f1r-2r, Simeoni to Corrigan, Rome, August 29, 1884: The Prefect of Propaganda Fide thanked Corrigan for his report and hoped that he might find a remedy.

48. *Acta et Decreta Concilii Plenarii Baltimorensis Tertii* (Baltimore: 1884), private edition, lxxi-lxxiii. Cf. Frederick Zweirlein, *The Life and Letters of Bishop McQuaid* (Rochester: 1926), II, 333-334.

49. AANY, C-2, Rev. John Farley to Corrigan, New York, November 1, 1883: Corrigan was instructed by Cardinal McCloskey to contact Don Bosco and to make arrangements with him to send his priests to work in New York with the Italians who were victims of the Protestant missionaries. The Franciscans, who were already working with the Italians, seemed totally inefficient. ACS, 38, New York Correspondence, 1883-1898, Corrigan to Don Bosco, Rome, December 15, 1883.

50. *Acta et Decreta Concilii Plenarii Baltimorensis Tertii* (Baltimore: 1886), Titulus VIII, *De Zelo Animarum*, Caput I. *De Colonis et Advenis*, 130-132.

51. Corrigan opposed this decision to address Propaganda instead of the pope, since the Italian bishops were not under Propaganda's jurisdiction. They were subject to the pope as suffragans. He was supported in this only by Bishops Becker of Wilmington and Muellen of Erie. Cf. Zweirlein, *McQuaid*, II, 335.

52. AANY, C-31, Corrigan to McCloskey, Baltimore, December 5, 1884.

53. ACMS, SRSR, #005, Box 1, Becker to Gibbons, Wilmington, December 17, 1884.

54. AANY, C-2, Becker to Corrigan, Wilmington, December 15, 1884. Becker mentioned that he was also being helped by the Jesuits, but no specific details were given.

55. APall, Newark/N.Y., SACante 1909, Kirner to Whitmee, New York, May 30, 1884.

56. WIA, Becker papers, Box 1, 1884-1885, Corrigan to Becker, New York, December 17, 1884.

57. AANY, C-2. Becker to Corrigan, Wilmington, December 17, 1884.

58. WIA, Becker papers, Box 1, 1884-1885, Corrigan to Becker, New York, December 18, 1884: "P.S. The presumption is, of course, that if the parents knew better, they would not send their children to these dangerous schools, but they are too ignorant to realize the difference and the enormous peril."

59. WIA, Becker papers, Box 1, 1884-1885, Corrigan to Becker, New York, December 23, 1884.

60. APF, S.O.C.G., 1885, vol. 1023, f848r-850r, Gibbons/Becker to Simeoni, Wilmington Idibus Ianuariis (*sic*), 1885. The key phrase is "crassam adeo supinam ignorantiam" and is a canonical description of the ignorance of religious truth and duties that the Italians displayed in America. It is an ignorance that "results from a total lack of requisite moral diligence, . . ." It is vincible, but the use of this term here is a strong accusation, stating clearly that the fathers of the council believed the Italians willfully chose not to practice their faith. Cf. John Abbo, Jerome Hannon, *The Sacred Canons* (St. Louis: 1960), I, 29.

Chapter 2 / Rome and the Catholic Immigrants

1. During the reign of Leo XIII, monthly meetings of the Prefect of Propaganda Fide and other cardinals were held in a *Congregatio Generalis* to discuss ecclesiastical matters of extreme importance. During the meetings, a presentation, or *ponenza*, would be made by the cardinal *ponens*, the cardinal designated to chair the discussions. There are three sections to each *ponenza*: (1) *Ristretto*: report of the cardinal; (2) *Sommario*: a documentary summary containing all important documents pertinent to the discussion; (3) *Rescriptum* or *Decretum*: the Congregation's decision.

2. APF, ACTA 1885, vol. 254, f333v, *Relazione con Sommario, Vota e Nota di Archivio sopra gli Atti e Decreti del III Concilio Plenario di Baltimora, 17, 24, 31 Agosto.*

3. APF, ACTA 1885, vol. 254, f334v.

4. APF, ACTA 1885, vol. 254, f352v. This was approved by the pope on October 4, 1885.

5. APF, S.O.C.G., 1885, vol. 1023, f848r-850r, Becker/Gibbons to Simeoni, Wilmington, Idibus Ianuariis (*sic*), 1885.

6. *Acta et Decreta Concilii Plenarii Baltimorensis Tertii* (Baltimore: 1886), Titulus VIII, Caput I, *De Colonis et Advenis*, paras. 233-234, 131.

7. Ellis, op. cit., I, 333-334: In 1886 the American hierarchy was composed of sixty-nine bishops. Their national origin, either by foreign birth or extraction was: Irish, 35; German (including Austrian and Swiss), 15; French, 11; English, 5; Dutch, Scots, and Spanish, 1 each. To many non-English speaking immigrants in America, anyone who spoke English was considered "Irish" even if born in the United States. *The Catholic News* of New York carried an article by John Gilmary Shea entitled "A Growing Danger" in its May 13, 1891 number. Shea wrote, "The insulting way in which all who do not come from Germany, Belgium, Austria, Sicily and Italy to this country are treated as Irish, shows the animus of the thing [Lucerne Memorial]. It treats this country as a mere camping ground, ignoring the existence of millions of native-born Catholics."

8. *American Catholic Quarterly Review*, VIII (July, 1883), 509-529.

9. *Pastoral Blatt*, XVII (November, 1883); XVIII (April, 1884), as quoted in Colman Barry, *The Catholic Church and the German Americans* (Milwaukee: 1953), 53-54.

10. APF, S.O.C.G., 1887, vol. 1026, f1024rv, German Priests of St. Louis to Simeoni, St. Louis, July 31, 1884.

11. McQuaid to Gilmour, Rochester, March 15, 1885, as quoted in Robert Curran, *Michael Augustine Corrigan and the Shaping of Conservative Catholicism in America, 1878-1902* (New York: 1978), 129.

12. Quoted in Barry, op. cit., 60.

13. Ibid.

14. ACMS, #019, Box 6, Series II, "Memorial presented by Monsignor Gilmour and Monsignor Moore to His Eminence Cardinal Simeoni Prefect

of Propaganda on the Question of the German Catholics in the Church in the United States," Rome, October 2, 1885.

15. APF, S.O.C.G., 1887, vol. 1026, f943r-944v, Flasch to Simeoni, LaCrosse, April 7, 1885.

16. APF, S.O.C.G., 1887, vol. 1026, f943r-944v, Gibbons to Simeoni, Baltimore, January 9, 1886.

17. APF, S.O.C.G., 1887, vol. 1026, f943r-944v, f886r-889v, Corrigan to Simeoni, New York, January 3, 1886. Both the Gibbons response and this letter of Corrigan played an important part in Propaganda's decision regarding national parishes. Cf. APF, ACTA 1883, vol. 257, f202r-205r, *Relazione con Sommario e Voto Intorno all'elezione di quasi-parrocchie distinte per nazionalità negli Stati Uniti d'America.*

18. APF, S.C. Amer. Cent., 1886, vol. 45, f657rv, Gibbons to Simeoni, Baltimore, October 9, 1886.

19. APF, S.C. Amer. Cent., 1886, vol. 45, f658r, Heiss to Simeoni, Milwaukee, October 2, 1886.

20. APF, S.C. Amer. Cent., 1886, vol. 44, f822r-823v, Färber to Grasselli, St. Louis, March 9, 1886.

21. APF, S.O.C.G., 1887, vol. 1026, f904r-942v.

22. AANY, C-16, Ireland and Keane to the U.S. Archbishops, Rome, December 10, 1886.

23. APF, S.O.C.G., 1887, vol. 1026, f1068r-1082r, Ireland and Keane to Simeoni, Rome, n.d.: *La Question Allemande dans l'Eglise des Etats-Units.* This document reproduces the report of the American archbishops' meeting in Philadelphia in December, 1886, along with the letters and telegrams sent by the American prelates in response to the letters and cables sent by Ireland, Keane, and O'Connell. Gibbons's wire, dated December 11, read, "Stay German action 'till we are heard." Corrigan wired on December 26, saying, "For this province I protest vehemently, and will write against these Teutonic calumnies."

24. AANY, C-16, Denis O'Connell to Corrigan, Rome, December 10, 1886.

25. APF, S.O.C.G., 1887, vol. 1026, f1109r-1143v, Ireland and Keane to Simeoni, Rome, December 9, 1886: *Observations sur la question Des Allemandes Catholiques dans l'Eglise aux Etats-Units.*

26. APF, S.O.C.G., 1887, vol. 1026, f1109r: "When we arrived in Rome we were surprised to find a representative of the German bishops. The American bishops of the English language, and some of the American bishops of the German language, had no knowledge of the presence of this representative in Rome."

27. AANY, C-16, Ireland and Keane to Corrigan, Rome, December 10, 1886: "There is a conspiracy wide-spread and well-organized against the English-speaking bishops and priests, the Consultors and Cardinals of the Propaganda, especially the Germans, have been filled with charges against them, as persecuting the Germans, depriving them of their rights, etc., etc."

28. APF, S.O.C.G., 1887, vol. 1026, f945r-948v, Corrigan to Simeoni, New York, December 17, 1886.

29. APF, S.O.C.G., 1887, vol. 1026, f1146r-1150v, Corrigan to Simeoni, New York, *Festa di S. Stefano*, 1886.

30. Corrigan revealed his statistical source as the *Missiones Catholicae Ritu Latini*, which, on page 358, gave the total Catholic population of the ecclesiastical Provinces of Baltimore, Boston, Philadelphia, and New York as 3,270,885.

31. APF, ACTA 1887, vol. 257, f186r-217v, *Relazione con Sommario e Voto Intorno all'elezione di quasi-parrocchie distinte per nazionalità negli Stati Uniti d'America.*

32. Barry, op. cit., 278-285.

33. Ibid., 268-288.

34. Ibid., 33.

35. Ibid., 35.

36. APF, S.C. Amer. Cent., 1883, vol. 38, f1000rv, Cahensly to Simeoni, Limburg an der Lahn, July 10, 1883. AANY, C-6, Simeoni to Corrigan, Rome, July 17, 1883.

37. APF, Coll. d'Italia, vol. 43, f1461r-1462v, Cahensly to Simeoni, Limburg an der Lahn, June 18, 1884.

38. Marco Caliaro, Mario Francesconi, *John Baptist Scalabrini, Apostle to Emigrants* (New York: 1977), 19-35.

39. APF, Coll. d'Italia, vol. 43, f1489r-1490r, Scalabrini to Simeoni, Piacenza, January 1, 1887.

40. APF, Coll. d'Italia, vol. 43, f1422r, Scalabrini to Simeoni, Piacenza, February 16, 1887.

41. Grazia Dore, *La Democrazia Italiana e l'Emigrazione in America* (Brescia: 1964), 56.

42. *London Times*, October 11, 1870.

43. Giacomo Martina, *La Chiesa nell'Età del Totalitarianismo* (Brescia: 1978), 10-11.

44. *Acta Sanctae Sedis* (Romae: 1877), X, 582-592. The above English translation is from Claudia Carlen, *The Papal Encyclicals, 1878-1903* (Wilmington, Del.: 1981), 8.

45. *L'Osservatore Romano*, March 22, 1879.

46. William Halperin, "Leo XIII and the Roman Question," Edward Gargan (ed.), *Leo XIII and the Modern World* (New York: 1961), 108-109.

47. APF, Coll. d'Italia, vol. 43, f1508r-1509v, Scalabrini to Zenchini, Piacenza, August 2, 1887.

48. APF, Lett. Occid. 1889, vol. 385, f16v-17v, Simeoni to Scalabrini, Rome, January 12, 1889.

49. APF, Coll. d'Italia, vol. 43, f1550r-1555v, Scalabrini to Simeoni, Piacenza, January 1, 1889.

50. APF, Coll. d'Italia, vol. 43, f1416r-1425v, Scalabrini to Simeoni, Piacenza, February 16, 1887.

51. Giovanni Battista Scalabrini, *L'Emigrazione Italiana in America*, An-

tonio Perotti, "La Società Italiana di fronte alle prime migrazioni di massa," *Studi Emigrazione* (Febbraio-Giugno: 1968), Anno V. N. 11-12, 204-205.

52. Ibid., 226.

53. Ibid., 230.

54. Silvano Tomasi, *Piety and Power* (New York: 1975), 54.

55. APF, ACTA 1885, vol. 254, f334v.

56. APF, ACTA 1887, vol. 257, f507r-529r: *Rapporto sull'Emigrazione Italiana con Sommario.*

57. APF, Lett. Occid., 1884, vol. 380, f3r, Simeoni to Archbishops of Naples and Genoa, Rome, January 1, 1884. Ibid., f181r, Simeoni to Archbishop of Palermo, Rome, April 7, 1884.

58. APF, Coll. d'Italia, vol. 43, f1436r-1437r, Archbishop of Naples to Simeoni, Naples, January 14, 1884. Ibid., f1438r-1439r, Archbishop of Genoa to Simeoni, Genoa, February 29, 1884. Ibid., f1440rv, Archbishop of Palermo to Simeoni, Palermo, April 26, 1884.

59. APF, Coll. d'Italia, vol. 43, f1442r-1444v, Corrigan to Simeoni, New York, August 4, 1884. This letter was important in influencing Propaganda's decision concerning the Italians, and is reproduced in the *ponenza* on Italian emigration. Cf. ACTA 1887, vol. 257, f521v-522r.

60. APF, Coll. d'Italia, vol. 43, f1445r-1446v, Rev. Thomas Lynch to Corrigan, New York, n.d., 1885. This report was sent by Corrigan to Propaganda and was important in influencing Propaganda's decision on Italian emigration. Cf. ACTA 1887, vol. 257, f522rv.

61. APF, ACTA 1887, vol. 257, f523r-525r, Morini to Rev. General of the Servants of Mary, Chicago, January 1, 1887. This letter influenced Propaganda in its decision concerning the Italians.

62. APF, Coll. d'Italia, vol. 43, f1455r-1456v, Corrigan to Jacobini, New York, March 30, 1886. This letter influenced Propaganda's decision concerning the Italians and is reproduced in ACTA 1887, vol. 257, f525v-526r.

63. APF, Coll. d'Italia, vol. 43, f1457r-1458v, Corrigan to Jacobini, New London, Connecticut, November 18, 1885.

64. APF, Coll. d'Italia, vol. 43, f1442r-1444v, Corrigan to Simeoni, New York, August 4, 1884. This letter only mentioned the work of the *padroni*, but mentions nothing about the labor boss's religious persuasions, let alone qualifying their hypothetical devotions as fanatical, as does the report. Propaganda Fide identified all evils to which the Italians were subjected in the United States with the doctrines of Protestantism, whose members all appeared to the distant Roman eye as "fanatical proselytizers."

65. APF, ACTA 1887, vol. 257, f518rv. The clerical institute was the Congregation of the Missionaries of St. Charles Borromeo, later known as the Scalabrinians. The lay institute was called the Società San Raffaele.

66. APF, Coll. d'Italia, vol. 43, f1568r-1569r, Scalabrini to Simeoni, Piacenza, April 4, 1889.

67. *Acta Sanctae Sedis* (Romae: 1888), vol. 21, pp. 258-260.

68. AGS, B, IV, 1888, N. 170, n.p., n.d., Scalabrini to Propaganda. Cf. Mario Francesconi, *Inizi della Congregazione Scalabriniana, 1886-1888* (Rome: 1969), 153 ff.

69. Giovanni Terragni, "Magistero Pontificio da Leone XIII a Paolo VI," *Studi Emigrazione*, V (September, 1979), 416.

70. N.Y. *Freeman's Journal*, January 5, 1889. The *New York Times* published three articles on the subject of Leo's letter: December 13, 1888; January 3, 1889; February 28, 1889.

71. APF, S.C. Amer. Cent., 1892, vol. 58, f995r-1007r, Corrigan to Simeoni, New York, May 21, 1891.

72. APF, S.C. Amer. Cent., 1891, vol. 57, f538r-539v, Cahensly to Simeoni, Limburg an der Lahn, November 18, 1891.

73. APF, S.C. Amer. Cent., 1892, vol. 58, f1037r-1050r. The above translation is from Barry, *German Americans*, 314.

74. APF, S.O.C.G. 1890, vol. 1037, f356r-491r: Documentation pertaining to the nomination of Frederick Katzer to Milwaukee and the actions of Ireland and his associates to secure the see for Spalding.

75. AANY, G-28, Corrigan to Mazzella (copy), New York, November 7, 1890.

76. APF, S.C. Amer. Cent., 1892, vol. 58, f1056rv, Corrigan to Simeoni, New York, May 25, 1891.

77. Ireland to Gibbons, St. Paul, May 30, 1891, quoted in Ellis, *Gibbons*, I, 369.

78. *New York Herald*, May 31, 1891.

79. *Philadelphia Press*, June 3, 1891, quoted in Barry, *German Americans*, 141.

80. APF, Lett. Occid., 1891, vol. 387, f481r, Simeoni to Corrigan, Rome, June 27, 1891.

81. AANY, C-17, Board of Directors of Leo House to Cahensly (copy), New York, July 1, 1891.

82. Shaunessy, *Has the Immigrant Kept the Faith?* (New York: 1925), 224-240: Cahensly estimated the total Catholic population in the United States to be 60,000,000 persons in 1889. This was impossible, since the total American population in 1889 was only 62,947,714 persons.

83. AANY, C-18, Corrigan to Cahensly, New York, July 22, 1891.

84. AGS, D, I, 1, Scalabrini to Corrigan (draft), Piacenza, August 10, 1891.

85. ACMS, SRSR, #005, Box 1, Corrigan to Scalabrini, New York, August 31, 1891.

86. Ibid.

87. APF, S.C. Amer. Cent., 1891, vol. 56, f414r-419r, Henri Mercier to Jacobini, n.p., May 5, 1891.

88. DeConcilio, a priest working in Newark, New Jersey, had written *On the Religious State of the Italians in the United States of America.*

89. APF, S.O.C.G. 1887, vol. 1027, f975ff: a collection of letters and petitions concerning the establishment of a Polish vicar-apostolic in the U.S.

90. ASV, SdiS 1893, R. 280, fasc. 1, f87r-88r, Leo XIII to Gibbons (draft), Rome, June 26, 1891. APF, S.C. Amer. Cent., 1892, vol. 58, f1075v, Leo XIII to Gibbons (copy), Rome, June 26, 1891.

91. ASV, SdiS 1893, R. 280, fasc. 1, f85r-86r, Gibbons to Rampolla, Baltimore, July 30, 1891. AANY, C-15, Gibbons to Corrigan, Cape May, July 11, 1891.

92. APF, S.C. Amer. Cent., 1891, vol. 57, f538r-539v, Cahensly to Simeoni, Limburg an der Lahn, November 18, 1891.

93. *Acta Sanctae Sedis* (Romae: 1891-92), XXIV, 684-686. AUND, Soderini Manuscript: Rampolla to Gibbons, Rome, June 28, 1892: Soderini mentions this letter as confirming the Holy See's stand against the possible favoring of any national interest by the Church.

Chapter 3 / Italian Priests in New York City

1. U.S. Bureau of the Census, *Historical Statistics of the United States, Colonial Times to 1957* (Washington, D.C.: 1969), Series A 195-209, 14.

2. ASV, DelApUSA, Emigrazione Italiana, 1, Charles Devlin to Satolli, Topeka, Kansas, May 30, 1894: Devlin was a mining representative and wrote asking the Apostolic Delegate's help for the Italians who were being made scapegoats "as are the Chinese and other minorities," for all the destruction, theft, and problems in the mining industry that was brought about by striking American-born laborers. The American press blamed the Italians and other immigrants for all the country's woes.

3. Edward George Hartman, *The Movement to Americanize the Immigrant* (New York: 1967), 17.

4. Ibid., 19.

5. Bernard A. Weisenberger, *The Life and History of the United States, 1890-1901: A Reaching for Empire* (New York: 1964), VIII, 67. The bill was passed but vetoed by President Grover Cleveland.

6. John A. Kouwenhoven, *The Columbia Historical Portrait of New York* (New York: 1953), 393-394.

7. Lloyd Morris, *Incredible New York; High Life and Low Life of the Last Hundred Years* (New York: 1951), 107.

8. Kouwenhoven, op. cit., 414.

9. APF, ACTA 1880, vol. 248, f473r, *Report with Summary on the election of a coadjutor with future right of succession to the Card. Archbishop of New York City, September, 1880.*

10. APF, ACTA 1880, vol. 248, f473r-477r. AANY, C-8, Ella Edes to Corrigan, Rome, September 28, 1880.

11. AANY, G-33, Corrigan to Archbishop Contieri, New York, April 15, 1884.

12. APF, S.C. Amer. Cent., 1890, vol. 54, f769r, Simeoni to the Vicar General of the Diocese Torquiensis, Rome, June 21, 1884. AABo, Williams Papers, 5.12, Simeoni to Archbishop Williams, Rome, August 31, 1886. *Epistola Circularis ad Episcopos Italos et Americanos, relate ad Sacerdotes Italos, Qui ad Americanas Regiones Emigrant, The American Ecclesiastical Review* (February, 1898), XVIII, 193-195.

13. APF, Coll. d'Italia, vol. 43, f1442r-1444v, Corrigan to Simeoni, New York, July 4, 1884.

14. APF, Coll. d'Italia, vol. 43, f1444r, Corrigan to Simeoni, New York, August 4, 1884.

15. AANY, G-30, Folder #7, Corrigan to McCloskey, Rome, December 2, 1883.

16. APF, Coll. d'Italia, vol. 43, f1480r, Corrigan to Simeoni, New York, March 3, 1885.

17. John A. Mooney, "The Most Rev. Michael Augustine Corrigan: A biographical sketch," *Memorial of the Most Rev. Michael Augustine Corrigan, D.D., Third Archbishop of New York* (New York: 1902).

18. AANY, C-19, Rev. Charles McDonnell to Corrigan, Paris, March 8, 1888. APF, S.C. Amer. Cent., 1888, vol. 49, f255r-256r, Corrigan to Simeoni, New York, August 3, 1888. AANY, C-31, Corrigan to the Fr. General of the Redemptorists (copy), New York, November 22, 1889. ARSI, Prov. Maryl. 1888-1897, Corrigan to Rev. Antonius Anderledy, New York, December 14, 1888.

19. APF, Coll. d'Italia, vol. 43, f1544r-1545v, Scalabrini to Simeoni, Piacenza, December 7, 1888.

20. AANY, C-13, Rev. Vincenzo DeParocco to Corrigan, Rome, May 21, 1887.

21. AANY, C-13, Msgr. Giovanni F. Lorenzo to Corrigan, Florence, December 31, 1880. AANY, C-13, DeParocco to Corrigan, Belgium, July 23, 1887. *N.Y. Times*, April 19, 1891: the Italian government extended the age for military service from thirty-nine to forty-two.

22. *N.Y. Times*, January 15, 1883.

23. *N.Y. Sun*, March 3, 1884. Aldo Merlino, *Il Patrimonio della Sacra Congregazione (dal secolo XIX ad oggi)*, Josef Metzler (ed.), *Sacrae Congregationis de Propaganda Fide Memoria Rerum* (Rome: 1975), III/1, 61-75.

24. Peter Guilday (ed.), *The National Pastorals of the American Hierarchy* (Washington, D.C.: 1923), 136.

25. APF, S.C. Amer. Cent., 1888, vol. 49, f255r-256r, Corrigan to Simeoni, New York, August 3, 1886.

26. APF, S.C. Amer. Cent., 1887, vol. 47, f196r-197v, Corrigan to Jacobini, New York, August 23, 1887.

27. APF, S.C. Amer. Cent., 1890, vol. 54, f801r-802r, Bonomelli to Corrigan (copy), Cremona, January 4, 1888.

28. APF, S.C. Amer. Cent., 1890, vol. 54, f803r, Corrigan to Simeoni (?), New York, January 19, 1888: a marginal note dated March 26, 1888 indicates Propaganda's response to Corrigan.

29. APF, Coll. d'Italia, vol. 43, f1511r, Scalabrini to Simeoni, Piacenza, September 21, 1887.

30. APF, Coll. d'Italia, vol. 43, f1421r, Scalabrini to Simeoni, Piacenza (?), n.d.

31. ACMS, SRSR, #005, Box 1, Corrigan to Scalabrini, New York, December 16, 1887.

32. Mario Francesconi, *Storia della Congregazione Scalabriniana* (Rome: 1973), pp. 190-191.

33. AANY, C-31, Corrigan to Raffaele Pietrostefano (copy), New York, January 8, 1889.

34. ACMS, #019, Box 1, Rev. Joseph Egan to Corrigan, Florence, October 19, 1894.

35. ANAC, Student Register, 1859-1932: from 1885, when Corrigan became the ordinary of the Archdiocese, until his death in 1902, Corrigan supported fifty-five students in Rome, forty-one of whom were ordained and returned to New York.

36. *The Catholic Church in the United States of America; undertaken to celebrate the Golden Jubilee of His Holiness, Pope Pius X* (New York: 1914), vol. III, 301. ACMS, SRSR, #005, Box 1, Corrigan to Martinelli, New York, September 16, 1899.

37. AANY, C-19, Rev. Thomas Lynch to Corrigan, New York, May 10, 1888.

38. ACMS, SRSR, #005, Box 1, Corrigan to Scalabrini, Newburgh, May 8, 1889.

39. APF, ACTA 1887, vol. 257, f525v, Corrigan to Jacobini, New York, March 30, 1886.

40. Ibid.

41. Nicholas J. Russo, *The Religious Acculturation of the Italian in New York City* (New York: 1968), 159. These churches were St. Anthony of Padua on Sullivan St., St. Raphael Church on W. 41st St., Holy Rosary on E. 119th St., Our Lady of Mount Carmel on 115th St., St. Brigid Church on Avenue B, Transfiguration Church on Mulberry St., Old St. Patrick Cathedral on Mott St.

42. APF, Coll. d'Italia, vol. 43, f1501r-1502v, Corrigan to Scalabrini, New York, October 28, 1887.

43. ACS, 38, New York Correspondence, 1883-1898, Rev. Edward M. Parocco to "Revmo e Carmo Sig. Vicario," Chateaugay, February 1, 1888. Parocco related that property in New York City cost between $40,000 and $50,000 for a building site suitable for a church.

44. The full title is *Fiat Lux sullo Stato Morale e Materiale Religioso d'Italiani Sbarcati a New York in Questi Ultimi Anni: Cause e Remedi* (sic) New York 1888. A copy may be found in ASV, DelApUSA, Emigrazione Italiana, 1.

45. Ibid., 24.

46. Ibid., 31.

47. Bernard J. Lynch, "The Italians in New York," *The Catholic World*,

XLVII (1888), 67-73. Lynch was the brother of the Rev. Thomas Lynch, rector of Transfiguration Church in New York City. This was an "annex" parish with one of the most rapidly growing Italian congregations in the city. Lynch's brother was the source of his information for the article.

48. Ibid., 68.
49. Ibid., 69.
50. Ibid., 70.
51. Ibid., 72.
52. A copy of this may be found in ASV, DelApUSA, Emigrazione Italiana, 1.
53. APF, S.C. Amer. Cent., 1890, vol. 54, f811r-812v, DeConcilio to Simeoni. DeConcilio wrote that this was a mere outline of a plan that he was willing to perfect if the pope would so require.
54. "Stato Religioso," 21.
55. Ibid., 21-23.
56. Ibid., 25: DeConcilio made a distinction between what he called the "mixed system," a church serving both the Irish-American and Italian communities simultaneously, and the "annex system," a primarily Irish-American church to which was joined "as an appendage or annex" the resident Italians living within the territorial boundaries of the parish. He cited Transfiguration Church on Mott Street in New York City as an example of an "annex" church, and claimed the Italian population to be between 12,000 and 15,000 persons annexed to the Irish-American congregation of only 3,000 or 4,000 persons.
57. "Delle condizioni religiose degli Emigrati Italiani negli Stati Uniti d'-America," *La Civiltà Cattolica*, XI (Settembre 15, 1888), 641-653: This article was nothing more than a rephrasing of DeConcilio's pamphlet, including his statistics and examples. The conclusions were the same as DeConcilio's: the solution to the Italian Problem was a nucleus of good priests, material subsidies, and national parishes.
58. These articles appeared in the April, May, and June numbers of the *Journal* in 1889. April 27, 1889: "The Only Italian Church in the State of Ohio." May 4, 1889: "The Italian Question." May 11, 1889: "The Italians as American Citizens." May 18, 1889: "The Italian Question." May 25, 1889: "The Italian Question." June 1, 1889: "The Italian Question." These were later translated and published in Cleveland in 1891 under the title *La Questione Italiana negli Stati Uniti d'America.*
59. "The Italians as American Citizens," May 11, 1889.
60. "The Italian Question," May 18, 1889.
61. Ibid., May 25, 1889.
62. Ibid., June 1, 1889.
63. Humphrey J. Desmond, "I Negletti Italiani: Memoriale alla Gerachia [sic] Italiana" (Milwaukee, September 30, 1899). An English translation was published in *The Catholic Citizen of Milwaukee* on September 30, 1899, numbers 4-10, entitled "Let Italy Awake." Desmond was the paper's editor.

64. Ibid., 5.
65. Ibid., 6.
66. Ibid., 8. There were, according to Desmond, 108 priests working for 114,292 Catholic Native Americans, and only 60 priests for 750,000 Catholic Italians in America.
67. Ibid., 9.
68. APF, S.C. Amer. Cent., 1890, vol. 54, f809r, Corrigan to Scalabrini, New York, February 10, 1888.
69. AANY, C-19, Rev. Charles McDonnell to Corrigan, Paris, March 8, 1888.
70. AANY, C-19, Rev. Thomas Lynch to Corrigan, New York, March 26, 1888. Corrigan had sent the plan to Lynch earlier in the year asking for his comments.
71. Gennaro DeConcilio, "Su lo Stato Religioso" (New York: 1888), 28: DeConcilio pointed out in his article that when the Italians were assured their pastor cared little for them, they in turn had little estimation for him in return. His example for this was what he termed the "exceptional case" of the Rev. Thomas Lynch, who allowed his brother, Bernard Lynch, to write such attacks against the Italians. DeConcilio continued, "There is no other pastor in New York City who would allow his brother to say this, so disparaging a remark, against 14,000 [sic] of his own."
72. AANY, G-33, Rev. Thomas Lynch to Jacobini (copy), New York, November 18, 1885. ACMS, #019, Box 1, Lynch to Rt. Rev. Msgr. Preston, New York, September 20, 1886.
73. AGS, D, I, 2, Comitato ecclesiastico collettori to Scalabrini, New York, March 27, 1888. There were at that time two Italian priests at Transfiguration Church: the Rev. Giuseppe Ansanello, from Salerno, and the Rev. Marcellino Moroni from Scalabrini's Institute.
74. APF, S.C. Amer. Cent., 1890, vol. 54, f816r-817v, Antonio Casazza and twelve members of the Comitato ecclesiastico collettori to Propaganda, New York, May 23, 1888.
75. APF, Lett. Occid., 1887, vol. 38, f214v, Simeoni to Bonomelli, Rome, September 16, 1887: Simeoni had written to various Italian bishops in search of priests for New York. S.C. Amer. Cent., 1887, vol. 47, f973r-974r, Bonomelli to Simeoni, Cremona, September 24, 1887: Bonomelli suggested Moroni. ACMS, SRSR, #005, Box 1, Simeoni to Corrigan, Rome, September 28, 1887: Letter of introduction for Moroni. APF, S.C. Amer. Cent., 1890, vol. 54, f773r, Corrigan to Simeoni, New York, October 28, 1887: Moroni was "already instituted as a vicar in the Church of the Transfiguration."
76. Lynch could have been referring to Corrigan's plan of affording the Italians independence from Transfiguration by securing Italian missionaries. If so, Lynch's move to have the Italians petition and hire some of Scalabrini's priests to work under Lynch would have undermined Corrigan's plans.

77. AGS, 551/1, Morelli to Scalabrini, New York, August 10, 1888: certain members of the New York clergy had circulated rumors that Scalabrini's priests would minister exclusively to the northern Italians. This report even appeared in some New York newspapers.

78. APF, S.C. Amer. Cent., 1890, vol. 54, f816v, Antonio Casazza and twelve members of the Comitato ecclesiastico collettori to Propaganda, New York, May 23, 1888.

79. AGS, D, I, 2, Rev. Marcellino Moroni to Simeoni, New York, May 16, 1888.

80. Moroni also offered Lynch a plan by which a house would be procured for the Italian missionaries within Lynch's territory. The priests would make a monthly offering to Lynch of $100 in order to freely function in the church basement. Lynch rejected the plan.

81. Moroni mentioned that the rector of Old St. Patrick had refused permission to his Italian assistant to teach catechism to Italian children or to perform any marriages for Italians within the parish.

82. John P. Marschall, "Diocesan and Religious Clergy: the History of a Relationship, 1789-1969," John Tracy Ellis, *The Catholic Priest in the United States: Historical Investigation* (Collegeville: 1971), 397.

83. Both Straniero and Mori were low-level Vatican employees who travelled around the United States giving interviews to the press and visiting American bishops, presenting themselves as high-ranking clerics sent by Rome on fact-finding missions.

84. Silvano Tomasi, "The Ethnic Church and the Integration of Italian Immigrants in the United States," in Silvano Tomasi, Madeline Engel, *The Italian Experience in the United States* (Staten Island: 1970), 180.

85. John T. Smith, *The Catholic Church in New York* (New York: 1905), II, 448-449.

86. Piacenza, March 15, 1892, Scalabrini to his New York missionaries, quoted in Marco Caliaro, Mario Francesconi, *John Baptist Scalabrini* (New York: 1977), 192.

87. ASV, DelApUSA, 18: "Del Anniversario 20 Settembre della presa di Roma." Satolli to "The Honorable Richard Olney, Secretary of State of the United States of America," Washington, D.C., May 25, 1895.

88. APNS 1895, Rub. 49, vol. 65, f755r, Bp. Winand Wigger to Ledóchowski, S. Orange, N.J., November 18, 1895.

89. ACMS, Scal. Frs. in North America, O.L. of Pompeii, Box 10, Circular Correspondence, Folder 1895-1912, Corrigan to all churches of the Archdiocese, New York, September 7, 1895.

90. Mario Francesconi, *Storia della Congregazione Scalabriniana* (Roma: 1973), III, 152-154.

91. Ibid., 157-159.

92. Ibid., Zaboglio to Scalabrini, Boston, July 5, 1889.

93. AANY, C-11, Rev. James Quinn to Corrigan, New York, April 14, 1887. Quinn was willing to take an Italian priest into his house in order that the two hundred Italians then in Tuxedo Park might make

their Easter duty. He wrote: "... but it would tend greatly to the preservation of the peace between such a priest and myself, were you to instruct him at the outset that his ministrations must be exclusively confined to the people of his own nationality."

94. AANY, C-28, Rev. Nicòla Russo, S.J., to Corrigan, New York, October 24, 1891.

95. *Acta et Decreta Concilii Plenarii Baltimorensis Tertii A.D. MDCCCLXXXIV* (Baltimorae: 1886), tit. v; par. 155; tit. vi; par. 199. *Synodus diocesana Neo-Eboracensis Quinta* (Neo-Eboraci: 1886), tit. iv; par. 22.

96. APF, S.C. Amer. Cent., 1891, vol. 56, f420r-421v, Corrigan to Simeoni, New York, May 8, 1891.

97. APF, APNS 1900, Rub. 153, vol. 194, f184r-230r, Corrigan to Simeoni, New York, May 21, 1900.

98. APF, S.C. Amer. Cent., 1890, vol. 52, f10r, Report of the Archdiocese of New York to Propaganda Fide, New York, January, 1890.

99. APF, S.C. Amer. Cent., 1892, vol. 58, f317r-320r, Corrigan to Ledóchowski, New York, March 7, 1892. The debts recorded were those exceeding $5,000.
Debts incurred by the extant "Italian" churches in New York City:
St. Anthony of Padua: $123,567.62
Our Lady of Mount Carmel:......................................$ 32,825.00
Debts incurred by new churches in New York City:
St. Joachim:..$120,240.00
Precious Blood: ....$ 77,500.00
Mount Carmel:..$121,000.00
The report contained other churches with debts. I have only reported on the Italian churches.

100. ASV, DelApUSA, New York, 52, Rev. Nicholas Ferretti to Satolli, New York, May 21, 1898: "The problem is not that the Archbishop is opposed to the new Italian parish," but, rather, that the opposition arose from New York rectors.

101. ACMS, SRSR, #005, Box 1, Corrigan to Scalabrini, New York, May 13, 1888.

102. APF, S.C. Amer. Cent., 1888, vol. 49, f255r-256r, Corrigan to Simeoni, New York, August 3, 1888.

103. ARSI, Prov. Maryl. 1888-1897, New York, Maryl. 1012-XVII, Corrigan to Rev. Antonius Anderledy, New York, December 14, 1888. Ibid., same to same, New York, January 14, 1889.

104. ARSI, Prov. Maryl. 1888-1897, New York, Maryl. 1012-XVII, Corrigan to Anderledy, New York, December 14, 1888.

Chapter 4 / Churches for the Italians in New York City

1. ACMS, SRSR, #005, Box 1, McSweeney to Corrigan, New York, November 26, 1900.

2. ACMS, #019, Box 1, Corrigan to Countess Teinitzel, New York, n.d.

Corrigan requested the Countess's assistance to aid her fellow Bohemians then in New York City. "We are now six Italian Churches, in the city, eleven German Churches, two French, one Spanish, one Bohemian and one Polish, so the city is becoming almost cosmopolitan. We have four hundred Catholic Arabs, a few Catholic Greeks, and in fact a sprinkling from every land under the sun."

3. Albert Giovanetti, *L'America degli Italiani* (Roma: 1975), 103. Cf. Jacob Riis, *The Making of an American* (New York: 1901), 275. "If the police want to find an Italian scamp, they find out first from what village he hails, then it is a simple matter, usually, to find where he is located in the city."

4. Nicholas J. Russo, *The Religious Acculturation of the Italians in New York City* (New York: 1968), 86. This colony was composed of immigrants from Sicily, Naples, Basilicata, Calabria, the Abruzzi, Apulia, and Genoa.

5. Jacob A. Riis, *How the Other Half Lives: Studies Among the Tenements of New York*, ed. Sam Bass (Cambridge, Mass.: 1970), 201-202. Henceforth referred to as *The Other Half*.

6. Ibid., xvii.

7. APF, Coll. d'Italia, vol. 43, f1445r-1446v, Rev. Thomas Lynch to Corrigan, New York, n.d.

8. Jacob A. Riis, *The Making of an American* (New York: 1901), 347-349. The Mott Street Barracks was mortgaged by a cemetery corporation.

9. Riis, *The Other Half*, 26.

10. Ibid., 27.

11. Maxwell F. Marcuse, *This Was New York* (New York: 1969), 61. The entire tenement area of "The Bend" was razed in 1892 and replaced by Columbus Park.

12. Riis, *The Other Half*, 45.

13. *Harper's Weekly*, June 29, 1895.

14. Russo, op. cit., 86.

15. Marcuse, op. cit., 58.

16. Russo, op. cit., 86.

17. Riis, *The Other Half*, 20, 21, 36.

18. *Saint Anthony of Padua Commemorative Book* (South Hackensack: 1967), 12.

19. Giovanni Schiavo, *Italian American History* (New York: 1949), 468.

20. *Saint Anthony of Padua Commemorative Book* (South Hackensack: 1967), 13. The north-south boundaries of the parish were W. Houston St. to Broome St.; the east-west boundaries were W. Broadway to West St.

21. Ibid., 16. Fr. Anacletus was also known as Anacletus da Roccagorga. APF, S.C. Amer. Cent., 1892, vol. 58, f317r-320r, Corrigan to Ledóchowski, New York, March 7, 1892: The new Church of St. Anthony had contracted a debt of $123,567.62 on the mortgage for construction of the new church.

22. Thomas Preston, "The Italian Mission," *The Catholic Review*, XXXV, n. 4 (January 26, 1889), 50-51.

23. AANY, C-2, Rev. John Farley to Corrigan, New York, November 1, 1883.

24. APF, S.O.C.G., 1887, vol. 1027, f766v, Mr. Raimondi to Propaganda, New York (?), February 1, 1883. The Italians in New York were given over to the care of the Franciscans who, according to this report, converted this Italian church into an "Irish church" for money. Ibid., f785v, Gennaro DeConcilio to Leo XIII, Jersey City, October 12, 1883: The Franciscans of St. Anthony's cared more for the Irish than the Italians. ARSI, Maryl. Neo-EB, vol. 1011, Pars 1a communia et miscellanea, fasc. Maryl. 11-r, Rev. Thomas Campbell, S.J., to Rev. Anthony Anderledy, S.J., New York, December 15, 1888: Campbell reported to the Father General of the Jesuits that Corrigan had requested the Society's help with the Italians of New York, and stated, "The Franciscans consider themselves to be in charge [of the Italian apostolate] but they do nothing."

25. APF, Coll. d'Italia, vol. 43, f1417r-1458v, Corrigan to Domenico Jacobini, New London, November 18, 1885.

26. ASV, DelApUSA, Emigrazione Italiana, 1, "P.P. Francescani Custodi della Immac. Concezione S.V.A. al Reverendissimo Padre Generale dell'Ordine dei Minori Convento di S. Antonio in via Merulana, Roma, Italia," New York, June 16, 1897.

27. APF, S.C. Coll. d'Italia, vol. 43, f1457r-1458v, Corrigan to Domenico Jacobini, New London, November 18, 1885.

28. ACFM, Immac. Concept., 1881-1888, vol. 3, f443-444, Corrigan to the Very Rev. Michael Richards, O.F.M., New York, June 4, 1886: "It would gratify me very much if the Franciscan Fathers in this City would observe the law of enclosures, and not permit females to enter the CLAUSURA. .... I trust also that you will succeed in enforcing regular discipline, which in my mind is very much needed in both houses, namely of Saint Anthony of Padua, Sullivan St., and Saint Francis, 31st St." AANY, C-13, Very Rev. Michael Richards, O.F.M., to Corrigan, Teutopolis, Ill., August 30, 1886. The visitation was made and new regulations formulated. The friars were instructed to make visitations to the Blessed Sacrament after meals, were prohibited from going into the city after supper, except for ministerial duties, and were not to drink in saloons or private homes. They were also prohibited from keeping money.

29. APF, S.C. Amer. Cent., 1883, vol. 38, f764rv, Five Italians to Simeoni, New York, February 10, 1882. APF, S.O.C.G., 1887, vol. 1027, f791r-792r. ASV, DelApUSA, Emigrazione Italiana, 1, P.P. Francescani to Reverendissimus Padre Gen., New York, June 16, 1897. *N.Y. Herald*, March 2, 1885.

30. John P. Marschall, "Diocesan and Religious Clergy: The History of a Relationship, 1789-1969," John Tracy Ellis, *The Catholic Priest in the United States: Historical Investigations* (Collegeville: 1971), 396.

31. Ibid., 409.

32. ARSI, Maryl. Neo-EB, vol. 1011, Pars 1a communia et miscellanea, 1888-1897, fasc. Prov. Maryl., Epist. comm. section I, Prae. Prov. Pa. Th. Campbell, 21 maii 1888-16 nov. 1893, Maryl. 11-I, 13, Rev. Thomas Campbell, S.J., to Rev. Anthony Anderledy, S.J., New York, March 20, 1889.

33. ACMS, #019, Box 1, Lynch to Preston, New York, September 20, 1886.

34. Cf. Robert Lord, John Sexton, and Edward Harrington, *History of the Archdiocese of Boston* (Boston: 1945), III, 224.

35. APF, S.C. Amer. Cent., 1890, vol. 54, f862r-863v, Rev. Vincent Morelli to "Illmo e Revmo Sig.," New York, November 6, 1889.

36. AABo, 5.13, Williams Papers, Cardinal John Simeoni, 1887-1888, Williams to Simeoni, Boston, January 12, 1888.

37. AGS, B. IV, n. 9, Scalabrini to Simeoni (draft), Piacenza, September 8, 1888.

38. APF, S.C. Amer. Cent., 1888, vol. 49, f1408r-1411r, Giuseppe Mazzi and other Italians to Leo XIII, Boston, n.d. AABo, 5.12, Simeoni, Card. John, 1886, Simeoni to Williams, Rome, June 6, 1886: The Italians had recourse to Propaganda for the sum of $8,000 for a new Italian church.

39. AGS, B. IV, 1888, n. 9, Scalabrini to Simeoni (draft), Piacenza, September 8, 1888.

40. APF, S.C. Amer. Cent., 1889, vol. 50, f217r-219v, Rev. Atanasio to Rev. Bonafacio da Verona, O.F.M., Boston, January 25, 1889.

41. APF, S.C. Amer. Cent., 1890, vol. 54, f862r-863v, Rev. Vincenzo Morelli to "Illmo e Revmo Sig.," New York, November 6, 1889.

42. APF, S.C. Amer. Cent., 1890, vol. 52, f85r-102v, Corrigan to Simeoni, New York, January 18, 1890. AOFM, Immac. Concept., 1889-1899, vol. IV, f239r-249r, Msgr. Donato Sbaretti to Rev. Luigi da Palma, Rome, February 21, 1890.

43. AANY, G-28, Corrigan to Simeoni, New York, September 24, 1891.

44. APF, Coll. d'Italia, vol. 43, f1583r-1548v, Scalabrini to Simeoni, Piacenza, November 30, 1889.

45. APF, S.C. Amer. Cent., 1889, vol. 50, f217r-219v, Rev. Atanasio, O.F.M. to Rev. Bonifacio da Verona, O.F.M., Boston, January 25, 1889. Folios 202r-273r of this volume of documents contain the entire correspondence concerning the dispute of the Franciscans and Scalabrinians in Boston and New York.

46. AANY, G-22, Rev. Anacletus, O.S.F., to Corrigan, New York, January 14, 1898.

47. AANY, C-12, Rev. William Whitmee to Corrigan, London, May 15, 1884.

48. AANY, C-17, Rev. William Whitmee to Corrigan, Rome, December 6, 1884.

49. AANY, G-33, Corrigan to Abp. Contieri (copy), New York, April 15, 1884.

50. AANY, C-17, Bp. John Vertin to Corrigan, Marquette, Michigan, May 20, 1886.

51. AANY, C-17, Bp. John Vertin to Corrigan, Marquette, Michigan, July 14, 1891.

52. APall, Newark/N.Y., SACante 1909, Fasc. 5, Rev. Emiliano Kirner to "Very Rev. Dear Fr.," New York, May 30, 1884.

53. Ibid.

54. Ibid. Kirner reported that Vento had been paid only $5 per week as a salary from the Italian congregation "and had to live on that and what he might get from a chance Mass or Baptism."

55. Ibid.

56. APF, Coll. d'Italia, vol. 43, f1455r-1456v, Corrigan to Domenico Jacobini, New York, March 30, 1886.

57. APall, SACante 1909, Newark/N.Y., Fasc. 5, New York, S.C. dei Religiosi 1884-1906, "Ex Audientia SSmi habita die 4 Aprilis 1886."

58. APF, Coll. d'Italia, vol. 43, f1502r, Corrigan to Scalabrini, New York, October 28, 1887.

59. Thomas Preston, "The Italian Missions," *The Catholic Review*, XXXV, n. 4 (January 6, 1889), 50: The Rev. Cahill arrived in January, 1886, and the Rev. Vincenzo Morelli in May, 1887.

60. APall, Newark/N.Y., SACante 1909, Fasc. 5, Kirner to "Very Rev. Dear Fr.," New York, May 30, 1884.

61. APF, Coll. d'Italia, vol. 43, f1442r-1444v, Corrigan to Simeoni, New York, August 4, 1884.

62. APF, S.C. Amer. Cent., 1887, vol. 46, f532rv, Corrigan to Simeoni, New York, March 29, 1887. Kirner was the source of information for Corrigan concerning the Italian immigrants which the Archbishop employed during Baltimore III and which served as background for the Becker letter to the pope following the Council.

63. AANY, C-19, Carmody to "Very Rev. Dear Fr.," New York, July 23, 1888.

64. APF, S.C. Amer. Cent., 1889, vol. 50, f301r-302v, Rev. William Whitmee to Simeoni, New York, March 2, 1889.

65. APF, S.C. Amer. Cent., 1892, vol. 58, f599r-601v, Corrigan to Ledóchowski, New York, June 3, 1892.

66. APF, S.C. Amer. Cent., 1891, vol. 57, f320r-322v, "Italian emigrants of New York City Parish of Our Lady of Mt. Carmel" to Simeoni, New York, n.d. The three other assistants, alleged by the Italians to be "Irish," were the Revs. McNeill, Kugelman, and Murray. All spoke Italian, but, according to a petition to Corrigan from the parish, were unable to speak the various Italian dialects.

67. *N.Y. Times*, August 29, 1892.

68. AANY, C-26, Sr. Mary Fidelis, P.S.V., to Corrigan, New York, March-September, 1891.

69. APF, S.C. Amer. Cent., 1891, vol. 57, f318r-319v, Corrigan to Simeoni, New York, September 12, 1891.

70. *N.Y. Times*, August 29, 1892.

71. APF, S.C. Amer. Cent., 1891, vol. 57, f320r-322v, "Italian emigrants of the New York City Parish of Our Lady of Mt. Carmel" to Simeoni, New York, n.d.

72. AANY, C-28, William O'Connor to Corrigan, New York, June 25, 1891: Ella Edes communicated the fact that Italian nuns were circulating stories in Rome concerning Italians being neglected by an Irish priest in New York. ACMS, #019, Box 1, Corrigan to Carmody, New York, June 26, 1891: "I understand that ugly stories are carried through Rome with regard to the persecution of Italian Sisters by an Irish priest."

73. ACMS, #019, Box 1, Corrigan to Carmody (copy), New York, August 25, 1891: Corrigan wrote, "I am shocked at the barbarous treatment of the Sisters."

74. *Synodus Dioecesana Neo-Eboracensis Quinta, November 17-18, 1886* (New York: 1886), 27, par. 97.

75. APall, Newark/N.Y., SACante 1909, Fasc. 4, Corrigan to Rev. Carlo Maria Orlandi, New York, August 31, 1891.

76. APF, Lett. Occid., 1891, vol. 387, f628r, Simeoni to Corrigan, Rome, August 22, 1891.

77. APall, Newark/N.Y., SACante 1909, Fasc. 4, Corrigan to Rev. Carlo Maria Orlandi, New York, October 6, 1891.

78. APall, Newark/N.Y., SACante 1909, Fasc. 4, Corrigan to Msgr. Sebastiani, New York, August 5, 1892.

79. APall, Newark/N.Y., SACante 1909, Fasc. 4, N.Y. Stampati e Resoconti, "Report of the Solidarities, Confraternities and Societies connected with the above mentioned church (Our Lady of Mount Carmel) for the year ending December 31, 1897," New York, December 3, 1897.

80. *N.Y. Times*, August 29, 1892.

81. APall, Newark/N.Y., SACante 1909, Fasc. 4, Corrigan to Sebastiani, New York, August 5, 1892.

82. APall, Newark/N.Y., SACante 1909, Fasc 4, N.Y. Stampati e Resoconti. Monsella to the Father General, "Financial Report of Our Lady of Mt. Carmel, 1892," New York, December 31, 1892; above reference, same to same, "Financial Report of Our Lady of Mt. Carmel, 1895."

	Jan. 1-Dec. 31, 1892	Jan. 1-Dec. 31, 1895
Total receipts:	$39,594.08	$20,705.67
Total expend., church and school:	$24,726.54	$20,705.67
Total debt:	$88,965.63	$88,905.08

(This includes a loan of $10,126.52 by the Pallotines.)

83. ACMS, #019, Box 1, Monsella to Corrigan, New York, April 3, 1894.

84. ACMS, #019, Box 1, Dolan to Corrigan, New York, October 1, 1900.

85. ACMS, #019, Box 1, Corrigan to Dolan, New York, December 12, 1900.

86. ACMS, SRSR, #005, Box 1, Corrigan to Scalabrini, New York, December 16, 1887.

87. APF, Coll. d'Italia, vol. 43, f1525r-1526v, Scalabrini to Simeoni, Piacenza, May 15, 1888.

88. AANY, C-19, Rev. Charles McDonnell to Corrigan, Paris, March 8, 1888.

89. AGS, D, I, 2, Moroni to Simeoni, New York, May 16, 1888. Since room assignments in Transfiguration were made according to seniority, Moroni was given an unheated attic room by Lynch. Moroni stayed until his mission was completed in June, 1888, returning to Italy with bronchial asthma.

90. AGS, D, I, 1, Corrigan to Scalabrini, New York, April 13, 1888.

91. AGS, D, I, 2, Moroni to Simeoni, New York, May 16, 1888.

92. AGS, D, I, 2, Moroni to Scalabrini, April 19, 1888.

93. AGS, D, I, 2, Moroni to Simeoni, May 16, 1888.

94. Scalabrini to Corrigan, Piacenza, June 2, 1888 as quoted in Mario Francesconi, *Storia della Congregazione Scalabriniana (1886-1888)* (Roma: 1969), II, 17-18.

95. Scalabrini to Corrigan, Piacenza, July 12, 1888, quoted in Francesconi, op. cit., III, 238-239.

96. Zaboglio to Scalabrini, New York, July 19, 1888, quoted in Francesconi, op. cit., III, 238-239.

97. AGS, D, I, 3, Zaboglio to Scalabrini, Jersey City, June 28, 1888.

98. AGS, D, I, 3, Zaboglio to Scalabrini, New York, July 19, 1888.

99. Ibid.

100. Scalabrini sent his missionaries earlier than planned because Propaganda had judged Corrigan's requests for priests to be urgent enough to outweigh any possible difficulties. The missionaries left Piacenza on July 12, 1888.

101. APF, S.C. Amer. Cent., 1890, vol. 54, f864r, Rev. Felice Morelli to Leo XIII, New York, November 27, 1888.

102. Thomas Preston, "The Italian Missions," *The Catholic Review* (January 26, 1889), XXXV, n. 4, 51.

103. AGS, D, I, 1, Corrigan to Scalabrini, August 10, 1888.

104. APF, S.C. Amer. Cent., 1890, vol. 54, f864r-866v, Morelli to Leo XIII, New York, November 27, 1889. The monthly rent was $400 (1,000 lire).

105. ACMS, SRSR, #005, Box 1, Corrigan to Scalabrini, Newburgh, May 8, 1889.

106. Francesconi, op. cit., III, 33.

107. AGS, 665, Astorri to Rolleri, New York, November 28, 1888.

108. *N.Y. Times*, January 2, 1895.

109. ACMS, SRSR, #005, Box 1, Corrigan to Scalabrini, Newburgh, May 8, 1889. Corrigan hoped to purchase the property for $63,000.

110. APF, S.C. Amer. Cent., 1890, vol. 54, f864v, Morelli to Leo XIII, New York, November 27, 1889.

111. AGS, D, I, 2, "Comitato Ecclesiastico Colletori," to Scalabrini, New York, March 27, 1888. The committee, attached to Transfiguration

Church, had turned the collection over to Corrigan, who deposited it in a bank under their name.

112. AGS, D, I, 2, Scalabrini to Corrigan, Piacenza, April 13, 1889.

113. ACMS, SRSR, #005, Box 1, Corrigan to Scalabrini, Newburgh, May 8, 1889.

114. APF, S.C. Amer. Cent., 1890, vol. 54, f758rv, Bp. Gentili Mattei to Simeoni, Larsina, April 26, 1889. Bp. Mattei, Morelli's ordinary, reported that Morelli abandoned his parish in Ravenna in December, 1887, as a result of a threatened lawsuit against him on the charge of forgery. Morelli fled the diocese and was accused in absentia of commercial forgery in the Court of Appeals of Bologna, on September 7, 1888, and ordered arrested. The Court of Assizes of Forlì postponed the case, but he was finally found guilty and sentenced. Morelli had also absconded with Church funds from a parish lumber mill.

115. *Storia della Parrocchia Italiana di S. Gioacchino in New York* (New York: 1938), 27. Henceforth referred to as *S. Gioacchino*.

116. Zaboglio to Scalabrini, Boston, April 13, 15, 1889, quoted in Francesconi, op. cit., III, 152-153.

117. AGS, 549, Scalabrini to Corrigan (copy), Piacenza, December 8, 1900.

118. *S. Gioacchino*, 27. Vicentini temporarily served as rector of the Church of the Most Precious Blood in early 1891, replacing Morelli, who was shifted from one post to another with great rapidity in an attempt to nullify his influence in the missions.

119. Vicentini to Rolleri, New York, February 28, 1894, quoted in Francesconi, op. cit., III, 269-271.

120. AGS, 665, Rev. A. Gibelli to Scalabrini, New York, October 14, 1890: One of the societies at St. Joachim demanded that the mortgage and debt-bound church be transformed into a hospital and threatened legal action if their demands were not met.

121. AANY, C-25, Preston to Corrigan, New York, May 23, 1890.

122. AGS, 665/2, Vicentini to Zaboglio, New York July 3, 1891.

123. AGS, 665/2, Vicentini to Rolleri, New York, July 3, 1891.

124. AGS, 665/2, Vicentini to Zaboglio, New York, July 7, 1891.

125. Scalabrini to Zaboglio, Piacenza, June 17, 1891, quoted in Francesconi, op. cit., III, 177.

126. AGS, 665/2, Vicentini to Rolleri, New York, December 3, 1891.

127. AGS, 302/2, Scalabrini to Vicentini, Piacenza, November 23, 1891. AGS, 549, Corrigan to Scalabrini, New York, July 29, 1893.

128. Francesconi, op. cit., III, 47.

129. Corrigan to Scalabrini, New York, September 29, 1893, quoted in Francesconi, op. cit., III, 255-260.

130. Corrigan to Scalabrini, New York, November 22, 1893, quoted in Francesconi, op. cit., III, 262.

131. Scalabrini to Zaboglio, Piacenza, September 11, 1891, quoted in Francesconi, op. cit., III, 178.

132. Ibid., 48.

133. Ibid., 287-288. AGS, 665/4, Strumia to Scalabrini, New York, July 19, 1894.
134. AGS, 665/3, "Declaration of P. F. Morelli, G. Carraro, G. Lippi, G. Poggi."
135. *S. Gioacchino*, 27.
136. AGS, 665/4, Strumia to Scalabrini, New York, December 28, 1894.
137. *S. Gioacchino*, 27.
138. AGS, 665/5, Rev. Oreste Alussi to Scalabrini, New York, January 26, 1899. ACMS, Scal. Frs. in N. Amer., Box 2, Folder #9, Financial Reports of St. Joachim.

1894	*1898*
Revenue:.........$ 9,822.59	Church revenue:.......$ 15,861.37
Expendit.:........$ 5,822.46	Church expendit.:.....$ 14,850.85
"Hypothetical	
debt"	House revenue:.........$ 3,211.92
(mortgage): $72,500.00	House expendit.:.......$ 3,594.34
	Total debt: $179,000.00

139. Zaboglio to Scalabrini, New Haven, August 30, 1895, quoted in Francesconi, op. cit., III, 210-211. AGS,665/4, Strumia to Rev. Giacomo Gambera, New York, February 4, 1898.
140. Zaboglio to Scalabrini, Boston, July 4, 1895, quoted in Francesconi, op. cit., III, 204-205.
141. AGS, 665/4, Strumia to Gambera, New York, February 4, 1898. AGS, 3023/2, Scalabrini to Alussi, Piacenza, February 12, 1899.
142. AANY, G-24, Gambera to Corrigan, Boston, March 9, 1898.
143. AGS, 665/5, Alussi to Scalabrini, New York, December 13, 1898.
144. Francesconi, op. cit., VI, 143.
145. ACMS, Scal. Frs. in N. Amer., Box 2, Folder #9, "Financial Report of St. Joachim, 1899."
146. ACMS, Box 5, Folder #6, "Contract between the Rev. Oreste Alussi, Rector of St. Joachim, and the Society of S. Vincenzo di Craso (Martyr)," New York, June 10, 1901.
147. ACMS, #019, Box 1, Rev. Bartolomeo Marenchino to Corrigan, New York, February 23, 1900.
148. AGS, 554/2, Novati to Scalabrini, Providence, November 28, 1902.
149. AGS, 551/1, Rev. Felice Morelli to Scalabrini, New York, August 10, 1888.
150. AGS, D, I, 2, Moroni to Simeoni (copy), New York, May 16, 1888.
151. ACMS, SRSR, #005, Box 1, Corrigan to Scalabrini, Newburgh, May 8, 1889.
152. ASV, DelApUSA, Emigrazione Italiana, 1, New York Chiesa di Baxter, Vicentini to Rolleri (copy), New York, February 28, 1894, "Cenno della Missione dei Missionari di S. Carlo per gli emigranti italiani in New York." Henceforth this report will be referred to as "Cenno."
153. "Cenno."
154. Ibid.

155. AGS, 665, Molinari to Rolleri, New York, April 2, 1891. AGS, 664, "Statistiche della Chiesa del Prez.mo Sangue, aperta il 27 Sett. 1891 nella Missione di New York."
156. "Cenno."
157. Francesconi, op. cit., III, 35.
158. AGS, 549, Corrigan to Scalabrini, New York, July 29, 1893.
159. APF, S.C. Amer. Cent., 1891, vol. 56, f653r, Corrigan to ? (copy), New York, June 16, 1891.
160. AGS, 549, Corrigan to Scalabrini, New York, August 29, 1893.
161. Scalabrini to Corrigan, Piacenza, September 9, 1893, quoted in Francesconi, op. cit., III, 258-259.
162. ASV, DelApUSA, Emigrazione Italiana, 1, Bandini to Ledóchowski, New York, May 3, 1893. Bandini to Satolli, New York, May 5, 1893.
163. ASV, DelApUSA, Emigrazione Italiana, 1, DeConcilio to Satolli, Jersey City, April 25, 1893.
164. ASV, DelApUSA, Emigrazione Italiana, 1, Satolli to Corrigan, Washington, D.C., April 28, 1893.
165. ASV, DelApUSA, Emigrazione Italiana, 1, Corrigan to Satolli, New York, May 1, 1893.
166. ASV, DelApUSA, Emigrazione Italiana, 1, Satolli to Ledóchowski (copy), Washington, D.C., May 5, 1893.
167. ASV, DelApUSA, Emigrazione Italiana, 1, Ledóchowski to Satolli, Rome, May 30, 1893.
168. ASV, DelApUSA, 3a, "Istruzione speciale a Msgr. Delegato Francesco Satolli an. 1892." Folder: "Persico to Satolli, Pres., Acad. Eccl." Title Sheet: "Pel visitatore Apostolico dell'America del Nord. . . ." This instruction is found under "Union among Bishops."
169. ASV, DelApUSA, Emigrazione Italiana, 1, Corrigan to Satolli, New York, May 11, 1893.
170. APF, S.C. Amer. Cent., 1886, vol. 44, f598r-599v, Corrigan to Simeoni, New York, February 14, 1886: "There is an Italian school in the City, but it is Protestant, to which King Umberto grants an annual subsidy. Could you not arrange that such assistance be converted rather to the Catholic Italian school?"
171. ACMS, SRSR, #005, Box 1, Satolli to Corrigan, Washington, D.C., April 28, 1893.
172. Vicentini to Scalabrini, New York, March 6, 1894, quoted in Francesconi, op. cit., III, 284.
173. AANY, G-3, Bp. Charles McDonnell to Corrigan, Brooklyn, May 19, 1893. McDonnell was Bishop of Brooklyn and reported to Corrigan on a recent meeting he had with Satolli concerning the Italians.
174. Corrigan to Scalabrini, New York, October 5, 1893, quoted in Francesconi, op. cit., III, 260-261. The church was sold for $60,000; the mortgage alone was $72,000, not including the other enormous debts. AOFM, Cust. Immac. Concept., 1889-1899, vol. IV, f390r-392v, Rev. Anacleto, O.F.M., to Ministro Generale, New York, February 2, 1894.

175. ASV, DelApUSA, Emigrazione Italiana, 1, New York, La Chiesa Italian di Baxter, "Cenno."

176. "Cenno." ASV DelApUSA, Emigrazione Italiana, 1, New York, La Chiesa Italiana di Baxter, Vicentini to Corrigan, New York, November 4, 1893. Vicentini to Corrigan, New York, December 27, 1893. Vicentini to Corrigan, New York, January 2, 1894.

177. AANY, G-5, Rev. Thomas Lynch to Corrigan, New York, January 23, 1894.

178. AANY, G-5, Rev. Thomas Lynch to Corrigan, February 3, 1894.

179. Corrigan to Scalabrini, S. Leone, Florida, February 22, 1894, quoted in Francesconi, op. cit., III, 264.

180. AOFM, Cust. Immac. Concept., 1889-1899, vol. IV, f390r-392v, Rev. Anacleto, O.F.M., to Ministro Generale, New York, February 2, 1894. Same to same, Pittsburgh, January 1, 1895, Satolli had been the author of the invitation to the Franciscans that they take over Most Precious Blood. He also pushed them to expand their Italian apostolate. Satolli's nephew was a Franciscan in Italy who wanted to come to America and enter into the work of the Custody of the Immaculate Conception. Satolli also requested Anacleto's assistance in this matter.

181. Scalabrini to Corrigan, Piacenza, February 5, 1894, quoted in Francesconi, op. cit., III, 262-263.

182. Corrigan to Scalabrini, S. Leone, Florida, February 22, 1894, quoted in Francesconi, op. cit., III, 264.

183. Cf. Francesconi, ibid., III, 172-179. ASV, DelApUSA, Emigrazione Italiana, 1, New York, La Chiesa Italiana di Baxter, "Cenno."

184. Corrigan to Scalabrini, New York, November 22, 1893, quoted in Francesconi, op. cit., III, 262.

185. Scalabrini to Corrigan, Piacenza, September 9, 1893, quoted in Francesconi, op. cit., III, 258-259.

186. AOFM, Cust. Immac. Concept., vol. IV, f394r-395v, Anacleto to "Rmo Padre," New York, February 6, 1894.

187. Ledóchowski to Scalabrini, Rome, February 23, 1894, quoted in Francesconi, op. cit., III, 281.

188. Even though the Franciscans were willing to take over the church debts, the Archdiocese required the Piacenzans to repay $15,000 lent them for construction by the Archdiocesan officials.

189. Scalabrini to Ledóchowski, Piacenza, February 26, 1894, quoted in Francesconi, op. cit., III, 273.

190. Corrigan to Ledóchowski, Rome, May 17, 1894, quoted in Francesconi, op. cit., III, 288.

191. Vicentini to Scalabrini, New York, May 4, 1894, quoted in Francesconi, op. cit., III, 289.

192. Vicentini to Scalabrini, New York, May 22, 1894, quoted in Francesconi, op. cit., III, 289-290. AANY, G-5, Vicentini to Corrigan, New York, May 22, 1894.

193. *The Catholic Church in the United States of America* (New York: 1908), I, 165: The total construction cost of the upper church was $83,000.

194. ARSI, Prov. Maryl. 1888-1897: Mary. 1012-XVII, 1, Corrigan to Rev. Antonius M. Anderledy, S.J., New York, December 14, 1888.

195. AANY, G-33, Corrigan to Abp. Contieri (copy), New York, April 15, 1884: Some Italian-speaking Jesuits were already employed in Italian work in the Archdiocese, along with the Franciscans, twenty-four diocesan Roman-trained priests, and twelve Italian diocesan priests.

196. ARSI, Maryl. Neo-EB, vol. 1011, Pars 1a communia et miscellanea, 21 May 1888-14 March 1897, fasc. Maryl. 11-I, Epistolarum Communium Pars Prima (Prae. Prov. Pa. Thoma J. Campbell), 26 maii 1888-16 nov. 1893, Campbell to Anderledy, New York, December 15, 1888.

197. Ibid. "Admittedly, I have some Italian Fathers here; however, they are too well educated in the English language and thereupon exists the danger of neglecting this specialized work."

198. ARSI, Prov. Maryl. 1888-1897, New York, "Residentia pro Italis et de cura Italorum in universum," Maryl. 1, 1012-XVII, 2, Corrigan to Anderledy, New York, January 14, 1889.

199. ARSI, Maryl. Neo-EB, vol. 1011, Pars 1a communia et miscellanea, 1888-1897, fasc. Prov. Maryl., epistolarum Comm. Pars Prima (Prae. Prov. Pa. Thoma J. Campbell), 21 maii 1886-16 nov. 1893, Maryl. 11-I, 13, Campbell to Anderledy, New York, March 20, 1889.

200. APF, S.C. Amer. Cent., 1891, vol. 56, f653r, Corrigan to ?, New York, June 16, 1891: ". . . the Piacenzans are not good for those people [southern Italians], and they have attempted to remedy this defect by employing bunglers (scagnozzi)."

201. ARSI, Maryl. Neo-EB, vol. 1011, Pars 1a communia et miscellanea, fasc. Maryl. 1011-I, 24, Campbell to Anderledy, New York, April 6, 1891.

202. ARSI, Maryl. Neo-EB, vol. 1011, Pars 1a communia et miscellanea, fasc. Maryl. 1011-I, 2, Campbell to Anderledy, New York, May 18, 1891.

203. Ibid.

204. ARSI, Prov. Maryl. 1888-1897, New York, "Res. pro Italis et de cura. . . .," Maryl. 1012, XVII, 3, Simeoni to Anderledy, Rome, August 21, 1891.

205. ARSI, Prov. Maryl. 1888-1897, New York, "Res. pro Italis et de cura. . . .," Maryl. 1012, XVII, 3, Simeoni to Anderledy, Rome, July 21, 1891.

206. APF, Lett. Occid., 1891, vol. 387, f537r, Simeoni to Corrigan, August 18, 1891.

207. Ibid.

208. ARSI, Prov. Maryl. 1886-1900, vol. III, Rev. Ludovico Martin to Campbell, Fiesole, June 12, 1891.

209. Nicholas J. Russo, "The Origin and Progress of Our Italian Mission," *The Woodstock Letters* (February, 1896), 134-143.

210. Ibid., 137.

211. ASV, DelApUSA, Emigrazione Italiana, 1, Russo to Corrigan (copy), New York, March 12, 1892.

212. ARSI, Maryl. Neo-EB, vol. 1011, Pars 1a communia et miscellanea, 1888-1897, fasc. Maryl. 1011-I, fasc. Maryl. 11-I, 48, Campbell to Martin, New York, February 3, 1893.

213. ARSI, New York, "Res. pro Italis et de cura. . . ," Maryl. 12-XVII, 8, Russo to Martin, New York, March 23, 1895.

214. AANY, C-28, Russo to Corrigan, New York, October 24, 1891.

215. AANY, C-30, Russo to Corrigan, New York, March 12, 1892.

216. AANY, C-30, Russo to Corrigan, New York, March 15, 1892.

217. Russo, op. cit., *Woodstock Letters*, 140.

218. ARSI, Prov. Maryl. 1888-1897, New York, "Res. pro Italis et de cura. . . ," Maryl. 12-XVIII, 4, Russo to Martin, New York, March 4, 1892.

219. Russo, op. cit., *Woodstock Letters*, 138 (emphasis in original).

220. Ibid.

221. ARSI, Prov. Maryl. 1888-1897, New York, "Res. pro Italis et de cura. . . ," Maryl. 12-XVIII, 8, Russo to Martin, New York, March 23, 1895.

222. ARSI, Prov. Maryl,, 1896-1900, vol. III, Martin to Russo (copy), Rome, May 11, 1895.

223. Russo, op. cit., *Woodstock Letters*, 142.

224. ARSI, Prov. Maryl. 1888-1897, New York, "Res. pro Italis et de cura. . . ," Maryl. 12-XVII, 8, Russo to Martin, New York, March 23, 1895.

225. ARSI, Maryl. Neo-EB, vol. 1013, 1897-1906, fasc. Maryl. 13-XVII, 2, Rev. Emmanuele DeCaro to Martin, Acireale, Sicily, October 9, 1901. ARSI, Prov. Maryl. Neo-EB, 1900-1911, vol. IV, Martin to Rev. William Gannon, S.J. (copy), Rome, September 28, 1901. This was the only "abuse" mentioned in this letter or in any other correspondence dealing with the Jesuit mission.

226. *N.Y. Times*, April 2, 1902.

227. ARSI, Maryl. Neo-EB, vol. 1013, 1897-1906, fasc. Maryl. 13, DVII, 1, Romano to Martin, New York, June 12, 1902.

228. Scalabrini to Corrigan, Piacenza, June 2, 1888, quoted in Francesconi, op. cit., III, 237.

229. ASV, DelApUSA, Emigrazione Italiana, 1, "Relazione della Società Italiana di San Raffaele in New York nel primo anno della fondazione (1 Luglio 1891 al 30 Giugno 1892)," Piacenza, 1892.

230. APF, S.C. Amer. Cent., 1891, vol. 57, f578r-579v, Scalabrini to Simeoni, Piacenza, February 20, 1891.

231. ASV, DelApUSA Emigrazione Italiana, 1, "Relazione della Società Italiana di San Raffaele in New York nel primo anno della sua fondazione (1 Luglio 1891 al 30 Giugno 1892)," Piacenza, 1892.

232. AANY, C-7, Cahensly to Corrigan, Limburg an der Lahn, December 4, 1885; same to same in above reference, January 12, 1886.

233. AANY, G-1, Bandini to Corrigan, New York, August 12, 1893.

234. APF, S.C. Amer. Cent., 1891, vol. 57, f528r-579v, Scalabrini to Simeoni, Piacenza, February 20, 1891.

235. Marco Caliaro, Mario Francesconi, *John Baptist Scalabrini* (New York: 1977), 229.
236. ASV, DelApUSA, Emigrazione Italiana, 1, "Relazione della Società Italiana di San Raffaele in New York nel primo anno della sua fondazione (1 Luglio 1891 al 30 Giugno 1892)," Piacenza 1892, 15. AGS, 110/10, Bandini to Scalabrini, New York, July 21, 1891.
237. AANY, C-10, Rev. John H. McGean to Corrigan, New York, December 16, 1885. AANY, C-11, Rev. John Joseph Riordan to Corrigan, Castle Garden, January 25, 1886.
238. ASV, DelApUSA, Emigrazione Italiana, 1, Bandini to Satolli, New York, April 4, 1893.
239. AGS, 583/2, Bandini to Scalabrini, New York, January 16, 1895.
240. AANY, G-1, Scalabrini to Corrigan, Piacenza, September 9, 1893.
241. Corrigan to Scalabrini, New York, October 5, 1893, quoted in Francesconi, op. cit., III, 260-261:
    Total income for the previous six months: $2,133.00
    Total expenditure for the previous six months: $2,120.14
    Balance: .... $ 12.86
242. Constantino Sassi, *Parrocchia della Madonna di Pompeii in New York* (Roma: 1944), 31: Contributions during the chapel's first four years totaled only $4,270.20.
243. ASV, DelApUSA, Emigrazione Italiana, 1, Gennaro DeConcilio to Satolli, Jersey City, April 25, 1893. DeConcilio claimed the Society's house to be indebted for $19,000. ASV, DelApUSA, Emigrazione Italiana, 1, Corrigan to Satolli, New York, May 11, 1893.
244. Corrigan to Scalabrini, New York, November 22, 1893, quoted in Francesconi, op. cit., III, 262.
245. Scalabrini to Corrigan, Piacenza, October 22, 1893, quoted in Francesconi, op. cit., 261-262.
246. ASV, DelApUSA, New York, 34, "Rev. Pietro Bandini Suo Caso," Bandini to Satolli, Ellis Island, January 7, 1895.
247. AGS, 583/2, Bandini to Scalabrini, New York, January 16, 1895. The actual asking price of the property was $52,000.
248. *N.Y. Times*, April 29, 1895.
249. AGS, 583/2, Bandini to Scalabrini, New York, January 16, 1895.
250. ASV, DelApUSA, New York, 34, "Rev. Pietro Bandini Suo Caso," Bandini to Satolli, New York, January 3, 1894 (*sic*). The actual date of the letter is 1895.
251. ASV, DelApUSA, New York, 34, "Rev. Pietro Bandini Suo Caso," Rev. C. G. O'Keefe to Satolli, Highland Falls, New York, January 3, 1895.
252. ASV, DelApUSA, New York, 34, "Rev. Pietro Bandini Suo Caso," Bandini to Satolli, March 16, 1895.
253. ASV, DelApUSA, New York, 34, "Rev. Pietro Bandini Suo Caso," Bandini to Satolli, March 27, 1895. Same to same, New York, March 29, 1895.
254. ASV, DelApUSA, New York, 34, "Rev. Pietro Bandini Suo Caso," Satolli to Bandini, Washington, D.C., March 28, 1895.

255. *N.Y. Times*, May 23, 1896.
256. ASV, DelApUSA, Emigrazione Italiana, 1, Zaboglio to Scalabrini, New Haven, January 12, 1896.
257. AANY, G-11, Connolly to Bandini (copy), New York, January 17, 1896.
258. ASV, DelApUSA, Emigrazione Italiana, 1, Zaboglio to Scalabrini, New Haven, January 12, 1896.
259. ASV, DelApUSA, Emigrazione Italiana, 1, Zaboglio to Satolli, New Haven, January 11, 1896.
260. ASV, DelApUSA, Emigrazione Italiana, 1, Zaboglio to Satolli, New Haven, January 7, 1896.
261. ASV, DelApUSA, Emigrazione Italiana, 1, Austin Corbin to Satolli, New York, January 10, 1896.
262. ASV, DelApUSA, Emigrazione Italiana, 1, Zaboglio to Satolli, New Haven, January 7, 1896.
263. ASV, DelApUSA, Emigrazione Italiana, 1, Zaboglio to Satolli, New Haven, January 11, 1896.
264. Zaboglio to Scalabrini, New Haven, January 12, 1896, quoted in Francesconi, op. cit., III, 220-221.
265. ASV, DelApUSA, Emigrazione Italiana, 1, Satolli to Zaboglio (copy), Washington, D.C., January 15, 1896.
266. ASV, DelApUSA, Emigrazione Italiana, 1, Satolli to Zaboglio (copy), Satolli to Bandini, Washington, D.C., January 20, 1896.
267. AANY, G-11, Connolly to Bandini, New York, January 30, 1896. ASV, DelApUSA, Emigrazione Italiana, 1, Bishop John Farley to Satolli, New York, April 15, 1896: The Archdiocese had paid "several thousand dollars of his [Bandini's] debts," since he had begun his administration. When Bandini left, against Farley's express prohibition, the Archdiocese found itself burdened with an additional $1,200 in debts owed by him.
268. AANY, G-11, Bandini to Connolly, Sunnyside, Arkansas, January 22, 1896.
269. AANY, G-13, Bandini to Corrigan, New York, March 19, 1896.
270. AANY, G-12, William P. O'Connor to Corrigan, New York, April 24, 1896.
271. AGS, 583/3, Zaboglio to Scalabrini, New York, May 7, 1896.
272. Ibid.
273. ASV, DelApUSA, Emigrazione Italiana, 1, Farley to Satolli, New York, April 24, 1896.
274. AGS, 583/3, Zaboglio to Scalabrini, New York, n.d.
275. *The Catholic Church in the United States* (New York: 1909), II, 195. Jacob Riis, *How the Other Half Lives* (Cambridge, Mass.: 1970 edition), 21: The Italians "overrunning the old Africa of Thompson Street, pushing . . . the Negroes uptown."
276. Zaboglio to Scalabrini, New Haven, April 12, 1896, quoted in Francesconi, op. cit., III, 225.
277. AGS, 583/3, Beccherini to Scalabrini, New York, July 29, 1896. Frs.

Zaboglio and Isola had smelled gas in the church basement during the late afternoon of July 14. Since it was difficult to see in the basement because of the failing light, the sexton lit a match, thus unwittingly igniting the escaping gas.

278. AGS, 553/2, Gambera to Scalabrini, Boston, May 30, 1899.

279. ACMS, Scal. Frs. in N. Amer., O.L. of Pompeii, Box 24, Folder: "Receipts," Gambera to Demo, Boston, July 8, 1899.

280. Costantino Sassi, *Parrocchia della Madonna di Pompeii in New York* (Roma: 1946), 53.

281. Michael Cosenza, *Our Lady of Pompeii in Greenwich Village: History of the Parish 1892-1967* and *St. Frances Xavier Cabrini's Story* (New York: 1967), 7-8.

282. Sassi, op. cit., 54: The Sunday schedule had included three Masses, celebrated at 8:00, 10:00, and 11:00 a.m., during which a nocturn of the dead was always sung along with the obsequies of the dead. This was suppressed by Demo, and the American schedule of seven Sunday Masses was instituted, the first celebrated at 6:00 a.m., and the last at 11:00 a.m.

283. Ibid., 53-54.

284. APF, APNS (1900), vol. 174, R. 8, f490r-491v, Gambera to Ledóchowski, Rome, September 4, 1900: Gambera wrote in the name of the bishops of North America, requesting permission for Scalabrini to visit the United States. Ibid., Ledóchowski to Scalabrini (draft), Rome, September 11, 1900.

285. *N.Y. Times*, August 11, 1901.

286. AANY, G-28, Corrigan to Farley, New York, November 6, 1901.

287. Scalabrini to Zaboglio, Piacenza, February 25, 1896, quoted in Francesconi, op. cit., III, 222.

288. ACMS, #019, Box 2, Rev. Gaudentius Rossi to Corrigan, Baltimore, July 31, 1883. APF, S.O.C.G. 1887, vol. 1027, f778r-781r, Rev. Luca Passionista to Simeoni, Carroll, Maryland, October 10, 1883.

289. AANY, C-2, Rev. John Farley to Corrigan, New York, November 1, 1883.

290. ACS, 38, New York, Correspondence, 1883-1898, Corrigan to Bosco, Rome, December 15, 1883.

291. ACS, 38, New York, Correspondence, 1883-1898, Corrigan to Don Bosco, New York, March 7, 1884.

292. ACS, 38, New York, Correspondence, 1883-1898, Rev. Edward M. Parocco to "Revmo e Carmo Sig. Vicario," Chateaugay, New York, February 1, 1888.

293. ACS, 38, New York, Correspondence, 1883-1898, Corrigan to the Salesian superior, New York, October 26, 1897.

294. ACS, 38, New York, Correspondence, 1883-1898, Corrigan to the Salesian superior, New York, October 26, 1897. On the "verso" side of this letter is a notation indicating the Salesian response, dated November 8, 1897.

295. ACS, 38, New York, Correspondence, 1883-1898, Corrigan to Rev. Michele Rua, New York, September 30, 1897.

296. ACS, 38, New York, Correspondence, 1883-1898, Corrigan to Rua, New York, February 24, 1898.

297. ACS, 38, New York, Correspondence, 1883-1898, Corrigan to Rua, New York, February 24, 1898: The "verso" side of the letter bears Rua's reply in note form, dated March 17, 1898: "I hope to have a sure date by October."

298. AANY, G-21, Rua to Corrigan, Torino, November 19, 1898. ACS, 38, New York, Correspondence, 1883-1898.

299. ACMS, #019, Box 6, "Documentation Indiv. Parishes: St. Bridgid's (NYC)," "Cronaca della Casa di Santa Brigida in New York City." This is an undated and unsigned diary, briefly tracing the history of the Salesians' arrival and work in New York from 1898 until the summer of 1903. Henceforth referred to as "Cronaca."

300. ACMS, #019, Box 6, "Cronaca."

301. ACS, 38, New York Correspondence, 1883-1898, Corrigan to Rua, New York, December 6, 1898.

302. ACMS, #019, Box 6, "Cronaca."

303. ACS, 38, New York Correspondence, 1883-1898, Corrigan to Rua, New York, December 6, 1898.

304. APF, S.C. Amer. Cent., 1884, vol. 41, f467r-468v, Corrigan to Simeoni, New York, September 16, 1884: McSweeney had been mentioned as a candidate for the position of auxiliary bishop of Pittsburgh.

305. APF, APNS (1896), vol. 77, R. 7, f910rv, McSweeney to Ledóchowski, New York, December 15, 1896. McSweeney had studied at Propaganda Fide in Rome. All alumni of Propaganda were obliged to submit reports to Rome about their work and diocese every two years.

306. Patrick D. O'Flaherty, *The History of St. Brigid's Parish in the City of New York under the Administration of the Rev. Patrick F. McSweeney* (New York: 1952), 70-71. This unpublished M.A. dissertation will henceforth be referred to as *History of St. Brigid.*

307. APF, APNS (1898), vol. 124, R. 7, f279r-280v, McSweeney to Ledóchowski, New York, October 19, 1898.

308. ACMS, #019, Box 6, "Cronaca."

309. Ibid.

310. AANY, G-2, McSweeney to Corrigan, New York, October 26, 1893 (*sic*).

311. ACMS, #019, Box 6, "Cronaca."

312. Coppo was a rather remarkable man and became involved in numerous activities in favor of the Italian immigrants in the city. He worked among the Italian prisoners in the city's jails. He, along with Corrigan, assisted the Italian Catholic newspaper *L'Italiano in America*, published in 1900 by l'Unione Italo-Americano Publishing Company. Coppo became the director of the Italian Catholic weekly by the beginning of 1902 which was later supported by the Salesian

parish of Our Lady Help of Christians, which the Salesians accepted in 1908.

313. New York, n.d., McSweeney to Corrigan, quoted in Patrick D. O'Flaherty, *St. Brigid*, 71.

314. AANY, G-23, Coppo to Corrigan, New York, December 13, 1900.

315. Ibid.

316. ACMS, #019, Box 6, "Cronaca."

317. ACMS, #019, Box 1, McLoughlin to Corrigan, New York, November 10, 1898.

318. ACMS, #019, Box 6, "Cronaca."

319. ACMS, #019, Box 1, McLoughlin to Corrigan, New York, March 5, 1902.

320. Ibid.

321. ACMS, #019, Box 1, McLoughlin to Corrigan, New York, April 9, 1902.

322. ACMS, #019, Box 1, "Cronaca." The neighborhood around Transfiguration Church continued to change ethnically, so that by 1909, the basement of the once predominately Irish church, which gave way to a predominately Italian congregation, was also used by the growing Catholic Chinese community, attended by the Rev. V. H. Montanar, under the direction of the Salesians. Cf. *The Catholic Church in the United States of America* (New York: 1908), II, 229.

323. There were other churches in the Archdiocese assisting the Italian immigrants during the years of Corrigan's administration. They were mixed congregations, allowing the Italians the use of church basements or halls for their services, with Italian or Roman-trained American priests attending them. Those churches that attended to the more numerous Italian congregations in the Archdiocese were the following:
Manhattan: St. Ann, St. Brigid, St. Catherine of Siena, St. Elizabeth, The Epiphany, Holy Rosary, Immaculate Conception, St. Lucy, The Nativity, St. Patrick's Old Cathedral, St. Peter, St. Rita.
Bronx: St. Philip Neri, St. Roch.
Richmond (Staten Island): St. Joseph.
Glasco: St. Joseph.
New Rochelle: St. Joseph.
Yonkers: St. Anthony.
Mount Vernon: Our Lady of Mount Carmel.
Cf. *Wiltzius Official Catholic Directory* (Milwaukee: 1903), 98-109.

324. ASV, DelApUSA, Emigrazione Italiana, 1, Corrigan to Satolli, New York, May 11, 1893.

Chapter 5 / Mother Cabrini: Early Years in New York

1. Mary Reid DiCesnola (1830-1902) was the second daughter of Mary Jennings and Captain Samuel C. Reid, hero of the War of 1812, and the designer of the present American flag. Mary was married to Luigi Palma DiCesnola, an American Civil War hero, Italian-born ar-

chaeologist, and controversial director of the New York Metropolitan Museum of Art.

2. APF, S.C. Amer. Cent., 1890, vol. 54, f798rv, Corrigan to "Dear Dr. [McDonnell]," New York, January 7, 9, 1888.

3. APF, S.C. Amer. Cent., 1886, vol. 44, f598r-599v, Corrigan to Simeoni, New York, February, 1886. S.C. Amer. Cent., 1890, vol. 54, f844r-845v, Corrigan to Simeoni.

4. APF, S.C. Amer. Cent., 1890, vol. 54, f834r; 842r, Mary DiCesnola to Corrigan, New Castle, New York, July 7, 1888.

5. APF, S.C. Amer. Cent., 1890, vol. 54, f837r; 840r, Mary DiCesnola to Corrigan, New Castle, New York, June 24, 1887. Same to same, New York, January 1, 1888, in the above reference, f798v-799v.

6. APF, S.C. Amer. Cent., 1890, vol. 54, f838r-839v, Mary DiCesnola to Corrigan, New Castle, New York, July 15, 1887. Same to same, New York, n.d., in the above reference, f847v. Same to same, New Castle, New York, July 7, 1888, in above reference, f834r; 842r.

7. AMSH, "Memorie della Casa in Bassa Città." This is a diary written by one of the sisters recording the daily activities of the sisters during the early years of the New York mission of Mother Cabrini. The record covers the period of their arrival in the city on March 31, 1889, and continues until mid-June, 1889. Henceforth referred to as *Memorie*.

8. Thomas Bender, *New York Intellect* (New York: 1987), pp. 168-171.

9. *N.Y. Times*, March 17, 24, 1882.

10. *N.Y. Times*, January 2, 1887.

11. Mary Louise Sullivan, *Mother Cabrini: "Italian Immigrant of the Century"* (New York: 1992), 89ff, offers another interpretation.

12. AANY, C-19, McDonnell to Corrigan, Paris, March, 8, 1888.

13. *Santa Francesca Saverio Cabrini* (Torino: 1962), 78-79. This is a reprinting of *La Madre Francesca Saverio Cabrini*, written by "Una delle sue figlie," in 1928. Most probably authored by Mother Antoniette Della Casa, who succeeded Mother Cabrini as superior general of the congregation. Henceforth referred to as *Cabrini*.

14. Ibid., 80-81.

15. New York, October 12, 1888, Morelli to Scalabrini, quoted in Francesconi, op. cit., III, 49-51.

16. New York, n.d., Morelli to Scalabrini, ibid., 51-52. New York, October 28, 1888, Zaboglio to Scalabrini, ibid., 141-142.

17. New York, October 28, 1888, Zaboglio to Scalabrini, ibid., 141-142.

18. APF, S.C. Amer. Cent. 1890, vol. 54, f798rv, Corrigan to "Dear Dr. [McDonnell]," New York, January 7, 1888.

19. APF, S.C. Amer. Cent. 1890, vol. 54, f844r-845v, Corrigan to Simeoni, New York, December 18, 1888.

20. Ibid.

21. New York, February 5, 1889, Corrigan to Scalabrini, quoted in Francesconi, op. cit., III, 243-244.

22. APF, S.C. Amer. Cent., 1890, vol. 54, f810r, Corrigan to Scalabrini, New York, April 24, 1888.

23. APF, S.C. Amer. Cent. 1890, vol. 54, f837r; 840r, Mary DiCesnola to Corrigan, New Castle, New York, June 24, 1887. Same to same in above reference, f838r-839v, New Castle, New York, July 15, 1887. Same to same in above reference, f798r-799r, New York, January 8, 1888. Same to same in above reference, f835r, New York, March 9, 1888. Same to same in above reference, f834r; 842r. New York (?) n.d. Corrigan to Simeoni, f844r-845v, New York, December 18, 1888.

24. New York, November 7, 1888, Corrigan to Scalabrini, quoted in Francesconi, op. cit., III, 242.

25. AGS, 102, Mary DiCesnola to Scalabrini, New York, January 3, 1889 (cable).

26. *Cabrini*, 85.

27. APF, S.C. Amer. Cent., 1890, vol. 54, f844r-845v, Corrigan to Scalabrini, New York, December 18, 1888.

28. Ibid.

29. Piacenza, January 23, 1889, Scalabrini to Corrigan, quoted in Francesconi, op. cit., III, 243.

30. AANY, C-18, Corrigan to Cabrini (copy), New York, March 8, 1889.

31. AMSH, *Memorie*, June 6, 1889, f180-181. Mother Cabrini never received this letter until June 6, since she departed Italy prior to its delivery.

32. Rome, March 8, 1889, Simeoni to the United States Bishops, quoted in *Sacra rituum Congregatione, Beatificationis et canonizationis Servae Dei Franciscae Xaverio Cabrini Fundatricis et Primae Antistitae Generalis Congregationis Sororum Missionarum A. S. Corde Jesu. Nova Positio Super Virtutibus* (Roma: 1973), I, 70. Henceforth referred to as *Rituum Congregatione*.

33. AMSH, *Memorie*, March 31, 1889, f28.

34. Ibid.

35. *Cabrini*, 97.

36. AMSH, *Memorie*, April 1, 1889, f28.

37. *Cabrini*, 97-98.

38. AMSH, *Memorie*, April 2, 1889, f33-34.

39. AMSH, *Memorie*, April 1, 1889, f31.

40. AMSH, *Memorie*, May 24, 1889, f80-82.

41. AMSH, *Memorie*, April 1, 1889, f32-33.

42. APF, Coll. d'Italia, vol. 43, f1571r-1572v, Cabrini to Scalabrini, New York, April 12, 1889.

43. AMSH, *Memorie*, April 2, 1889, f33-34. Morelli was to serve as the nuns' confessor. He was opposed to Corrigan's decision concerning the orphanage project, seeing it as a part of the alleged Irish hatred for the Italians.

44. AMSH, *Memorie*, April 5, 1889, f36-37.

45. AMSH, *Memorie*, April 5, 1889, f36-40.

46. AMSH, *Memorie*, April 2, 1889, f34; April 5, 1889, f31; April 6, 1889, f41.

47. AMSH, CL-2-198, f568r-571r, Mother Cabrini to the Sisters in New York, New York, April 5, 1889.

48. APF, Coll. d'Italia, vol. 43, f1571r-1572v, Mother Cabrini to Scalabrini, New York, April 12, 1889.

49. AMSH, *Memorie*, April 10, 1889, f46-47.

50. APF, S.C. Amer. Cent., 1891, vol. 56, f420r-421v, Corrigan to Simeoni, New York, May 8, 1891.

51. ACMS, Scal. Frs. in N. Amer., O.L. of Pompeii, Box 10, Circular letter of Corrigan to the clergy of New York, New York, October 16, 1896.

52. *Cabrini*, 107.

53. AMSH, *Memorie*, April 17, 1889, f55.

54. AMSH, *Memorie*, April 21, 1889, f60-61.

55. AMSH, *Memorie*, April 27, 1889, f65.

56. ACMS, SRSR, #055, Box 1, Corrigan to Scalabrini, Newburgh, May 8, 1889.

57. Ibid.

58. AGS, 551/2, Morelli to Scalabrini, New York, June 9, 1889.

59. *Cabrini*, 108-109.

60. AMSH, *Memorie*, June 3, 1889, f151-152.

61. AMSH, *Memorie*, June 4, 1889, f152.

62. AMSH, *Memorie*, June 6, 1889, f153.

63. AMSH, *Memorie*, June 8, 1889, f153.

64. AGS, 551/2, Morelli to Scalabrini, New York, June 9, 1889.

65. AGS, 102, Cabrini to Scalabrini, New York, June 10, 1889.

66. Francesconi, op. cit., III, 58.

67. AMSH, *Memorie della Casa di 43 East 59th Street*, vol. III, 1889, f3. Henceforth referred to as *Memorie 43 E. 59th St.*

68. AGS, 551/2, Morelli to Scalabrini, New York, June 9, 1889.

69. APF, S.C. Amer. Cent., 1890, vol. 53, f718r-721v, Mother Cabrini to Simeoni, Manresa, July 31, 1890.

70. AMSH, *Memorie*, April 10, 1889, f46-49.

71. AMSH, *Memorie*, June 15, 1889, f191-192.

72. Quoted in William Rhinelander Stewart, *The Philanthropic Work of Josephine Shaw Lowell* (New York: 1911), 250-251.

73. AMSH, CL-2-229, f679r-682r, Mother Cabrini to the New York sisters, Rome, February 22, 1890.

74. Theodore Maynard, *Too Small a World* (Milwaukee: 1947), 103-104; 114-115.

75. AANY, C-25, Msgr. Thomas Preston to Corrigan, New York, June 20, 1890.

76. APF, S.C. Amer. Cent., 1890, vol. 53, f718r-721v, Mother Cabrini to Simeoni, Manresa, July 31, 1890.

77. *Sadlier's Catholic Directory, 1894* (New York: 1894), 148: The orphanage reception house moved to 251 West 14th Street. The or-

phanage cared for approximately forty children at this time. By 1898, the reception house again moved to Fort Washington Ave. and West 190th St.

78. George Paul Jacoby, *Catholic Child Care in Nineteenth Century New York* (New York: 1974), 220.

79. APF, Lett. Occid., 1890, vol. 386, f587r, Simeoni to Mthr. Cabrini, Rome, July 27, 1890.

80. *N.Y. Times*, February 9, 1891. *N.Y. Herald*, February 9, 10, 1891.

81. APF, S.C. Amer. Cent., 1890, vol. 52, f101r, Morelli to Corrigan, New York, September 29, 1888.

82. AGS, 664/1, Corrigan to Morelli, New York, December 3, 1890.

83. AGS, 664/1, Rev. Giuseppe Molinari to Rev. Carlo Molinari, New York, March 5, 1891.

84. ACMS, SRSR, #005, Box 1, Scal. Frs. Papers, Rev. Felice Morelli, *Memoria*. This unpublished work, written about 1912, records Morelli's version of the beginnings of the apostolate in New York.

85. AANY, C-28, William O'Connor to Corrigan, New York, April 23, 1891.

86. Giuseppe Dall'Ongaro, *Francesca Cabrini La Suora che Conquistò L'America* (Milan: 1982), 174.

87. AMSH, CL-2-234, Mother Cabrini to New York sisters, Codogno, April 2, 1890.

88. APF, APNS (1893), vol. 8, R. 13, f55v, Mother Cabrini to Ledóchowski, Codogno, January 20, 1893.

89. AANY, C-17, Simeoni to Corrigan, Rome, July 16, 1891.

90. AANY, G-28, Folder #9, Corrigan to Parocchi (draft), New York, September 24, 1891.

91. AMSH, CL-2-275, Mother Cabrini to New York sisters, Codogno, June 20, 1891.

92. APF, APNS (1893), vol. 8, R. 13, f55v, Mother Cabrini to Ledóchowski, Codogno, January 20, 1893.

93. Dall'Ongaro, op. cit., 176-177.

94. AMSH, *Memorie 43 E. 59th St.* The first president of the medical corps was Dr. Stephen Smith. The first patrons were Corrigan, Giovanni Branchi, the Italian Consul in New York, General Palma DiCesnola, and General Ferrero.

95. AMSH, Columbus Hospital Statistics:

	1896	1898	1899
Patients treated	615	912	994
Patients cured	323	612	605
Patients improved	156	120	156
Patients died	29	37	51
Patients transferred	8	14	14
Patients treated without charge	530	768	784
Patients treated for partial fee	50	69	108
Patients paying full board	38	34	48

Out-Patient Dispensary	1896	1898	1899
Total out-patients	6,171	12,185	13,670
Total prescriptions given	4,981	10,401	11,629

The majority of the patients treated during these years were Italian, but the hospital was not restricted by its constitution to Italians alone.

96. AMSH, *Memorie 43 E. 59th St.*
97. APF, APNS (1895), vol. 74, R. 153, f2r-3v, Mother Cabrini to Ledóchowski, New York, December 20, 1894.
98. Ibid.
99. APF, ACTA 1885, vol. 254, f333v, *Relazione con Sommario Vota e Nota di Archivio sopra gli Atti e Decreti del III Concilio Plenario di Baltimora, 17, 24, 31, Agosto.*
100. AMSH, CL-7-882, f3392r-3399v, Mother Cabrini to New York sisters, Codogno, October 24, 1901.
101. APF, S.C. Amer. Cent., 1890, vol. 53, f718r-721v, Mother Cabrini to Ledóchowski, Manresa, July 31, 1890. AMSH, CL-2-229, f679r-682r, Mother Cabrini to New York sisters, Rome, February 22, 1893 (?), APF, APNS (1895), vol. 74, R. 153, f2r-3v, Mother Cabrini to Ledóchowski, New York, December 20, 1894.

Chapter 6 / Aspects of Italian Parish Life in New York
1. *Official Catholic Directory* (Milwaukee: 1903), 98-109.
2. ASV, DelApUSA, 3a, *Istruzioni speciali a Mgr. Delegato Francesco Satolli an 1892.*
3. AANY, G-6, Giorgio Cerio to Corrigan, New York, November 13, 1895.
4. ASV, DelApUSA, Emigrazione Italiana, 1, Corrigan to Satolli, New York, May 11, 1893.
5. AANY, G-16, Corrigan to Rev. J. Owens (copy), New York, November 12, 1900.
6. AANY, G-1, Rev. Thomas J. Campbell, S.J., to Corrigan, n.p., n.d.
7. APF, Coll. d'Italia, vol. 43, f1501r-1502v, Corrigan to Scalabrini, New York, October 28, 1887.
8. AANY, G-33, Corrigan to "Emo. e Rmo. Signore," New York, November 18, 1885. APF, APNS (1900), vol. 194, R. 153, f206r, "Report of the Archdiocese of New York," New York, May 21, 1900.
9. ASV, DelApUSA, Emigrazione Italiana, 1, Corrigan to Satolli, New York, May 11, 1893.
10. Costantino Sassi, *Parrochia della Madonna di Pompeii* (Marino: 1946), 53-54.
11. ACMS, Scal. Frs. in N. Amer., Box 16, *Costituzione del Circolo della Madonna di Pompeii in New York. Costituzione della Società San Giuseppe. Costituzione della Società Sant'Antonio di Padova, di Mutuo Soccorso in New York.* All these societies belonged to the Church of Our Lady of Pompeii.
12. APF, S.C. Amer. Cent., 1884, vol. 41, f467r-468v, Corrigan to

Simeoni, New York, September 16, 1884: So important was the Italian patronal feast day that Corrigan requested permission to allow the Italians in St. Brigid Parish to transfer their patronal feast to a Sunday, since the members of the congregation were laborers, unable to attend the celebration if the feast were celebrated on a weekday.

13. ACMS, Box 5, Folder #6, "Contract between the Rev. Oreste Alussi, Rector of St. Joachim, and the Society of S. Vincenzo di Craso (martyr)," New York, June 10, 1901.
14. ACMS, Scal. Frs. in N. Amer., Box 20, O.L. of Pompeii, "Avvisi in Chiesa, 1894-1895."
15. Silvano Tomasi, *Piety and Power* (New York: 1975), 124.
16. Cf. Appendix I, containing the church announcements of the Church of Our Lady of Pompeii, for the year 1894-1895. These announcements give a clear view of the religious life of a growing national Italian parish in New York, which worshipped in a style very Italian, but which was slowly changing and altering its practices in response to the surrounding American culture and practice of the Church in America.
17. AGS, 583/3, Zaboglio to Scalabrini, New York, n.d.
18. ACMS, Scal. Frs. in N. Amer., Box 20, "Avvisi in Chiesa, 1894-1895," August 11, 18, 1894.
19. ACMS, Scal. Frs. in N. Amer., Box 20, "Avvisi in Chiesa, 1894-1895," December 2, 1895.
20. Nicholas J. Russo, *The Religious Acculturation of the Italians in New York City* (New York: 1968), 53.

Appendix

1. ACMS, "Avvisi in Chiesa, 1894-1895," Book 1, Scal. Frs. in N. Amer., Box 20, O.L. of Pompeii. The Church of Our Lady of Pompeii was begun by the Scalabrinian missionaries on May 8, 1892, in a small chapel on Waverly Place, attached to the original house of the Società San Raffaele for the assistance of Italian immigrants. The congregation moved during 1894-1895 to an abandoned Protestant church on Sullivan Street, which opened on April 28, 1895. The rector of the church was the Reverend Pietro Bandini.

These church announcements provide an interesting look into the daily life of an immigrant parish in New York City at the turn of the century. The announcements were originally in Italian. I have loosely translated them. Any direct, precise quotations are marked off in quotation marks, while any comments of my own are shown in parentheses (or in brackets within quoted matter). All repetitions originally found in the announcements have here been removed for the sake of brevity. Only the initial citation or announcement for any activity is noted here, such as notices for monthly first Friday devotions and society meetings. Any Sundays with no recorded announcements here were those simply repeating earlier announcements and have not been repeated here.

All church societies met monthly. The following schedule was followed at Our Lady of Pompeii:

First Sunday of each month: Societies of Sacro Cuore and of San Giuseppe.

Second Sunday of each month: Society of San Luigi.

Third Sunday of each month: Society of the Madonna of Pompeii.

Fourth Sunday of each month: Society of the Figlie de Maria.

Index